Uncorked

A CORKSCREW COLLECTION

FOR IVAN, AMIE AND JESSE,
JOINT VENTURERS ON THIS
CORKSCREW PATH

MARILYNN GELFMAN KARP
AND JEREMY FRANKLIN BROOKE

Uncorked

A CORKSCREW COLLECTION

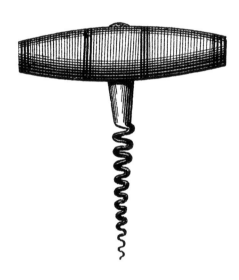

ABBEVILLE PRESS PUBLISHERS
NEW YORK   LONDON

Grape

Barrel

Bung-hole

Bung

Gimlet

Contents

Engravings on endpapers
and title page:

From *The Growth of
Industrial Art*,
Washington, DC, 1886.
Page 81. Compiled under
the supervision of Hon.
Benjamin Butterworth,
Commissioner of Patents.

Engravings on page 2,
and on page 7 (at right):

From W.C. Kantner,
*Illustrated Book of
Objects: English and
German Self-Educator*,
Reading, PA, 1888.
Pages 50, 70, 77, 16, 95,
148, 74, 19, 83, 104, 139.

Demijohn

Bottle

Cork

Corkscrew

Label

1 *The Coming of the Corkscrew*
LORE

I grew up in apartment 1B at 2121 St. Raymond Avenue, Bronx 62, New York, across the street from P.S. 106, which I attended from kindergarten through the sixth grade. Mom was a wholehearted mother and a dedicated housewife. She cleaned the apartment, did the laundry and marketed while my brother, Bill, and I were in school. My father returned from his Garment Center employment at 6:45 PM, washed up and we all sat down to a well-balanced, thoughtfully constructed dinner at 7:00 PM every night of my childhood, except for Sundays. That's when we went to Toy Sun Chinese Restaurant to enjoy exotic splendors of the East, including wonton soup and egg rolls, or to Sam's Kosher Delicatessen for corned beef sandwiches. We had a mixed case of Hoffman's sodas delivered to our apartment weekly by Irving the Seltzer Man. That was what we drank with our dinners. Bill and I had three dinner responsibilities: discovering new flavor sensations by mixing different sodas in the glass, washing up and wiping the dishes. The closest we ever got to wine was Welch's grape juice and we combined that with seltzer or Tom Collins mixer.

Wine was either sacramental or something Hollywood types drank in society movies. By the time I was a teenager, I had shared enough dinners in my friends' homes to realize that their Greek and Italian parents enjoyed red wine with dinner…and offered it to everyone at the table. Not wanting to offend, I often tasted it. Like cabbage soup and other in-your-face foods they offered, I gradually became accustomed to its hearty, yeasty, sour aggressiveness; enjoyment had nothing to do with it. These were rough homemade wines.

My palate evolved as I grew into my mature-ish self, and I found that wine at gallery openings and at dinner with friends was enjoyable and later, even preferable to other beverages. When I married Ivan, my (late) art dealer husband, we became seriously involved in the interplay between wine and food; we ate and drank very well throughout our lives together. In 1968 we were feeling

At left:
Giotto di Bondone, *Marriage at Cana* (detail), Cappella Scrovegni, Padua, 1304–06.

downright wine-intelligent and adventurous and ordered a mixed case of 1965–66 Château Margaux, Château Haut-Brion, Château Latour and Romanée-St.-Vivant. Alas, had we let them age ten to fifty years, they could have reached their full potential. I made fine French dinners to accompany them and we drank them all in the year we bought them, believing that they just weren't as great as they were reputed to be. We live and yearn.

Wine came first. Corkscrews came much later. In Neolithic times (around six thousand years ago), wine was made, stored and served in clay pots between the geographic locations currently called Turkey and Iran. Clay tablets from the first millennium BCE (around three thousand years ago), record the partial payment of wages in wine rations to workers in Assyrian royal employ. Biblical Noah planted the first recorded post-flood grapevines on Mt. Ararat. In early wine-producing societies, the areas where wine was grown, its consumption was routine and it was also used for ritual purposes—libation, consecration and as an essential part of the baggage on the life-after-death voyage. Beer and wine developed along a parallel timeline, but beer was produced widely, in as many locations as grain was cultivated. Made only in climates where grapes could be grown, wine was stored in open or loosely capped containers and was consumed shortly after pressing, as it was more palatable when fresh.

In earliest Mesopotamia, where bruised or crushed grapes were stored in clay jars, wine made itself. Left undisturbed, the natural yeast on the grape skins converted the natural sugars into alcohol. The qualities of flavor, nuance, body, palatability, drinkability and elegance are about timing and varietal variations of this one basic process. The concept of aging wines hadn't yet occurred.

Early Greek and Roman wine artifacts are on permanent exhibition in regiments of showcases at the Metropolitan Museum of Art. Nestled among other early necessities of life are stone and

Above:
This clay wine strainer with an applied handle, deep bowl and pierced perforations was found near the Dead Sea excavations amidst other pottery, fourth to third century BCE. Clay, 2.25" high, 5.25" wide. Made in Israel.

At right:
Duccio di Buoninsegna, *Marriage at Cana*, Museo dell'Opera del Duomo, Siena, 1308–11.

clay vessels that were used to make, serve and consume wine. These include Cycladic marble bowls from 3200 BCE and Cretan and Cycladic terra-cotta spouted jugs from 2800 to 2300 BCE. There are Minoan chlorite and steatite spouted bowls, terracotta vessels and diorite and marble bowls from 2700 to 1600 BCE and Mycenaean and Helladic terracotta stemmed cups and stirrup jars from 1400 to 1100 BCE, some with delicate murex (mollusk dye) decoration. They are part of a continuous wine artifactual line, narratively decorated, leading to stemmed terracotta wine bowls with handles (kylix), terracotta wine jugs (oinochoe), wine/water mixing vessels (krater) and terracotta amphorae from 560 to 460 BCE in Roman culture.

Through early Greek society and pervasive Roman culture, commercial quantities of wine were stored and shipped in terra-cotta amphorae stopped up with wood bungs, clay stoppers or cork plugs that were covered with fiber, wadding, leather, textiles or grape leaves and sealed with beeswax, tallow, pitch, resin, pine tar, clay, gypsum or crude building mortar. Breaking these seals was literal. Wine residuum found in grave goods bears testament to airtight closing in early times. Potable wine for portable personal consumption was frequently stored in wineskins and clay jars. In finer households, wine for consumption was kept in large storage vessels and transferred to more easily manageable wine pitchers, decorated clay jugs or glass or ornamented metal pitchers at the dining table.

The Marriage at Cana, where Jesus Christ performed his first miracle—turning water into wine—predates the corkscrew. John 2:6 describes the vessels that held the wine as "six stone water jars… each holding from twenty to thirty gallons" (Gateway Bible, New International Version, 2007). This scene is the subject of many paintings. One of the finest is in Giotto's painting cycle of the Virgin Mary in the Scrovegni (Arena) Chapel in Padua, which

 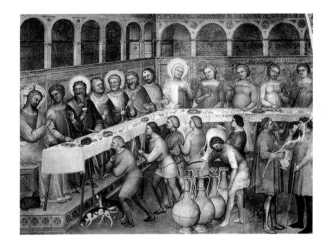

he finished in 1306. In this version, the stone jars are exquisitely and prominently depicted. A household retainer is pouring water from a clay ewer into one of them, and the wine steward is sampling the resulting wine from a glass pitcher. Filled wine glasses are set before the guests. During Giotto's time, wine was stored in clay amphorae, barrels, wooden casks and wine skins and served from pitchers into silver, gold, wood or clay bowls, flagons, blown-glass drinking vessels, rock crystal chalices and other ornate goblets and vessels suitable for imbibing this celebratory and convivial drink.

Starting in sixteenth-century England, wine was conveyed to the drinker from the cask in dark glass bottles. These bottles were globular, long necked and irregularly shaped. On the occasion that they were corked, it was easier to truncate or behead the bottle than to draw the cork out. Two centuries later, the manufacture of glass bottles became standardized with respect to shape (cylindrical), thickness (strength) and size (amount of contents). Clay pots, stone bowls, wine skins, urns, amphorae, stone jars, wooden casks, flagons and stoneware vessels were replaced by glass bottles, for transit to the consumer.

Above, left to right:

Giotto di Bondone, *Marriage at Cana*, Cappella Scrovegni, Padua, 1304–06.

Giusto de' Menabuoi, *Marriage at Cana*, Cathedral Baptistry, Padua, 1376–78.

Gerard David, *Marriage at Cana*, Musée du Louvre, 1503.

This revolutionized the transport of wine, simplifying storage and shipping as well. Sealed bottles could be brought to the table at any location, from diverse places of origin. A happy side effect of bottling was that wine would now be aged in the bottle.

Beer and cider, being naturally carbonated, required a tight cap reinforced with wire to keep it in place. Cork had been one material of choice for the cap since antiquity and was quickly adopted by wine makers once bottles had become standardized. This renewable resource grew as the bark of the Quercus suber or cork oak tree, native to Portugal, one of England's trade partners. England exported woolens and imported port and cork.

In France, cork sealing of wine was readily adopted early for storage and transport. *Tire-bouchon*, the French term for corkscrew, literally means cork-pull. Sealed bottles could be brought to the kitchen or to the dining room in the appropriate quantity for the number of diners without the chance of the serving staff helping themselves to a sip en route.

The glass bottle and cork necessitated the development of the corkscrew.

There is little doubt that teeth and hands were the earliest uncorking tools, for corks extended past the lip of many early cork-capped bottles. Common tools were used to pry corks from bottle. During the middle of the eighteenth century in England, "gun worms," also called "gun screws," were manufactured to remove wadding and cartridges from gun barrels. It is generally believed that these tools, with their double- or triple-pointed spiral arms on a ramrod, were the prototype for the corkscrew, but anything at hand was fair game for cork removal. Transitional and provisional tools, including common nails and skewers, were opportunistically used to pry, gouge, lever, twist or just plain dig.

Nicholas Amhurst, the English poet, wrote *The Bottle-Scrue: A Tale* published in his *Poems on Several Occasions* in both the 1720 and the 1723 editions. The comic poem describes Sir Roger, a jolly vicar who faced the "hoary Bottle" and

> *...seem'd to tell,*
> *that all within was Ripe and Well;*
> *When studious to extract the Cork,*
> *Sir Roger set his teeth to work;*
> *This way and that the Cork he ply'd,*
> *And wrench'd in vain from side to side;*
> *In vain his ivory Grinders strain'd,*
> *For still unmove'd the cork remain'd...*

Strained and tired, he "meditates a second war" and

> *Firm on the spungy Cork he plac'd*
> *His doubty Thumb, and downward press'd*
> *The yielding Wood;—But oh! dire luck!*
> *Fast in its place his own thumb stuck.*
> *Loudly the pleas'd Spectators laugh'd,*
> *With Pain and Shame the Parson chaf'd,*
> *Long did he strive with adverse Fate,*
> *His captive Thumb to extricate,*
> *Nor could his Liberty regain,*
> *'Till hammer broke the glassy Chain...*

1   This finger-pull corkscrew has a cut-steel key handle and shank, tapered shaft, tapered helical worm, c. 1820. Steel, 2.75" high. Made in England or France.

2   This blown green glass bottle, likely used to transport both wine and beer, has a rough pontil mark in the depression at the bottom and an applied lip. An early attempt at standardization, groups of such bottles could be somewhat stabilized in shipment by locking the top of one bottle into the bottom of another and, as the natural carbonation in beer often became explosive when jostled, the applied lip aided the wiring of the cork to stay in place, 1780–1810. Glass, 10" high. Made in England.

1

2

That night he dreamed a fitful dream of Bacchus offering release from shame and grief in the form of a "crooked instrument" and with a smile Bacchus

> *...in his Hand the Weapon took,*
> *He slip't it o'er his Finger-joint,*
> *And to the Cork apply'd the Point,*
> *Gently he turn'd it round and round,*
> *'Till in the Midst its Spires were wound,*
> *Then bending earthward low, betwixt*
> *His Knees the Bottle firmly fix't;*
> *And giving it a sudden Jerk,*
> *From its close Prison wrench'd the Cork...*

Upon waking he was inspired to replicate the "Bottle-scrue"; committed to the "mighty task," he sets

> *His Hands, and o'er the Anvil sweats,*
> *First puts the Iron in the Fire,*
> *And hammers out the glowing Wire,*
> *Then tortures it in Curls around,*
> *As Tendrils on the Vine are found,*
> *Sharpens the Bottom, rounds the Top,*
> *And finish'd bears it from the Shop;*
> *Well-pleas'd, a Bottle-scrue he names it,*
> *And sacred to the God proclaims it.*

While considering that "This curious Engine, says the Priest, Shall stretch my Fame from West to East", he muses

> *By me shall Birmingham become*
> *In future Days, more fam'd than Rome,*
> *Shall owe to me her Reputation,*
> *And serve with Bottle-scrue the Nation.*

Although corkscrews were certainly in use previous to 1795, the origins of the earliest corkscrews are shrouded in poetry, legend and surmise. While the first corkscrew patent was awarded to Samuel Henshall in England in 1795, the devices were certainly in use before then. Henshall added a "button," a small circular disk, to the shaft of a basic T-shaped corkscrew, breaking the cork's tenacious, crusted hold, and easing its extraction.

Function is the grounding reality of tools and usability is their proof. Consider the corkscrew. It has more permutations than the proverbial "better mousetrap" and a shorter history.

I love tools and have spent hours in hardware stores, flea markets and antique shows contemplating their culture and evolution and respecting their singular purposes. The tool that I collect most passionately is the corkscrew.

Corkscrews define humankind's ingenious and cumulative effort to draw the cork and get to the elixir with an element of grace. The territory of this collection is originality of principle, inventiveness of concept, inspired improvement on a preceding format and singular decorative adaptation. Accrued ingenuity is the continuous thread that binds the collection. This book is not an encyclopedia; it was never destined to include examples of every corkscrew ever made. My collection is not about quantity or rarity or mint condition. I value evident tracks of use, as well as eccentricity of design and good functional condition.

Being embraced in my collection means that each corkscrew is identified in the context of material culture. For each, a description, composition and size, country of manufacture, placement in time, specific operation, and manufacturer and patentee (when known) are included in the captions, which are also intended to assist readers in identifying their own corkscrews. The arrangement of the whole collection and this volume is about identifying discrete and fluid categories of form and function within the evolutionary narrative of the corkscrew, which is succumbing to the advent of the screw-top.

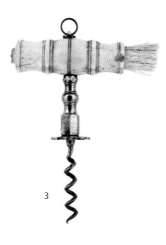

3

3 Straight pull corkscrew with brush-tipped turned bone handle and a cut-steel shaft supporting a concave daisy button secured by a steel pin running through the handle to a steel loop fitting atop, tapered helical worm, Henshall 1795 patent, 1850–70. Bone, vegetal fiber and steel, 6" high. Made in England.

4   Folding figural cork-
screw with bottle handle
stamped "Williamson Co.
Manfrs Newark, NJ" on
bottom and featuring a
brass faux label engraved
with "Anheuser Busch"
and logo, shown in open
position, pivoting helical
worm, Williamson patent,
1897. Worn nickel-plated
brass, engraved brass
and nickel-plated steel,
2.5" high. Made in USA.

5   Straight pull corkscrew
with printed wood dowel
handle advertising
"Schlitz" on center globe,
"Schlitz Milwaukee U.S.A."
on both sides and stamped
"E.S.M. Co. Erie, PA
Walker Pat. Applied For"
on dowel end. A smooth
shaft, attached by a steel
rod through the handle
lengthwise end-to-end,
supports a short fixed cast
steel demi-globe bell

with three feet stamped
"Schlitz" over a grid
pattern. As the worm is
screwed into the cork,
the legs of the bell put
pressure on the bottle
rim, continued rotation
of the shaft draws the
cork upward and out of
the bottle, bladed center
worm, Walker patent,
1893. Wood and steel,
5.5" high. Made in USA.

6   Mechanical cast steel
bar corkscrew with turned
hardwood handle and
screw-mounted lever
arm and with circular
rack action. Beginning
with the handle in the
raised position, the worm
is lowered, rotating to
penetrate the cork.
Continued downward
motion forces the
contoured lift arm to raise

the cork, helical worm,
Gilchrist patent, 1888.
Steel and wood, 16" high
with lever arm raised.
Made in USA.

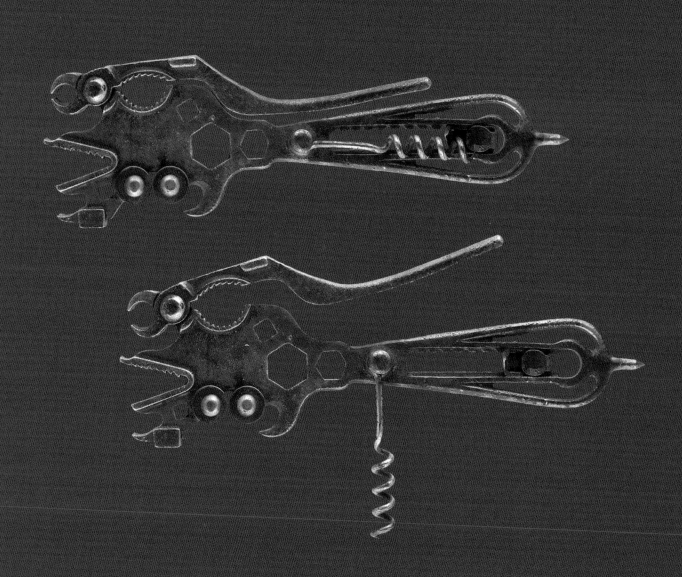

2 *Turn of the Screw*
THE ANATOMY OF THE CORKSCREW

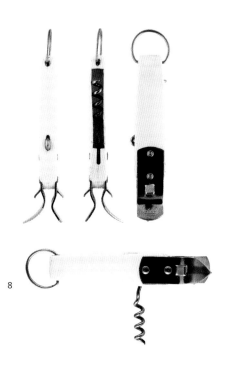

8

I shared a bottle of wine each dinnertime with Ivan for forty-nine years. Our first corkscrew came from the kitchen aisle of a supermarket, proffered between the measuring spoons and the manual can openers. This corkscrew was designed to pivot out from the center of a white plastic handle, making a simple T shape. The twinned nickel-plated steel can opener and cap-lifter at one end of the handle was balanced by a nickel-plated loop for wall hanging at the other. It was a handy kitchen tool in a pre-pop-top era, enabling easy access to canned beer, soda pop or wine. It is stamped "EKCO USA".

My 361st corkscrew acquisition is at the center of a multi-purpose cast-iron and steel tool from 1909 that offers wire nippers, an alligator wrench, a pipe wrench which performs as a compressor for cork reinsertion, a pocketknife sharpener, four prying tools (one of which slides with ten stops and clips the corkscrew into place when not in use), two hex wrenches and two square bolt wrenches. It was made in the United States and although "PAT 09" has been cast into it, there is no manufacturer's mark. The essential end, that pointed screw called the worm, is of the same helical type of worm as my first corkscrew and pivots similarly.

---

7   (at left) Corkscrew with multi-tool handle including pipe wrench, nail lifter and hammer square at botatom, scissors sharpener, knife sharpener, wire breaker, nippers and nutcracker at top, as well as wrench holes and a sliding can opener with adjustable stops. The can opener is also used to lock the pivoting corkscrew, wire pivot shaft, helical worm, maker's mark "PAT 1909", Nylin patent (first version), 1909. Cast iron and steel, 7.25" long. Made in USA.

8   Nesting corkscrew in plastic multi-tool handle with cap-lifter (stamped "EKCO USA") and can piercer back-to-back on one end, hanging loop release at center, in four positions. LaForte patent, pivot shaft, helical worm, c. 1953. Plastic and nickel-plated steel, 5" long. Made in USA.

A selection of helical worms

THE WORM TURNS
(TURN, TURN, TURN)

While the variety of corkscrews is legion, the worm is the least varied and the most unchanging part of the corkscrew's anatomy. It usually curls clockwise (called right-handed), infrequently counterclockwise (called left-handed) and is of one of three forms: helical, center or Archimedean, referring to technical subtleties of the thread or spiral.

Helical worms are like a strand of DNA, which means that the curl winds around an empty central axis, a core of space. The helical spiral is a (sometimes tapering) steel wire, usually round in cross section, which is sometimes threaded with a continuous running groove. The length of the spiral section, or helix, and the space between turns varies from one worm to another.

Center worms have a steel center core around which a ridge spirals. There is variety to the length of the worms and the angle or pitch of the sharpened threads; the sharpest are called bladed worms. When the pitch is extreme and the diameter tight, it is called a speed worm, connoting the comparative swiftness of cork entry. Center worms are manufactured from one solid spiral of steel and the pointed end may be on or off center to the core.

Named for the third century BCE Greek mathematician and inventor of the spiral water pump, Archimedean worms have a central steel core tapered to a point, around which a spiraling tapering bladed strip is soldered or welded. The point is always on center to the core, which is its tip, but the length of the threaded section and pitch or angle of the spiral varies. This is the rarest of the three types of worms.

9

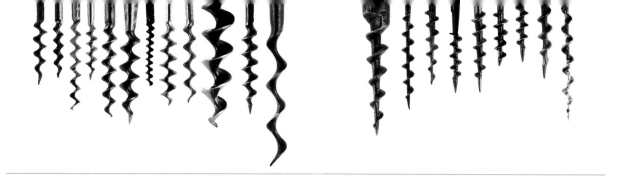

A range of center worms

An assortment of Archimedean worms

9   Mechanical corkscrew with turned wood handle connected to a fixed spring-assisted smooth shaft pinned beneath the top of an open frame to stabilize it. With the frame placed on the bottle lip, the handle is rotated to penetrate the cork, causing the fixed stop to compress the spring, building pressure to aid cork extraction. The open frame enables easy removal of the cork from the bladed center worm, Dunisch & Scholer patent, c. 1883. Wood and steel with traces of silver paint, 6.75" high. Made in Germany.

10   Straight pull corkscrew with cruciform steel handle and loop atop for insertion of tool for cork removal, Armand Walfard patent, layered steel shaft, Archimedean worm, 1888. Steel, 4.25" high. Made in France.

10

HOLD FAST: HANDLES (STURDINESS, COMFORT, FASHION)

By contrast with the three kinds of worms, handles are the most various and decorated part of even the simplest corkscrews, yet their forms must be secondary to their essential grip; they are where the rubber meets the road. If the handle meets the palm's requirement of comfort, the cork may be extracted efficiently, without stress, awkwardness or pain. It may be as beautiful, whimsical, primitive, elegant, fashionable, graceful and complex as the maker's sensibility allows. Handles have been made of steel, bone, horn, Bakelite, mother-of-pearl, brass, ivory, wood, silver, bronze, Celluloid and gold. They are straight, contoured, cruciform, tipped, folding, winged, levered, figural, scissored, cased, perforated, bowed, collapsing, finger-pulls and multi-tooled and have been carved, cast, cut, pressed, turned, laminated, inlaid and capped.

The handles of mechanical corkscrews have to attend to the dictates of weight and the specific functions of the device. These additional constraints require such adaptations as streamlining, telescoping, compressing, pivoting, sheathing, contracting or cranking, which have further challenged makers' imagineering.

11

11 Figural eyebrow handle corkscrew with baby holding grape bunches, smooth shaft, bladed center worm, 1920s. Nickel-plated steel, 5.25" high. Made in Sweden. (See other view on page 41.)

An array of handles

A sampling of shafts

ENABLING: SHAFTS
(CONNECTING BOTH BUSINESS ENDS)

Shafts and shanks are the parts of a corkscrew that connect the handle to the worm. I own corkscrews with shafts from a quarter inch to ten inches long. In the simplest cases, as in basic T corkscrews, the shaft may be smooth or decorated, cylindrical, squared, twisted, tapered, cut, turned, balustered, layered or buttoned.

In corkscrews with a mechanical connection of the worm to the handle, shafts may be spring-assisted.

Corkscrews with complicated mechanics—Kings Screws, 2 barrels and concertinas—may have telescoping or pivoting shanks as well as shafts. Not to confuse the two, I prefer to think of the shaft as unequivocally wedded to the worm (sometimes not obviously) and of the shank as allied with the barrel, frame or handle. This makes understanding how they work somewhat easier.

An astonishing variety of forms arise despite the requirement that the worm be placed at the bottom of every contraption. The harmony with which handle, shaft and worm combine, may result in corkscrews of primitive splendor, poignant practicality, roughshod beauty, constrained simplicity, functional grace, quirky complexity, unexpected flourish or make-do bluntness. Each of the corkscrews to follow transcends functionality; each is an operatic tribute to eccentric ponderings and musings on how to get that intractable cork extracted.

12　Mechanical closed-barrel corkscrew with turned wood handle attached through the center to a threaded steel shaft by a loop fitting atop. A counterthreaded brass shank telescopes into a bronze barrel with maker's plate depicting an oval "Patent" shield flanked by a rising lion and a recumbent unicorn. With the barrel resting on the bottle lip, the Thomason patent enabled the penetration, drawing, extraction and removal of the cork from the worm (without handling the cork) in one continuous counterclockwise then clockwise motion, center worm, 1802. Wood, brass, bronze and steel, 7.25" fully compressed. Made in England.

12

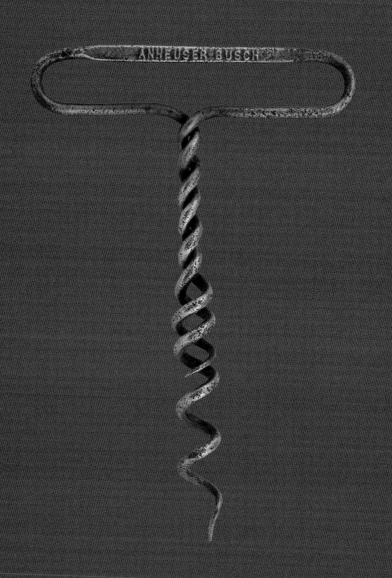

3 Twist and Shout

YOUR WRIST IS THE ONLY MOVING PART

My annual childhood birthday treat was to be taken to a Broadway show. The ritual included passing the Californian, a twenty-four-hour diner/dive on Broadway, in the theater district. Each year from 1946 to 1958, there was a not-too-clean short order cook I could see through the window, deftly wielding an ordinary stainless steel fork in a bruised frying pan, making perfect inverted spiraling cones of scrambled eggs for the diners within. He looked like a hobo and I imagined him perfecting his style over a campfire beside railroad tracks. The skill with which he twisted that fork and mesmerized those eggs into standing at attention in the middle of an oval platter, awaiting fries and toast, had my complete attention. In fact, I looked forward with more anticipation to this performance than to *My Fair Lady* or *South Pacific*. A deft hand with the fork myself, I have never been able to replicate the magical maneuver, so smoothly enacted by the down-and-outer in the window's frame. My father's annual dismissal of my gape-jawed admiration was, "It's all in the wrist."

Some things are. Another truism that pertains to this chapter is: that *necessity is the mother of invention*. Before corkscrews were common items, there was no standard tool for the removal of the impacted corks necessary for the preservation of the integrity of bottled wine. Basic T and finger pull corkscrews were model adaptive reuses of gun-cleaning hardware: wadding extractors with ramrods. Necessity was the dynamic that made it happen. Simple implements were adapted in the service of a new use, cork extraction. Straight pull, basic T and finger pull corkscrews require strength and purpose; they are "still" corkscrews, in the sense that there are no moving parts to facilitate the pull, one's wrist is the only moving part.

13 (at left) Straight pull or basic T corkscrew made from one steel wire with "Anheuser-Busch" stamped on obverse of handle and blank reverse, Clough patent, twisted wire shaft, double helical worm, Williamson manufacturer, 1876. Steel, 4.25" high. Made in USA.

14

15

14   Handwrought gun screw with double helical worm. Gun screws such as this were prototypes for early corkscrews, no markings, c. 1850. Steel, 1.5" high. Made in USA.

15   Enfield sergeant's T-shaped steel musket tool with double helical worm in place on the threaded left arm, right screwdriver arm is stamped "T&CG". An oil compartment with a threaded cap, short dropper and threaded screw in the base, the length of which supports a pivoting nipple pick and a cast clamp, acts as handle for insertion, Thomas & Charles Gilbert manufacturers, 1853. Steel, 4.75" high. Made in England.

16

17

16 Handwrought gun screw with double helical worm, no markings, c. 1850. Steel, 3.5" high. Made in USA.

17 Enfield private's Y-shaped steel musket tool shown assembled with double helical worm in place on the right threaded arm, stamped "395", left screwdriver arm is stamped "T&CG". The base of the Y is a socket wrench and between arms is an oil compartment with a threaded cap and dropper, the length of which supports a pivoting nipple pick, Thomas & Charles Gilbert manufacturers, 1853. Steel, 4.75" high. Made in England.

STRAIGHT PULLS

BASIC T ALL STEEL

Once the wedged cork has been penetrated, we assume that one has the vigor and purpose to wrest it from the neck of the bottle. Basic T corkscrews demand the whole hand's grasp around a handle. Finger pulls require one, two, three or four fingers through a loop handle. With all types the same direct action is requisite: rotate, penetrate and pull—it is all in the wrist.

The multiplicity of form within this genre speaks to more than the mutability of fashion. Basic T corkscrews are still manufactured. They are the most abundantly present sort of corkscrew to be found at flea markets, antiques shops and shows, yard, barn and lawn sales. They are the simplest of tools with which to remove the impediment to the enjoying the wine.

18

19

20

18   Basic T corkscrew made from one steel wire, twisted wire shaft, helical double helical worm, Clough patent, Williamson manufacturer, 1876. Steel, 4" high. Made in USA.

19   Basic T corkscrew made from one steel wire, twisted wire shaft, helical worm, Clough patent, Williamson manufacturer, 1876. Steel, 4" high. Made in USA.

20   Basic T corkscrew made from one steel wire with "Rhum Black" stamped on obverse of handle and "Liqueur Kermann" on reverse, twisted wire shaft with button, helical worm, Clough patent, Williamson manufacturer, 1876. Steel, 3.75" high. Made in USA.

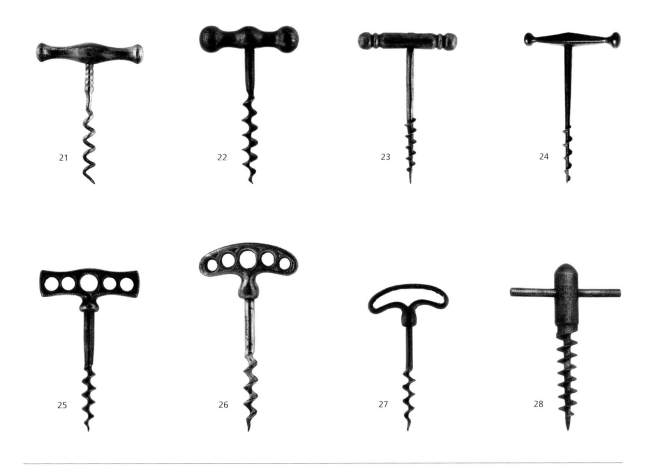

21   Basic T corkscrew with shaped steel handle, turned steel shaft, and tapered, reverse helical worm, c. 1870. Nickel-plated steel, 3.5" high. Made in England.

22   Basic T corkscrew with ball-tipped turned steel handle, tapered steel shaft, wide bladed center worm, c. 1890. Steel, 3.75" high. Made in France.

23   Basic T corkscrew with ball-tipped turned steel handle fixed to a smooth peened steel shaft, Archimedean worm, c. 1850. Steel, 4.25" high. Made in Italy.

24   Basic T all steel corkscrew with four-sided handle with knob ends and a long tapered steel shaft secured through the handle by peening at the top, Archimedean worm, c. 1830. Steel, 4.25" high. Made in France.

25   All steel basic T corkscrew, applied stamp of Perille factory on the perforated handle, tapered shaft, center worm, c. 1890. Steel, 3.5" high. Made in France.

26   All steel basic T corkscrew, applied stamp of Perille factory on the perforated handle, tapered shaft, bladed center worm, c. 1880. Steel, 4.25" high. Made in France.

27   Basic T corkscrew with two finger indents on bottom of crescent shaped skeleton handle, smooth steel shaft secured at the handle base, bladed center worm, 1880–90. Steel, 3.75" high. Made in France.

28   Basic T Bossin Champagne corkscrew with rod handle fixed through a machined shaft. This corkscrew was fitted into a Champagne cork extracting apparatus used during the disgorgement phase of Champagne making, cylindrical shaft, Archimedean worm, c. 1900. Steel, 4" high. Made in France.

ALL STEEL FINGER PULLS

29   Finger-pull corkscrew with miniature cut-steel key handle and cut-steel shank, tapered shaft, tapered helical worm, c. 1820. Steel, 2.75" high. Made in England or France.

30   Single wire finger pull corkscrew with ring handle and twisted shaft with button, Clough patent, helical worm, c. 1874. Steel wire, 3" high. Made in USA.

31   Single wire finger pull corkscrew with ring handle and twisted shaft with button, Clough patent, helical worm, c. 1874. Steel wire, 3" high. Made in USA.

32   Single wire finger pull corkscrew with ring handle and twisted shaft with button, Clough patent, helical worm, c. 1874. Steel wire, 3.5" high. Made in USA.

33   Multi-tool finger pull "Williamson Flash" corkscrew with stamped cap-lifter in handle and looped wire shaft, helical worm, 1929. Nickel-plated steel, 3.5" high. Made in USA.

34   Multi-tool finger pull corkscrew with single-wire handle and shaft and stamped cap-lifter in loop, Walker patent, helical worm, 1910. Nickel-plated steel, 3.25" high. Made in USA.

35   Four-finger pull, or "cellarman," corkscrew with applied steel handle and turned steel shank, short tapered shaft, bladed center worm, steeply angled speed worm, c. 1900. Steel, 5.5" high. Made in England.

36   Cellarman three-finger pull corkscrew with loop handle cast with shank (marked "UNIVERSAL" and "G.F. HIPKINS") ending with a button, cylindrical shaft, tapered helical worm, c. 1880. Steel, 5.25" high. Made in England.

37   Three-finger pull "La Vrille" (or gimlet) corkscrew made from a single steel wire by Tony Dussieux, straight shaft with wire twists, bladed center worm, c. 1900. Steel, 5.5" high. Made in France.

STEEL EYEBROW HANDLES

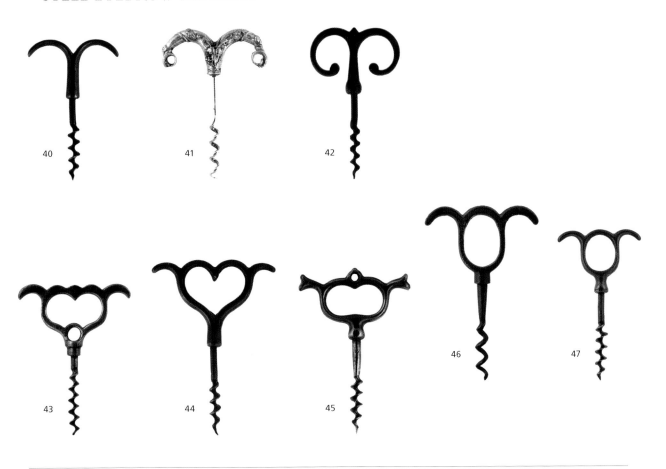

38 Three-finger pull multi-tool corkscrew with applied cap-lifter handle and "Walker Collar" wire breaker prong below, Walker patent, smooth shaft, speed worm, 1910. Nickel-plated steel, 6.25" high. Made in USA.

39 Two-finger pull corkscrew made from one steel wire with stamped cap-lifter handle and a long shaft engraved "Ste Laitiere Maggi Bte SGDG"* with a slot for opening sardine tins, bladed center worm, c. 1900. Steel, 8.25" high. Made in France.

40 Two-finger eyebrow corkscrew with applied handle and smooth shaft, bladed center worm, c. 1890. Steel, 4" high. Made in France.

41 Two-finger eyebrow corkscrew with applied cast pewter handle in grapevine motif, smooth shaft, and helical worm, c. 1960. Pewter and steel, 4.25" high. Made in France.

42 Two-finger eyebrow corkscrew with applied handle, smooth shaft and bladed center worm, c. 1890. Steel, 4.25" high. Made in France.

43 Four-finger eyebrow corkscrew with applied cut-steel handle and lever hole, short smooth shaft and bladed center worm, c. 1890. Steel, 4.25" high. Made in England.

44 Four-finger eyebrow corkscrew with applied handle, smooth shaft and bladed center worm, c. 1890. Steel, 5" high. Made in France.

45 Eyebrow corkscrew with four-finger decorative applied handle and tapered shaft stamped with Perille trademark, bladed center worm, 1819 patent. Steel, 4.75" high. Made in France.

46 Three-finger eyebrow corkscrew with applied handle, tapered shaft and helical worm, c. 1890. Steel, 5" high. Made in France.

47 Three-finger eyebrow corkscrew with applied handle, smooth shaft and bladed center worm, c. 1880. Steel, 4.25" high. Made in France.

* Bte SGDG stands for Breveté Sans Garantie Du Gouvernement.

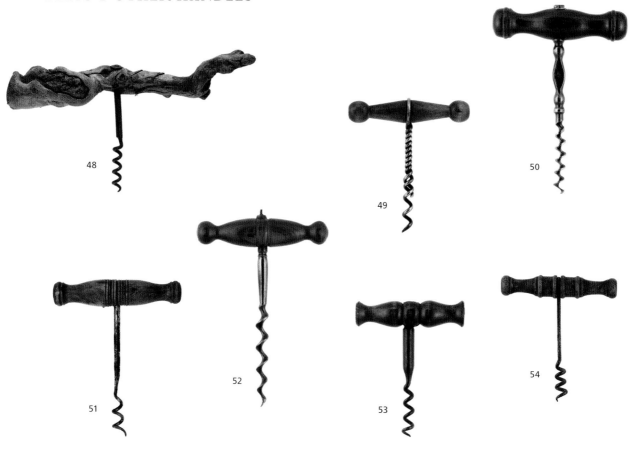

48

49

50

51

52

53

54

48   Basic T corkscrew with 8.25"-long grapevine handle, smooth rectangular shaft and helical worm, twentieth century. Grape wood, 4" high. Made in France.

49   Basic T corkscrew with ball-tipped turned wood handle, shaft and duplex worm made from one steel wire wrapped around midsection of the handle, twisted wire shaft, double helical worm,

Clough patent, made by Williamson, 1876. Wood and steel, 4.25" high. Made in USA.

50   Basic T corkscrew with acorn-tipped turned wood handle and turned flattened threaded steel shaft secured through handle by brass washer and threaded hexagonal bolt, center worm, c. 1870. Steel, brass and wood, 6" high. Made in USA.

51   Basic T corkscrew with turned boxwood handle secured to a cylindrical steel shaft, short helical worm, c. 1876. Wood and steel, 5" high. Made in USA.

52   Basic T corkscrew with ball-tipped turned wood handle secured to threaded turned steel shaft by steel fitting and hole for ring atop, speed center worm, 1890. Wood and steel, 6.25" high. Made in England.

53   Basic T corkscrew with turned wood handle secured by threaded smooth shaft peened atop, helical worm, nineteenth century. Steel and wood, 4.25" high. Made in England.

54   Basic T corkscrew with turned wood handle with center groove for wire wrap of wire shaft, tight short helical worm, nineteenth century. Steel and wood, 4" high. Made in USA.

55   Basic T corkscrew with carved eight-faceted wood handle secured by a smooth inset wire shaft, helical worm, nineteenth century. Steel and wood, 3.25" high. Made in France.

56   Basic T corkscrew with wood dowel handle secured by a twisted wire shaft with button, helical worm, Clough patent, Williamson manufacturer, 1876. Steel, 4.5" high. Made in USA.

57 Basic T corkscrew with wood dowel handle secured through center by a threaded smooth shaft peened atop a brass washer, bladed speed worm, twentieth century. Steel, brass and wood, 5" high. Made in England.

58 Basic T corkscrew with simple turned wood handle secured to dimpled steel shaft by a long pin through the length of the handle tip to tip, center worm, twentieth century. Steel and wood, 4.5" high. Made in Germany.

59 Basic T corkscrew with turned wood handle and turned, flattened and threaded steel shaft pinned through the sides of handle and secured by steel washer and fitting for a hanging loop atop, center worm, c. 1870. Steel, brass and wood, 5.5" high. Made in USA.

60 Basic T corkscrew with simple turned wood handle attached by a threaded square steel shaft peened atop a steel washer, grooved helical worm, nineteenth century. Steel and wood, 4.5" high. Made in England.

61 Basic T corkscrew with simple turned wood handle secured to a dimpled steel shaft by a long pin through the length of the handle tip to tip, flattened helical worm, twentieth century. Steel and wood, 5" high. Made in Germany.

62 Basic T corkscrew with simple turned wood handle attached by a threaded square steel shaft peened atop a steel washer, tapered helical worm, nineteenth century. Steel and wood, 4.25" high. Made in England.

63 Basic T corkscrew with simple turned wood handle secured by a threaded smooth shaft peened atop, bladed center worm, nineteenth century. Steel and wood, 4" high. Made in England.

64 Basic T corkscrew with turned acorn-tipped wood handle secured to a threaded turned steel shaft, speed center worm, c. 1890. Wood and steel, 4.75" high. Made in USA.

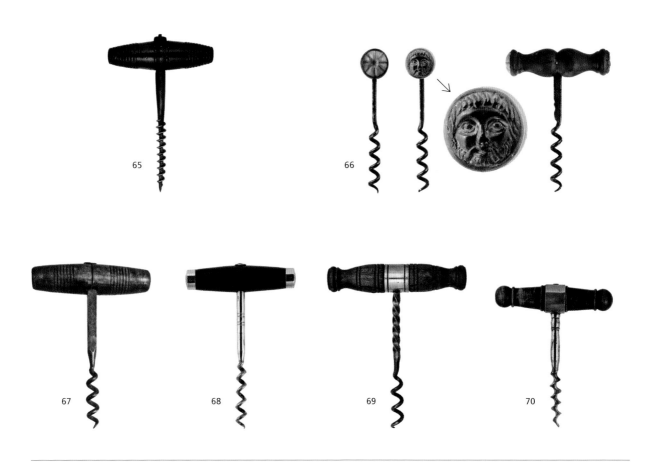

65

66

67   68   69   70

65   Basic T corkscrew with turned wood handle attached by a threaded tapered steel shaft, steel washer and a drilled tab for a loop, tapered Archimedean worm, c. 1870. Steel and wood, 4.75" high. Made in England.

66   Basic T corkscrew with carved stone button tipped turned horn handle secured to a notched rectangular steel shaft by peened steel pin through sides, grooved helical worm, nineteenth century. Horn and carved stone, 4.25" high. Made in France.

67   Basic T corkscrew with turned wood handle attached by a threaded steel shaft peened atop a brass washer, square shaft (stamped "JOHN WATTS SHEFFIELD") tapering to a helical worm, c. 1870. Steel, brass and wood, 5" high. Made in England.

68   Basic T corkscrew with resin handle with nickel-plated tip bands and stamped "1SG" secured by peened, threaded turned nickel-plated steel shaft and copper fitting, triangular helical worm, twentieth century. Steel, copper and resin, 5" high. Made in England.

69   Basic T corkscrew with turned wood handle secured to a twisted steel shaft by steel band stamped "Patent Applied For", helical worm, Haff patent, c. 1880. Wood and steel, 5" high. Made in USA.

70   Basic T corkscrew with ball-tipped turned wood handle secured to a threaded turned nickel-plated steel shaft by peened top and brass band, bladed center worm, c. 1890. Steel, wood and brass, 4.25" high. Made in France.

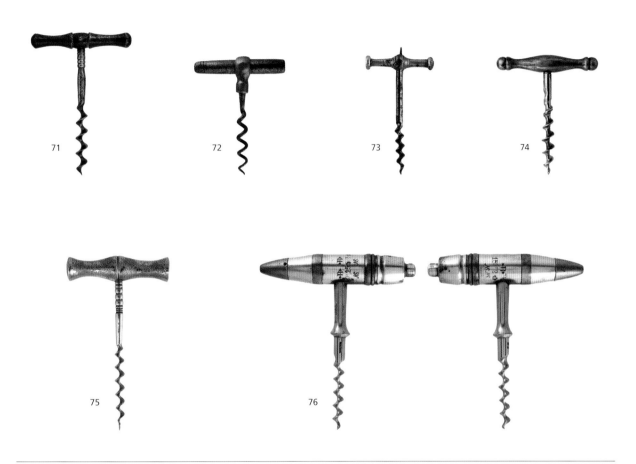

71　Basic T corkscrew with turned brass handle with rounded ends and turned steel shaft (stamped "W.H.Loftus" on one side and "140 Oxford S" on the other) secured through the center of the handle with threaded peened end, center worm, 1840. Steel and brass, 4.25" high. Made in England.

72　Basic T corkscrew, resembling a sheath and worm, with turned steel handle fixed to a tapered smooth steel shaft by a brass shank, tapered helical worm, c. 1880. Steel, 3.25" high. Made in England.

73　Basic T corkscrew with turned brass handle with knob ends and a long smooth steel shaft secured through the handle through sides and top with a fitting for loop, center worm, nineteenth century. Steel and brass, 3.5" high. Made in France.

74　Basic T corkscrew with acorn-tipped turned nickel-plated brass handle stamped "Rainond, ITALY" on top. A smooth nickel-plated steel shaft is secured to the center of the handle with a threaded end, Archimedean worm, c. 1920.

Nickel-plated steel and brass, 3.25" high. Made in Italy.

75　Basic T corkscrew with chased silver-plated handle engraved with grapes and grape leaves and a turned nickel-plated threaded steel shaft secured through handle lengthwise, long center speed worm, c. 1920. Silver, nickel and steel, 5.25" high. Made in England.

76　Basic T corkscrew with brass-tipped stainless steel and copper anti-aircraft bullet stamped "27" and engraved on both sides with arrows piercing "B B" (for Bofors Cannon Works), "15 1/2", crown logo and script "NS", turned steel shaft stamped "ROSTFREI" and "PH", bladed center worm, c. 1935. Stainless steel, copper and brass, 4.5" high. Made in Sweden.

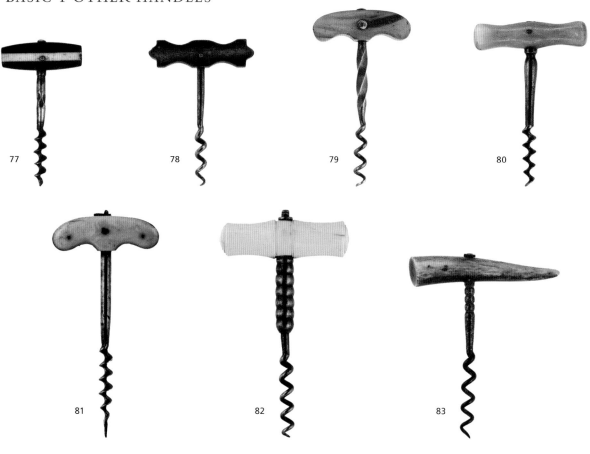

77   Basic T corkscrew with rounded, polished horn and bone handle with squared ends secured to a turned and dimpled steel shaft by a peened fitting atop and a steel pin through the center, bladed center worm, c. 1875. Steel, bone and buffalo horn, 3.5" high. Made in France.

78   Basic T corkscrew with decoratively cut horn handle secured to a threaded turned steel shaft by steel pin through sides, tapered helical worm, c. 1870. Horn and steel, 3.5" high. Made in France.

79   Basic T corkscrew with contoured cut horn handle secured to a threaded twisted steel shaft by peened top and brass washers and steel pin through sides, helical worm, c. 1880. Steel and horn, 4.25" high. Made in France.

80   Basic T corkscrew with blond buffalo horn handle secured to a threaded turned steel shaft by peened top and steel pin through sides, bladed center worm, nineteenth century. Steel and horn, 4" high. Made in France.

81   Basic T corkscrew with contoured horn handle secured to a threaded smooth steel shaft by fitting and loop atop and three steel pins through sides, bladed center worm, nineteenth century. Steel and horn, 5.5" high. Made in France.

82   Basic T corkscrew with turned bone handle with checker ends and a turned steel shaft secured through the handle with a threaded nut, tapered helical worm, nineteenth century. Steel and horn, 5.5" high. Made in England.

83   Basic T corkscrew with stag-horn handle secured to a threaded turned steel shaft by peened top and copper washer, tapered helical worm, nineteenth century. Steel and horn, 4.5" high. Made in England.

84   Basic T corkscrew with horn handle secured to a threaded turned steel shaft peened atop and brass washers and steel pin through sides, tapered helical worm, c. 1870. Horn and steel, 2.75" high. Made in France.

84

85

86

87

88

89

90

91

85 Basic T corkscrew with horn handle secured to a threaded turned steel shaft peened atop and brass washers and steel pin through sides, helical worm, nineteenth century. Steel and horn, 3" high. Made in France.

86 Basic T corkscrew with brass handle inlaid with horn secured to a threaded turned steel shaft, helical worm, nineteenth century. Brass,

horn and steel, 3" high. Made in France.

87 Basic T corkscrew with green Celluloid and wood laminated handle secured to a threaded turned steel shaft by a steel pin through the handle sides, shaft stamped "A C Paris" (A. Credot), flattened helical worm, c. 1900. Celluloid, wood and steel, 3.75" high. Made in France.

88 Basic T corkscrew with layered steel and horn contoured handle advertising "SIXTINE" on one side and "QUINA BRUNIER" on the other. Handle is secured to a threaded turned steel shaft with three steel pins through sides, helical worm, nineteenth century. Steel and horn, 4" high. Made in France.

89 Basic T corkscrew with shell-inlaid horn handle with two finger indents on bottom and a turned steel shaft secured with a brass washer atop the handle, bladed center worm, late eighteenth century. Buffalo horn, seashell, brass and steel, 4.5" high. Made in France.

90 Basic T corkscrew with contoured cut horn handle secured to a threaded twisted steel

shaft peened atop and brass washers and steel pin through sides, bladed center worm, c. 1880. Steel and horn, 4" high. Made in France.

91 Basic T corkscrew with cut contoured horn handle secured to a threaded turned steel shaft by a steel pin through sides, center worm, nineteenth century. Steel and horn, 4" high. Made in France.

92

93

94

95

92   Straight pull figural handle of Napoleon's bust in hat and overcoat, long rectangular shaft, bladed tapered helical worm, c. 1820. Carved ivory and steel, 6.75" high. Made in France.

93   Figural handle corkscrew with angry cat crouching, smooth shaft, bladed center worm, 1920s. Nickel-plated steel, 5" high. Made in Denmark.

94   Figural handle corkscrew with Bacchus eating grapes, short smooth shaft, bladed center worm, 1920s. Steel, 5" high. Made in Sweden or Denmark.

95   Straight pull corkscrew with carved fruitwood figural boot handle and a silver spur in the shape of a helical worm with smooth shaft, 1955–60. Fruitwood,

silver and steel, 4" toe to spur tip, 3.5" high. "Made in France" stamped on boot sole.

96   Two-finger pull figural corkscrew with cuffed hand holding wreath handle affixed to shaft, cuff ending in brass Henshall button, tapered helical worm, c. 1880. Steel and brass, 5.5" high. Made in England.

97   Two-finger pull figural corkscrew with cast brass buffoon face handle and hole for wall hanging, short tapered shaft, tapered helical worm, twentieth century. Steel and brass, 6" high. Made in England.

98   Figural eyebrow handle corkscrew with baby holding grape bunches, smooth shaft, bladed center worm,

1920s. Nickel-plated steel, 5.25" high. Made in Sweden.

99   Figural straight pull corkscrew with goat-eared horned devil with tail and finely modeled body as handle, rectangular shaft, helical worm as an exaggerated male member, 1999. Silver-plated steel, 5" high. Made in USA.

96

97

98

100 Figural multi-tool corkscrew with Art Deco terrier handle, open mouth as cap-lifter and short shaft with helical worm as the tail. The dog's back foot is stamped with "WHW" in a circle, the Hagenauer symbol and "Made in Vienna Austria", 1930s. Nickel-plated steel, 3.25" high. Made in Austria.

99

100

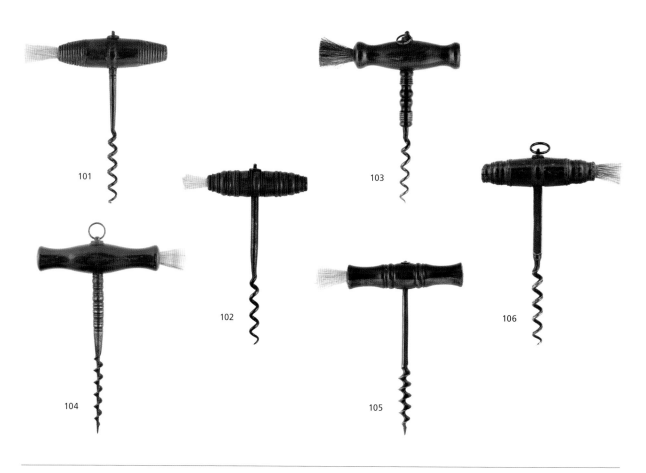

101

103

102

106

104

105

101　Basic T corkscrew with brush-end turned wood handle secured to a threaded tapered turned steel shaft, steel fitting and hole for ring atop, grooved tapered helical worm, nineteenth century. Wood, vegetal fiber and steel, 5.5" high. Made in England.

102　Basic T corkscrew with brush-end turned wood handle secured to a threaded tapered smooth steel shaft, steel fitting and hole for ring atop, tapered helical worm, c. 1860. Wood, vegetal fiber and steel, 5.75" high. Made in England.

103　Basic T corkscrew with brush-end turned wood handle secured to a threaded turned steel shaft, steel fitting and hanging loop atop, tapered helical worm, nineteenth century. Wood, animal fiber and steel, 5.5" high. Made in England.

104　Basic T corkscrew with brush-end turned wood handle secured to a turned steel shaft by a steel washer and a hanging loop atop, Archimedean worm, c. 1850. Wood, vegetal fiber and steel, 6.75" high. Made in England.

105　Basic T corkscrew with brush-end turned wood handle and a long, smooth, steel shaft peened atop a brass washer, bladed center worm, nineteenth century. Wood, vegetal fiber and steel, 5.5" high. Made in England.

106　Basic T corkscrew with brush-end turned wood handle secured to a threaded square steel shaft (stamped "warranted"), steel fitting and hanging loop atop, tapered grooved helical worm, c. 1860. Wood, vegetal fiber and steel, 6.5" high. Made in England.

107　(at right) Basic T corkscrew with brush-end turned wood handle secured to a turned steel shaft, steel washer atop, Archimedean worm, c. 1850. Boxwood, vegetal fiber and steel, 5.5" high. Made in England.

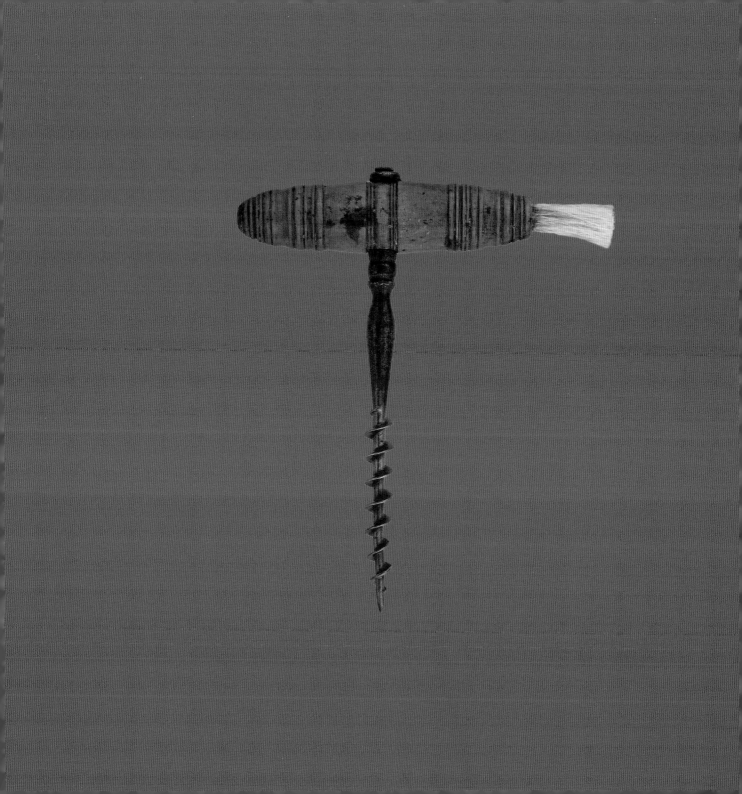

BASIC T TOOL FEATURE HANDLES

Each of the corkscrews on this spread have a tool or tools on the handle or shaft to assist in opening a bottle.

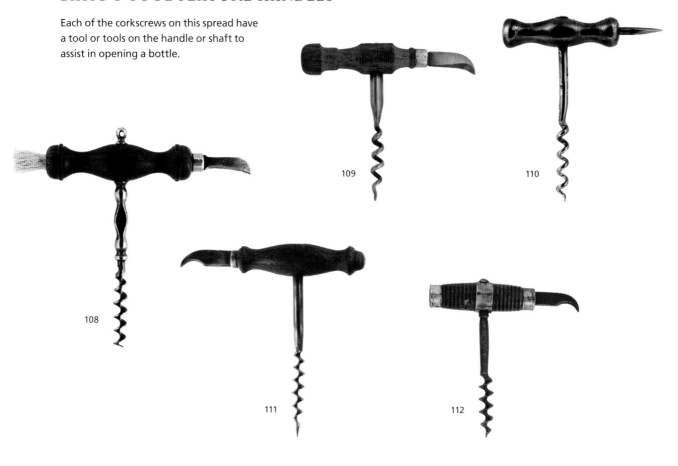

108   Basic T corkscrew with acorn-tipped turned wood handle (inset brush on one end and brass collared foil cutter knife on the other) and a threaded turned steel shaft attached by a brass loop fitting atop, bladed center worm, nineteenth century. Wood, fiber, brass and steel, 6.5" high. Made in USA.

109   Basic T corkscrew with turned wood handle and brass-collared, serrated foil cutter knife stamped "S.H.CO. [Simmons Hardware Company, St. Louis, Missouri] No 1 Original Package", tapered steel shaft secured by a steel pin running through center of the handle with peened fitting, helical worm, 1890. Wood, brass and steel, 4.5" high. Made in USA.

110   Basic T corkscrew with steel handle with pick tip on one end, the other to be used to tap the cork back into the bottle, smooth steel shaft and washer peened atop, tapered helical worm, c. 1890. Nickel-plated steel, 5.25" high. Made in England.

111   Basic T corkscrew with turned wood handle and steel-collared foil cutter knife on one end, slightly tapered steel shaft secured by a long steel pin running from tip to tip of the handle, bladed center worm, nineteenth century. Wood, brass and steel, 5.5" high. Made in USA.

112   Basic T corkscrew with turned boxwood handle with a nickel-plated, brass-collared, steel foil cutter knife on one end, a nickel-plated brass cap on the other and a nickel-plated brass band at center. The turned shaft is secured through the handle by a peened fitting, bladed center worm, c. 1900. Wood, brass and steel, 4.5" high. Made in France.

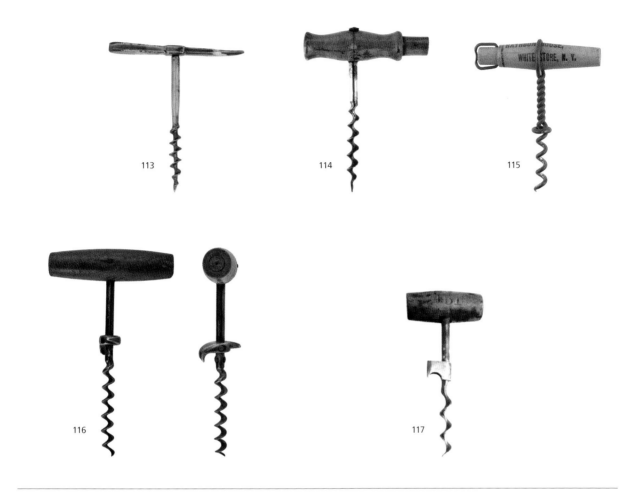

113 Basic T corkscrew
with left-handed foil
cutter knife blade on a
steel handle, smooth
tapered shaft, Archime-
dean worm, made by
J. Perille, Paris, c. 1890.
Nickel-plated steel,
4.25" high. Made in
France.

114 Basic T corkscrew
with Codd bottle opener
on one end of a turned
wood handle secured to a
smooth steel shaft peened

atop a steel washer. The
Codd bottling system
employed a molded
bottle neck to keep a glass
marble and rubber gasket
in place when filled
with carbonated liquids.
Pouring the beverage
entailed pressing down
on the marble and gasket
to break the seal, bladed
center worm, Roper
patent, 1881. Boxwood
and steel, 4.75" high.
Made in England.

115 Basic T corkscrew
made from one steel
wire. The printed turned
wood handle has a Codd
bottle opener and wire
cap-lifter on one end and
advertises "RATHBUN
HOUSE WHITESTORE, N.Y."
also stamped "TRADE
(DECAPITATOR) MARK"
and "WRC WIRE
CAPLIFTER PAT. MAR,1
1910", twisted wire shaft
with button, helical worm,
Clough patent, Williamson

manufacturer, 1910. Steel
and wood, 4.25" high.
Made in USA.

116 Basic T corkscrew
with wood handle secured
to a threaded smooth steel
shaft stamped "WILLIAM-
SON'S". A wire breaker
and cap-lifter is fitted just
above the center worm,
c. 1900. Wood and steel,
6" high. Made in USA.

117 Basic T "Walker
Hallboy" corkscrew with
plain turned wood handle
stamped "TOT" and a
smooth shaft with steel
cap-lifter affixed, speed
worm, 1897. Steel and
wood, 4.75" high. Made
in USA.

4 *Take Me Along*
FOLDING AND POCKET PORTABLE

As an avid observer of the New York City scene, I am frequently captivated by birds nesting in the slim interstices between signs and buildings, tiny spaces afforded by fire escape attachments, holes in the decorative tin cornices of nineteenth-century apartment houses and unimaginable apertures in new buildings. These are all above the reach of pedestrians, sometimes by a slim margin. Some birds are risk takers. I am keenly aware of this phenomenon; it's a preoccupation that can be likened to my radar for finding corkscrews that show a surprising nuance of ingenuity.

On a Saturday afternoon walk in April 2001, my daughter, Amie, and I stopped in a drugstore on Broadway in busy SoHo. The store's door was propped open. We made our selections and while we were standing on one of five checkout lines at the front of the store, a sparrow flew in and took a left turn between my face and the back of the head of the woman in front of me, then dropped in a kamikaze dive into the basket of merchandise on the floor that was about to be shelved. Amie incredulously said, "Did you see that?" I was astonished, mesmerized. The woman in front of us said, "See what?" I said, "A bird flew in the door, into that basket and died." The line moved up and the woman didn't even glance toward the basket. She must have thought she should have kept her mouth shut, proving to herself, once again, that talking to strangers was risky business. Only Amie and I saw that bird's polyvalent moment, which I treasure as one of the extreme visuals of my life.

I liken that revelation to my dumbstruck response and great luck at finding, in a coffee can filled with pieces of metal hardware, bolts and wingnuts, at a flea market for four dollars, an eighteenth-century folding double-hinged, cut-steel pipe-tamp corkscrew with a firestriker pattern on its handle. To date, this is one of the earliest pocket corkscrews in my collection.

118 (at left) Folding figural corkscrew with mermaid with long tresses, scales and hands at her breast as handle, lever stamped "Henry Boker", pivot shaft, helical worm, c. 1890. Steel and pressed Celluloid with paint, 4.25" high. Made in Germany. (See other views on page 57.)

Many inventive adjustments to handles and shafts to accommodate the worm for portage in one's pocket (without piercing anything but the intended cork) occurred after the shortcomings of the basic T and Finger Pull concepts became apparent. Of course the earlier corkscrews were a godsend for those who enjoyed wine, but improvements could be made, and they were. This chapter looks closely at orders and suborders of ingenuity from folding bows and folding finger pulls, pegs and worms, sheaths and worms, collapsing case handles, to roundlets, slides, folding multi-tools, folding scissors styles and pocket figurals, all of which rendered their bearers ready to open a bottle and consequently equipped to be the life of the party. Ever handy, Waiter's Friends, with their folding lever assists, brought—and are still bringing—most restaurant occasions to the peak of their potential.

EARLY FOLDING DOUBLE HINGE

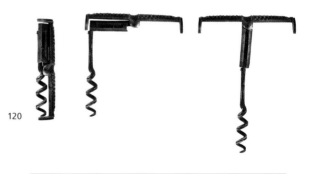

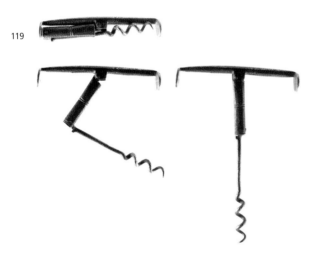

119 Folding double-hinged corkscrew with pipe tamp ends and traces of cut steel firestriker pattern on handle and incised steel shaft, helical worm, c. 1810. Steel, 4.5" high in fully open position. Made in England.

120 Folding double-hinged corkscrew with pipe tamp ends and cut steel firestriker pattern on handle and incised steel shaft, grooved helical worm, c. 1810. Steel, 3.75" high in fully open position. Made in England.

FOLDING BOWS

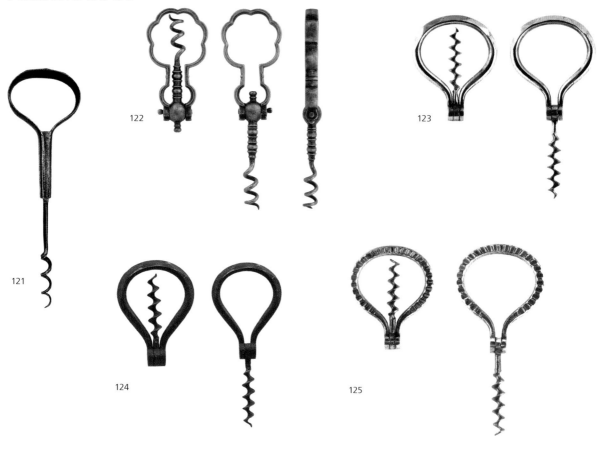

121   Folding bow corkscrew with handle faceted at top, incised bands at long sides and a locking tapered pivot shaft, grooved helical worm, c. 1740. Steel, 6" open. Made in England.

122   Folding ornate bow corkscrew with decorative scalloped grooves accommodating two fingers, pinned ball and turned steel shaft ending in concave handle pivots, short tapered helical worm, c. 1770. Steel, 2.75" closed, 4.75" open. Made in France.

123   Folding faceted nickel-plated steel bow corkscrew, grooved locking cylinder shaft, bladed center worm with close pitch, c. 1880. Nickel-plated steel, 2.75" closed, 4.25" open. Made in England.

124   Folding bow corkscrew with faceted handle and grooved locking hinge, locking pivot shaft, bladed center worm, early nineteenth century. Steel, 2.25" closed, 3.5" open. Made in England.

125   Folding nickel-plated steel bow corkscrew with coggled handle and grooved locking cylinder shaft, bladed center worm with close pitch, c. 1880. Nickel-plated steel, 2.5" closed, 4.5" open. Made in England.

FOLDING BOWS

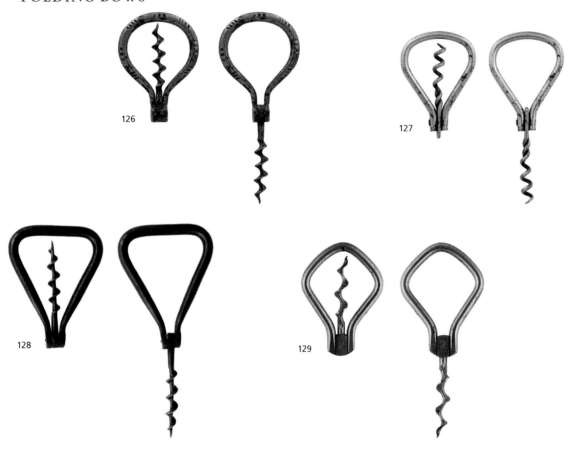

126 Folding bow corkscrew with cut steel glyphs on handle and a grooved locking hinge, locking pivot shaft, center worm, early nineteenth century. Steel, 3.75" closed, 5" open. Made in England.

127 Folding bow corkscrew with pinned locking hinge and twisted wire shaft, helical worm, nineteenth century. Steel, 3" closed, 4.5" open. Made in England.

128 Folding bow corkscrew with grooved locking hinge, locking pivot shaft, tapered Archimedean worm, nineteenth century. Steel, 3.25" closed, 5.5" open. Made in England.

129 Folding bow corkscrew with pinned and grooved rectangular locking shaft with maker's monogram "AKA", speed worm, twentieth century. Nickel-plated steel, 3" closed, 5" open. Made in Germany.

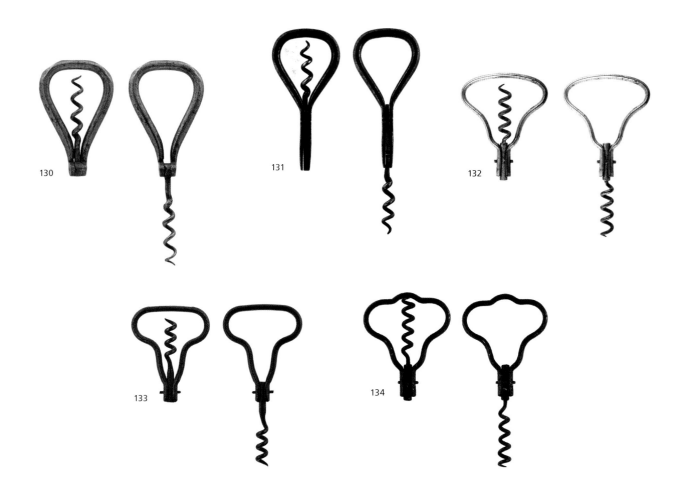

130   Folding bow corkscrew with faceted handle and grooved locking hinge, locking pivot shaft, tapered helical worm, early nineteenth century. Steel, 3" closed, 5.25" open. Made in England.

131   Cut steel folding bow corkscrew with pivoting hinge and a cut steel pivot shaft. In closed position, the shaft and handle are a carriage key, tapered helical worm, early nineteenth century. Steel, 3.75" closed, 5.25" open. Made in England.

132   Folding bow corkscrew with three-finger space in handle and a pinned cylinder shaft ending in a concave handle pivot, helical worm, Havell patent, 1855. Steel, 2.75" closed, 4.25" open. Made in USA.

133   Folding bow corkscrew with pinned cylinder shaft ending in concave handle pivot, helical worm, Havell patent, 1855. Steel, 2.75" closed, 4.25" open. Made in USA.

134   Folding bow corkscrew with three finger grooves and a pinned cylinder shaft ending in a concave handle pivot, helical worm, Havell patent, 1855. Steel, 2.75" closed, 4.5" open. Made in USA.

FOLDING BOW MULTI-TOOLS

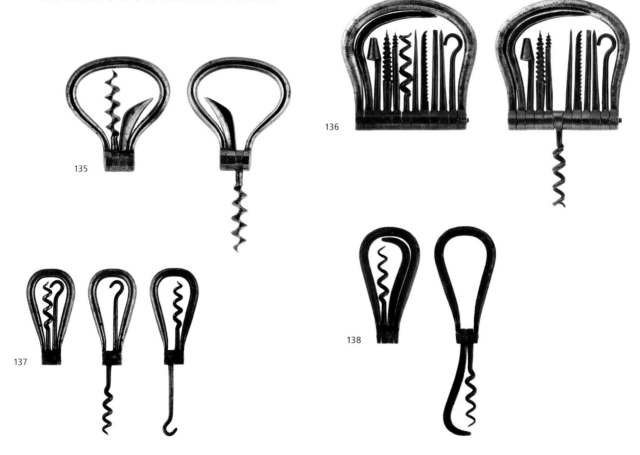

135   Folding nickel-plated steel bow corkscrew with hawkbill foil cutter, pivot shaft locked by pinned grooved hinges, bladed center worm, nineteenth century. Steel, 2.75" closed, 4.5" open. Made in England.

136   Folding steel bow multi-tool corkscrew stamped "Edwards & Sons 161 Regent St." with ten tools (hoof pick, leather punch, auger, gimlet, worm, awl, saw, chisel, screwdriver, button hook), pinned grooved locking hinges, locking pivot shaft, grooved helical worm, nineteenth century. Steel, 2.75" closed, 5" open. Made in England.

137   Folding steel bow corkscrew with button hook, pinned grooved locking hinges, locking pivot shaft, tapered helical worm, nineteenth century. Steel, 2.25" closed, 3.5" open. Made in England.

138   Folding steel bow corkscrew with hoof pick, pinned grooved locking hinges, locking pivot shaft, tapered helical worm, nineteenth century. Steel, 2.25" closed, 5" open. Made in England.

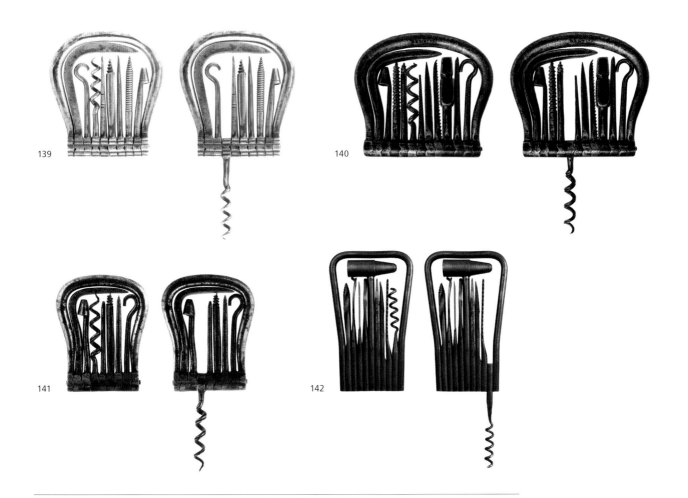

139   Folding faceted steel bow corkscrew with eight tools (hoof pick, button hook, worm, screwdriver, gimlet, awl, auger, leather punch), pinned grooved locking hinges, locking pivot shaft, helical worm, nineteenth century. Steel, 2.75" closed, 5" open. Made in England.

140   Folding steel bow multi-tool corkscrew stamped "BB Wells" (Benjamin Blake Wells) with eleven tools (hoof pick, leather punch, auger, gimlet, grooved worm, awl, squared point, saw, carriage key, chisel, button hook), pinned grooved locking hinges, locking pivot shaft, grooved helical worm, nineteenth century. Steel, 2.75" closed, 5" open. Made in England.

141   Folding steel bow corkscrew stamped "53 Haymarket Holzapfel" with seven tools (hoof pick, leather punch, worm, pick, gimlet, screwdriver, button hook), pinned grooved locking hinges, locking pivot shaft, tapered grooved helical worm, nineteenth century. Steel, 3" closed, 4.75" open. Made in England.

142   Folding steel bow multi-tool corkscrew with nine tools (gimlet, nail puller, knife, cap-lifter, hammer, slot screwdriver, punch, saw, worm), pinned grooved locking hinges, locking pivot shaft, helical worm, Strauss patent, 1949. Steel, 3.5" closed, 5.25" open. Made in Germany.

FOLDING SINGLE LEVERS & WAITER'S FRIENDS

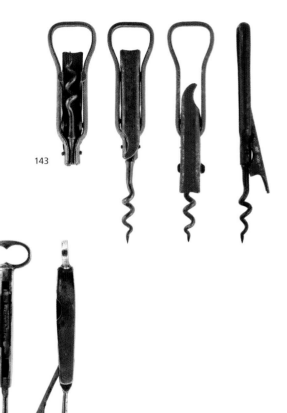

143

144

145

143 Folding lever corkscrew stamped "Universal" with pinned locking cylinder pivot shaft and worm which folds into a pivoting footed lever/foil cutter stamped "Universal JUNE27 '05–JULY3 '06". After the footed lever has been firmly planted on the bottle lip and the worm has penetrated the cork, downward pressure must be exerted on the handle to raise the cork. The finger-pull may then be used to lift the cork away from the bottle, helical worm, Noyes patent, c. 1906. Steel, 4.5" closed, 6.5" open. Made in USA.

144 Folding finger-pull corkscrew with long hollow center shank housing, footed lever with pivot shaft and worm with locking cylinder pivot shaft, bladed center worm, c. 1900. Steel, 4.5" closed, 6.5" open. Made in France.

145 Folding finger-pull corkscrew with lever and worm nested in long hollow center shank with two pivots, smooth pivot shaft, close pitch bladed center worm overlaying footed lever stamped "Bechon-Morel B.S.G.D.G.",* 1877. Steel, 4.5" closed, 6.75" open. Made in France.

* B.S.G.D.G. stands for Breveté Sans Garantie Du Gouvernement.

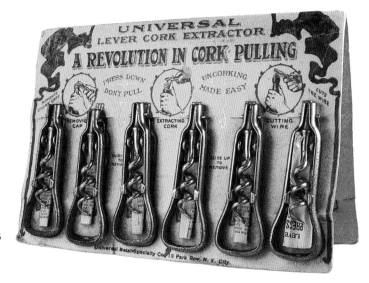

146

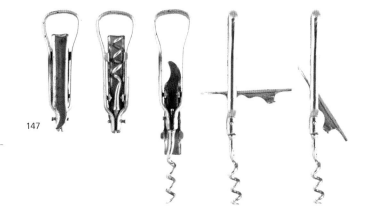

147

146   Twelve "UNIVERSAL" folding lever corkscrews and instructions on two-sided display card, 1910. 9" high. Made in USA.

147   Folding lever corkscrew stamped "Universal" with pinned locking cylinder pivot shaft, pivoting footed lever/foil cutter stamped "Universal JUNE27 '05–JULY3 '06". After the footed lever has been firmly planted on the bottle lip and the worm has penetrated the cork, downward pressure must be exerted on the handle to raise the cork. The finger-pull may then be used to lift the cork away from the bottle, Noyes patent, c. 1910. Steel, 3.5" closed, 5.75" open. Made in USA.

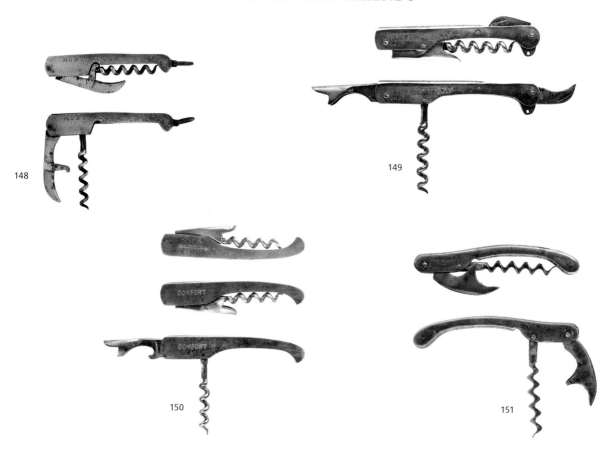

148

149

150

151

148   Folding corkscrew with steel handle and pivot link, advertising "MONT ROUGE WINES", footed foil cutter and worm nest in handle, pivoting rectangular shaft, helical worm, Steinfeld patent, c. 1899. Steel, 4.5" closed, 3" open. Made in Germany (for California winemaker that was in business from mid-nineteenth century through Prohibition).

149   Folding corkscrew advertising "Piper Heidsieck BRUT" with a contoured steel handle, in which the foil cutter and worm nest, and a link fitting for hanging ring affixed. The worm and pivot shaft are locked into place when the footed neckstand lever (stamped "Germany") is closed, helical worm, 1885. Steel, 5" closed, 3" open. Made in Germany.

150   Folding corkscrew with neckstand lever and a contoured handle stamped on arrow shaft "SDR" (Severin R. Doescher, NYC importer) on one side and "COMFORT" on the other, pivot shaft, helical worm locked in place when neckstand lever is closed, 1883. Steel, 4.25" closed, 3" open. Made in Germany.

151   Folding corkscrew with neckstand lever and a contoured handle stamped "The Davis Cork Screw Pat'd July 14, 1891", pivot shaft, center worm, 1891. Steel, 4.25" closed, 3.25" open. Made in USA.

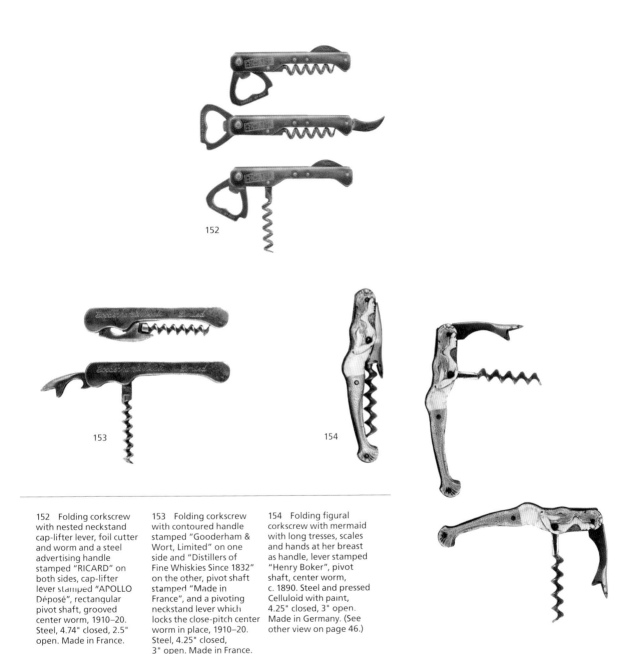

152   Folding corkscrew
with nested neckstand
cap-lifter lever, foil cutter
and worm and a steel
advertising handle
stamped "RICARD" on
both sides, cap-lifter
lever stamped "APOLLO
Déposé", rectangular
pivot shaft, grooved
center worm, 1910–20.
Steel, 4.74" closed, 2.5"
open. Made in France.

153   Folding corkscrew
with contoured handle
stamped "Gooderham &
Wort, Limited" on one
side and "Distillers of
Fine Whiskies Since 1832"
on the other, pivot shaft
stamped "Made in
France", and a pivoting
neckstand lever which
locks the close-pitch center
worm in place, 1910–20.
Steel, 4.25" closed,
3" open. Made in France.

154   Folding figural
corkscrew with mermaid
with long tresses, scales
and hands at her breast
as handle, lever stamped
"Henry Boker", pivot
shaft, center worm,
c. 1890. Steel and pressed
Celluloid with paint,
4.25" closed, 3" open.
Made in Germany. (See
other view on page 46.)

FOLDING MULTI-TOOLS

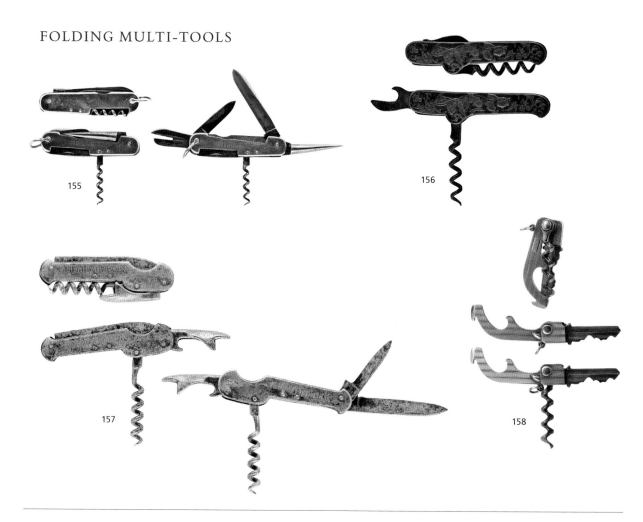

155   Corkscrew in steel folding multi-tool handle with loop for hanging from belt (two knife blades, screwdriver, nail puller, pointed punch), blades stamped "Henry Barnascone, Sheffield", rectangular pivot shaft, tapered helical worm, handle stamped "Girl Guides", early twentieth century. Steel, 3.75" closed, 2.5" open. Made in England.

156   Corkscrew in folding, well-used cast brass multi-tool handle (two knife blades, foil cutter/ cap-lifter and corkscrew), square pivoting shaft, grooved helical worm, c. 1890. Brass and steel, 3.5" closed, 2.75" open. Made in France.

157   Corkscrew in steel folding multi-tool handle (two knife blades, screwdriver, cap-lifter/ lever), rectangular pivot shaft, grooved helical worm, handle stamped "St Raphael Quinquina", early twentieth century. Steel, 3.5" closed, 3" open. Made in France.

158   Folding corkscrew with a handle in two parts, a steel key half and a 14K gold cap-lifter/cigar box pry half (engraved "WDM" and stamped "PAT. FEB. 23, 1926") with a key chain ring, pivoting shaft, center worm, McLean patent, 1926. Steel, 2" closed, 1.75" open. Made in USA.

159   (at right) Corkscrew in ivory covered steel folding multi-tool handle (two knife blades, button hook, gimlet, pick), blades stamped "Vulcan Sheffield", rectangular pivot shaft, grooved helical worm, nineteenth century. Ivory and steel, 2" closed. Made in England.

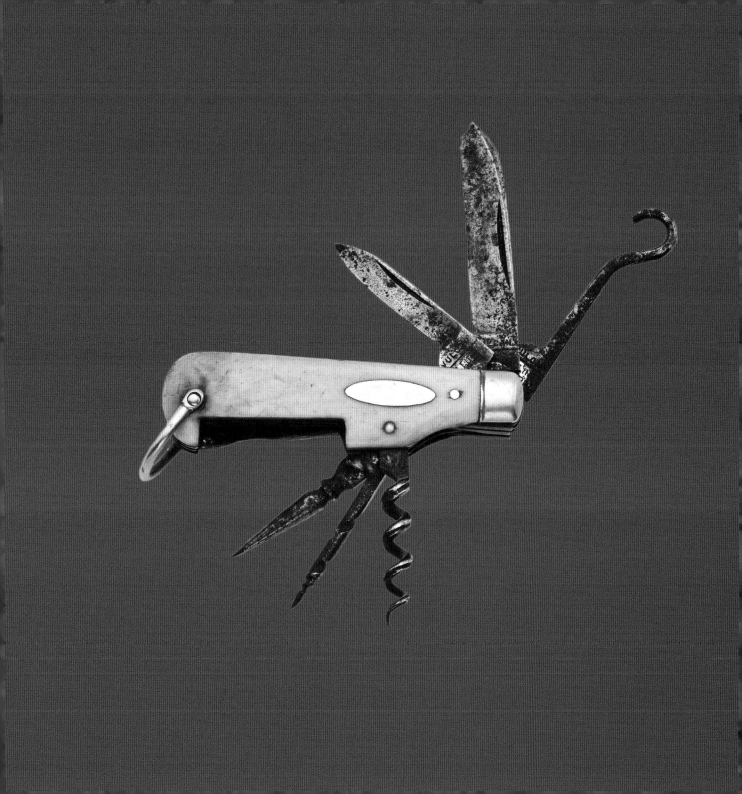

FOLDING MULTI-TOOLS

160   Corkscrew in steel folding multi-tool handle (foil cutter serrated knife blade, triggered serrated screw-top opener, neckstand, cap-lifter, worm), rectangular pivot shaft, helical worm, handle printed "DRYLANDS", 2008. Stainless steel, 7.5" closed, 7.5" high open. Made in USA.

161   Folding corkscrew with teaspoon handle advertising remedies, stamped "Tabloids of compressed drugs, Hazeltine Cream, Kepler Extract & Essence of Malt. Kepler Solution of Cod Liver Oil. Digestive, Demulgent, Strengthening. Hazeltine Beef and Iron Wine", pivot shaft, helical worm, Williamson patent, 1882. Stamped nickel-plated steel, 2.75" closed, 4" open. Made in USA.

162   Folding Williamson corkscrew with cap-lifter handle advertising liquor store, stamped "DIAL 3-3410 - M. & T LIQUORS, INC.", pivot shaft, helical worm, 1900. Stamped nickel-plated steel, 2.5" closed, 2.75" open. Made in USA.

163   Folding multi-tool corkscrew with carriage key and foil cutter handle, double pivot shaft, helical worm, c. 1900. Nickel-plated steel, 2.25" closed, 2.25" open. Made in England.

FOLDING SCISSORS STYLE

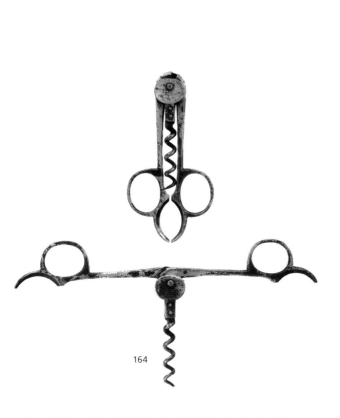

164

165

166

164 Folding steel corkscrew with scissors-style notched wire/foil cutter handles, pinned pivot shaft, helical worm, Wesche & Ruppelt patent, 1904. Nickel-plated steel, 4.25" closed, 4.25" open. Made in Germany.

165 Folding steel corkscrew with scissors-style notched handles marked "BERTON" and "Déposé", which (with corkscrew pivoted into position) becomes wire cutter and cigar cutter, pivot shaft, tapered helical worm, nineteenth century. Steel, 4" closed, 6.75" open. Made in France.

166 Folding steel corkscrew with scissors-style notched wire cutter handles, pinned pivot shaft marked "GMS No10985", helical worm, Thiel & Kull patent, c. 1890. Steel, 4" closed, 3.25" open. Made in Germany.

167

167   Cut steel sheath handle corkscrew with turned steel shaft and a close pitch tapered helical worm; sheath and shaft are threaded to screw closed, c. 1800. Steel, 3" high assembled for use, 3.5" high closed. Made in England.

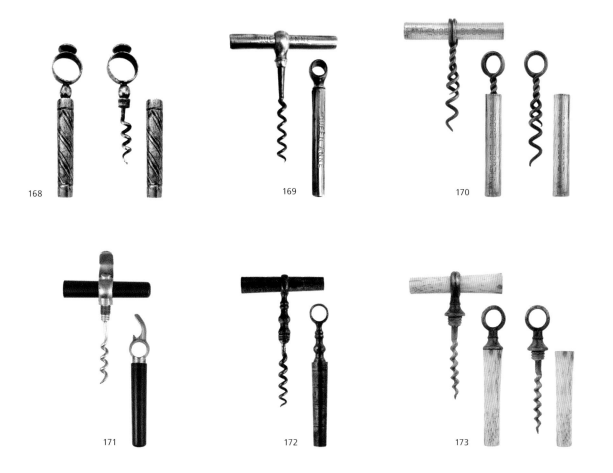

168   Ring pull sheath and worm corkscrew, intaglio seal of mounted swordsman with drawn sword attached to top of ring, ball and threaded shank, smooth shaft and tapered helical worm. The threaded sheath is turned in a spiral design, c. 1780–1820. Steel, 4" closed, 3.25" ring & worm. Made in England.

169   Sheath handle corkscrew stamped "QUEEN ANNE SCOTCH WHISKEY" with brass sheath handle and nickel-plated steel ring, smooth shaft, tapered helical worm, Clough patent, c. 1920. Steel, nickel-plated steel, brass, 3.75" assembled for use. Made in USA.

170   Brass sheath handle corkscrew, advertising "Anheuser-Busch", with nickel-plated steel ring, twisted wire shaft and duplex helix worm, Clough patent, c. 1920. Steel, nickel-plated steel and brass, 3" assembled for use. Made in USA.

171   Bakelite sheath handle corkscrew, threaded steel shaft with ring and cap-lifter end, helical worm, c. 1920. Bakelite and steel, 3.25" assembled for use. Made in England.

172   Sheath handle corkscrew, turned steel shaft with ring and close pitch tapered helical worm, c. 1800. Steel, 4" assembled for use. Made in England.

173   Bone sheath handle (with threaded end) and corkscrew with steel ring, threaded shank, smooth round shaft and center worm, c. 1890. Steel and bone, 3.25" assembled for use. Made in England.

174

175

176

174 Finger-pull corkscrew with printed wood sheath advertising "D. Germanus, Family Liquor Dealer 228 Morrison Avenue Portland, Oregon" with telephone numbers, nickel-plated steel single-wire corkscrew, twisted wire shaft, helical worm, Clough patent, c. 1920. Wood and nickel-plated steel, 3" closed. Made in USA.

175 Single-wire finger-pull corkscrew within printed wood sheath advertising "TRY DAVIS 100 PERCENT PURE RYE IT'S ALL WHISKEY DAVIS BIG MAIL ORDER HOUSE OAKLAND, MD. THE CINCI BOTTLERS SUPPLY CO. CIN.", twisted wire shaft with button, helical worm, Clough patent, c. 1920. Wood and nickel-plated steel, 3.75" closed. Made in USA.

176 Two-finger pull corkscrew made from one wire, wire handle, twisted shaft with button, helical worm, cylinder sheath stamped "Germany", Clough patent, c. 1874. Nickel-plated steel, 3.25" closed. Made in Germany.

177 (at right) "All-ways" combination corkscrew with single-wire finger-pull in printed wood sheath advertising "Compliments of FOURTH AVENUE BOTTLE HOUSE, ANDREW NELSON, Prop. 2714 North Avenue, MILWAUKEE, WIS." and in very small type "J.M. Miller Milwaukee, Wis. patented April 30 1901", and doubling as handle when inserted into the pull ring; multi-tool (stopper lifter, foil cutter and cap-lifter) at one end, twisted wire shaft, helical worm, Miller patent, Clough patent, 1901. Wood and nickel-plated steel, 2.75" assembled for use. Made in USA. The remains of the box from "The 'ALL-WAYS' HANDY COMBINATION Bottle Opener & Corkscrew" describe the multiple uses.

PAT. APRIL 30, 1901, OCT. 16, 1900.

THE
"ALL-WAYS"
HANDY
COMBINATION
BOTTLE OPENER & CORKSCREW.

CORK
SCREW

Pulling a Cork

Taking out
Aluminum Stopper

Removing a Seal

Lifting a Crown Cap

NO TWO WAYS
ABOUT THIS BEING USEFUL, IT'S USEFUL
FOUR WAYS

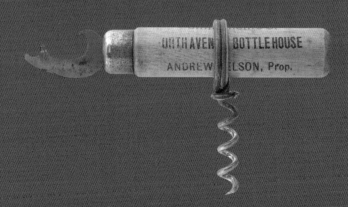

10TH AVENUE BOTTLE HOUSE

ANDREW NELSON, Prop.

179

178

178   Figural key sheath and worm corkscrew with three-finger pull handle, threaded shaft and sheath with built-in cap-lifter, bottom of sheath marked "Aubock", bladed center worm, c. 1950. Copper and steel, 4.75". Made in Austria.

179   Key to the City of Bremen sheath and worm corkscrew with key top handle, smooth shaft, and bladed center worm, c. 1950. Silver and steel, 5". Made in Germany.

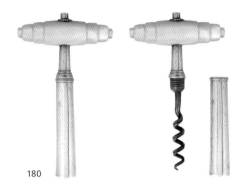

180

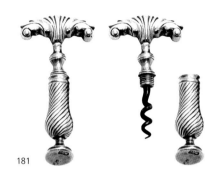

181

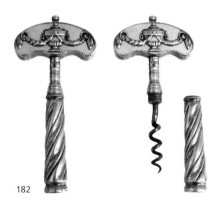

182

183

180 Basic T corkscrew with symmetrically stepped carved mother-of-pearl handle and silver sheath (with finely decorated neck) for pocket portability. The handle has a silver shank and a finely decorated silver cap atop, threaded steel shaft, tapered grooved helical worm, c. 1800. Silver, steel and mother-of-pearl, 3.25" closed, 3" open. Made in England.

181 Silver corkscrew with scroll-tipped contoured fluted handle, turned silver shank, smooth steel shaft and tapered helical worm, maker's mark stamped on bottom of threaded pipe tamp sheath, c. 1780. Silver and steel, 3" closed, 2" open. Made in Holland.

182 Silver corkscrew with contoured crescent shaped handle inset with mother-of-pearl and applied silver urn and swags, turned threaded silver shank, smooth steel shaft and tapered helical worm, maker's mark on twisted rope-pattern sheath, 1830. Steel, silver and mother-of-pearl, 3.5" closed, 3" open. Made in England.

183 Silver corkscrew with turned green-stained ivory handle with silver bands, turned silver shank, threaded steel shaft and a tapered grooved helical worm, likely made by Samuel Pemberton of Birmingham, c. 1820. Silver, ivory and steel, 3.5" closed, 3.25" open. Made in England.

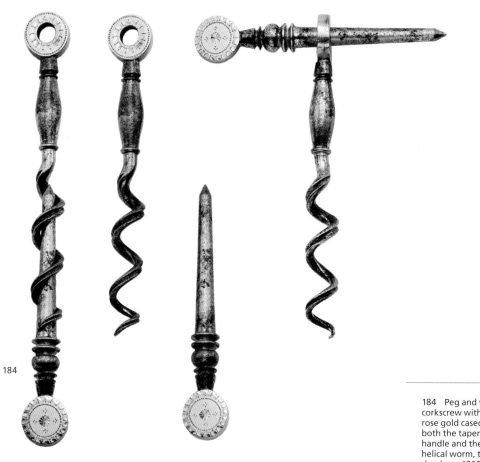

184

184 Peg and worm corkscrew with bright, cut rose gold cased finials on both the tapered peg handle and the grooved helical worm, turned steel shanks, c. 1800. Gold & steel, 3.25" with peg inserted into worm, 2.25" assembled for use. Made in England.

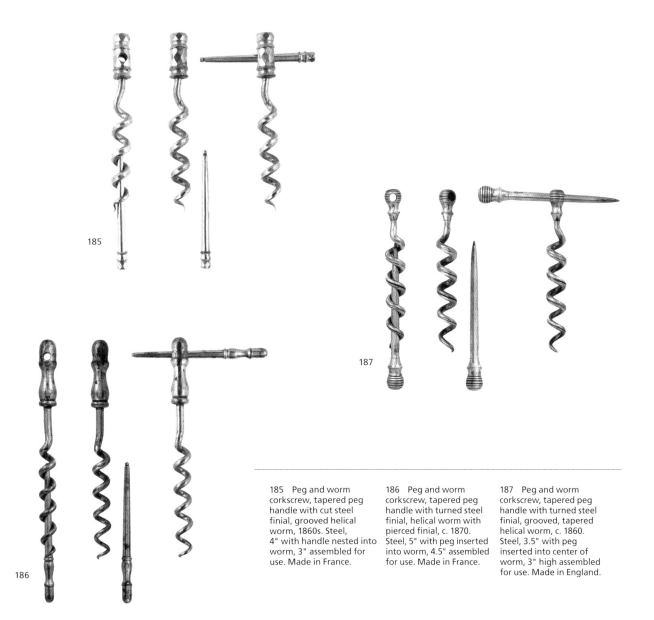

185 Peg and worm corkscrew, tapered peg handle with cut steel finial, grooved helical worm, 1860s. Steel, 4" with handle nested into worm, 3" assembled for use. Made in France.

186 Peg and worm corkscrew, tapered peg handle with turned steel finial, helical worm with pierced finial, c. 1870. Steel, 5" with peg inserted into worm, 4.5" assembled for use. Made in France.

187 Peg and worm corkscrew, tapered peg handle with turned steel finial, grooved, tapered helical worm, c. 1860. Steel, 3.5" with peg inserted into center of worm, 3" high assembled for use. Made in England.

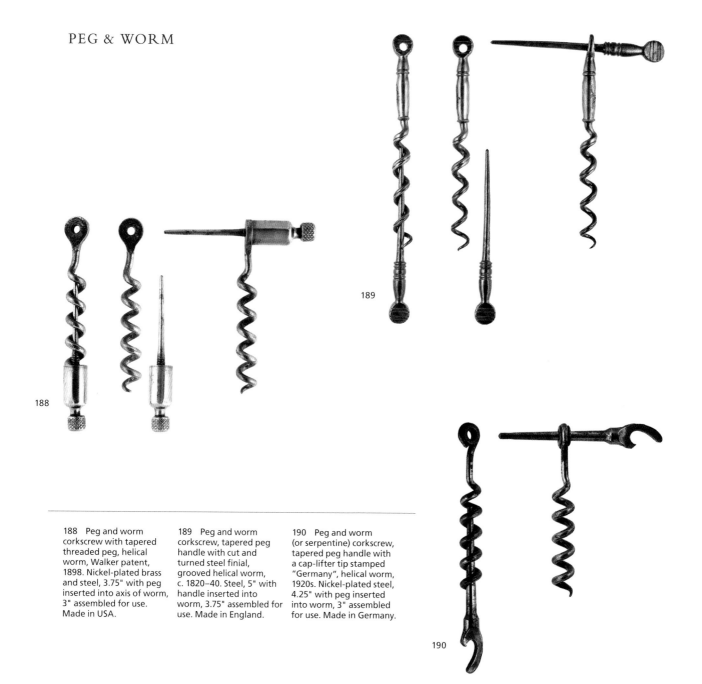

189

188

190

188 Peg and worm corkscrew with tapered threaded peg, helical worm, Walker patent, 1898. Nickel-plated brass and steel, 3.75" with peg inserted into axis of worm, 3" assembled for use. Made in USA.

189 Peg and worm corkscrew, tapered peg handle with cut and turned steel finial, grooved helical worm, c. 1820–40. Steel, 5" with handle inserted into worm, 3.75" assembled for use. Made in England.

190 Peg and worm (or serpentine) corkscrew, tapered peg handle with a cap-lifter tip stamped "Germany", helical worm, 1920s. Nickel-plated steel, 4.25" with peg inserted into worm, 3" assembled for use. Made in Germany.

FOLDING CASE HANDLES

191

192

193

194

191   Folding T corkscrew with case handle stamped "Patent Angemeldet, Made Abroad, Patent Applied For", square pivot shaft with a double pivot top, center worm, Hollweg patent, 1891. Nickel-plated steel, 2.75" closed, 2.75" assembled for use. Made in Germany.

192   Folding corkscrew with clamping brass clamshell case handles, turned steel shaft with

knob finial, and helical worm, 1880s. Brass and steel, 2.75" closed, 2.5" assembled for use. Made in USA.

193   Folding steel case handle T corkscrew, stamped advertising "PABST Milwaukee", tapered smooth pivot shaft with double pivot top, bladed center worm, Hollweg patent, 1891. Steel, 3.25" closed, 3.25" assembled for use. Made in Germany.

194   Folding corkscrew with rosewood and steel case handles, double pivot shaft stamped on one side "THEO G STONER Washington DC" and "GERMANY" on the other side, bladed center worm, 1894. Rosewood and steel, 2.5" closed, 2.5" assembled for use. Made in Germany.

FOLDING CASE HANDLES

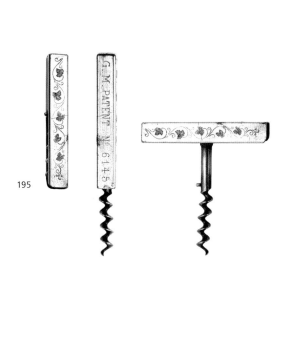

195

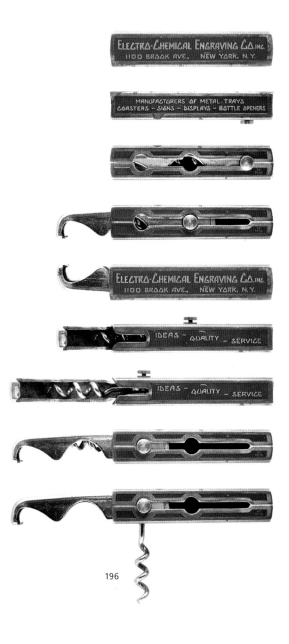

196

195 Folding retractile case handle corkscrew showing and engraved grape leaf pattern and "G.M. No 6145" on sides. The retracting bladed center worm, when exposed, slides into a functional right angle to the handle, Jansen patent, 1892. Steel, 3" closed, 3" assembled for use. Made in Germany.

196 Folding retractile corkscrew with enameled case handle (release button on one face and advertising on others) and extendable slide with a finger indent (and cap-lifter) as the second half of the handle,

pivoting smooth shaft attached to the button, retracting helical worm, Andrews patent pending, 1932. Enameled steel, 2.5" closed, 1.75" high with 4" handle assembled for use. Made in USA.

197 (at right) Roundlet, or barrel, corkscrew with two-part threaded silver floral handle (stamped "Cartier" [hallmark] and "STERLING") which locks the steel shaft and tapered helical worm into a square notch, its functional place at right angles to the handle, 1873. Silver, brass steel, 3.5" high, 3.5" long. Made in USA.

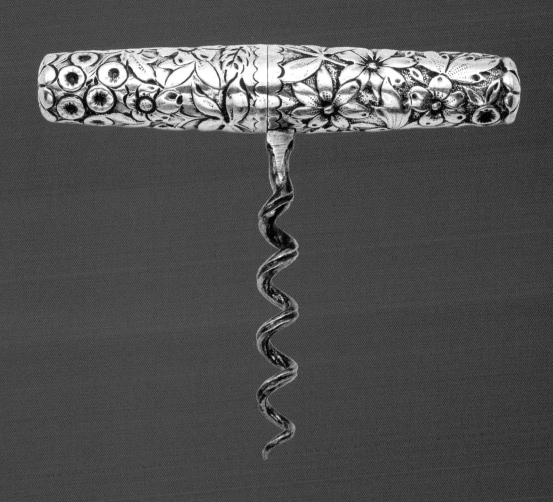

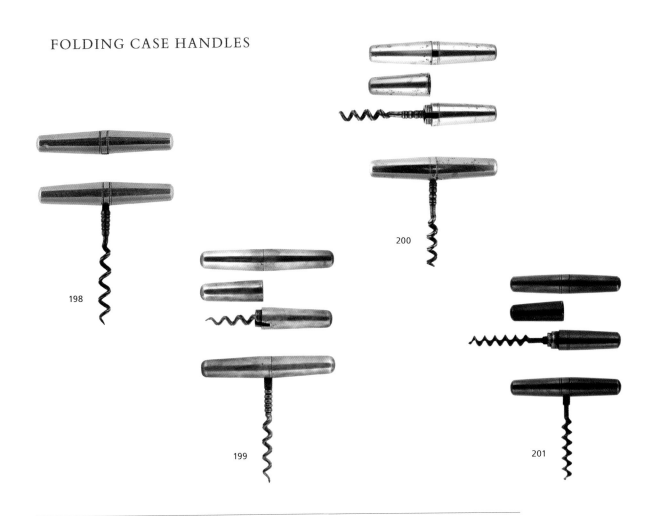

198

199

200

201

198 Roundlet, or barrel, corkscrew with two-part threaded handle with central square notch at the bottom edge. A turned steel shaft, grooved helical worm pivots from a brass flange in one side of the handle into the central notch, locking it into its functional place at right angles to handle, 1873. Steel, brass and nickel-plated steel, 3.5" closed, 3.5" assembled for use. Made in England.

199 Roundlet, or barrel, corkscrew with two-part threaded silver handle and a turned steel shaft, grooved helical worm. The worm pivots from a brass flange in one side of barrel, locking into its functional place at right angles to handle, 1873. Silver, brass and steel, 3.25" closed, 3.5" assembled for use. Made in England.

200 Roundlet, or barrel, corkscrew with two-part threaded silver handle and a turned steel shaft, grooved helical worm. The worm pivots from a brass flange in one side of barrel, locking into its functional place at right angles to handle, 1873. Silver and brass steel, 3.25" closed, 2.75" assembled for use. Made in England.

201 Roundlet, or barrel, corkscrew with two-part threaded handle and a center worm which pivots from steel flange in one side of barrel, locking into its functional place at right angles to handle, 1873. Steel, 2.75" closed, 2.5" assembled for use. Made in England.

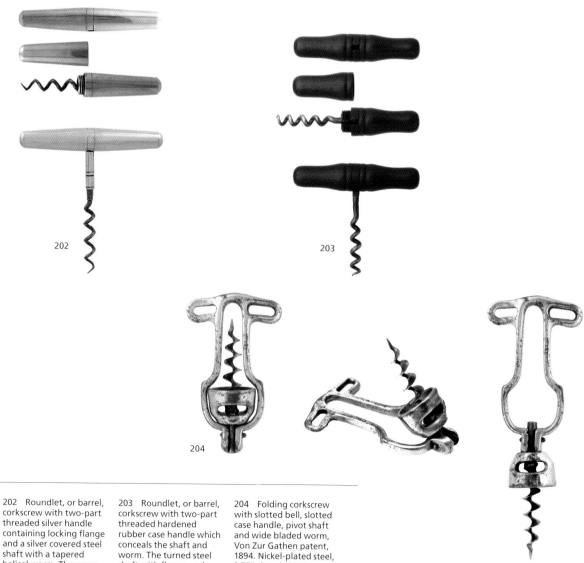

202   Roundlet, or barrel, corkscrew with two-part threaded silver handle containing locking flange and a silver covered steel shaft with a tapered helical worm. The worm fits into a square notch at right angles to handle, 1873. Silver and brass steel, 3.5" closed, 3.5" assembled for use. Made in England.

203   Roundlet, or barrel, corkscrew with two-part threaded hardened rubber case handle which conceals the shaft and worm. The turned steel shaft with flange and helical worm pivot into a square notch at right angles to handle for use, Goodyear patent, 1851. Hardened rubber and steel, 2.75" closed, 2.75" assembled for use. Made in USA.

204   Folding corkscrew with slotted bell, slotted case handle, pivot shaft and wide bladed worm, Von Zur Gathen patent, 1894. Nickel-plated steel, 3.75" closed, 6.75" assembled for use. Made in Germany.

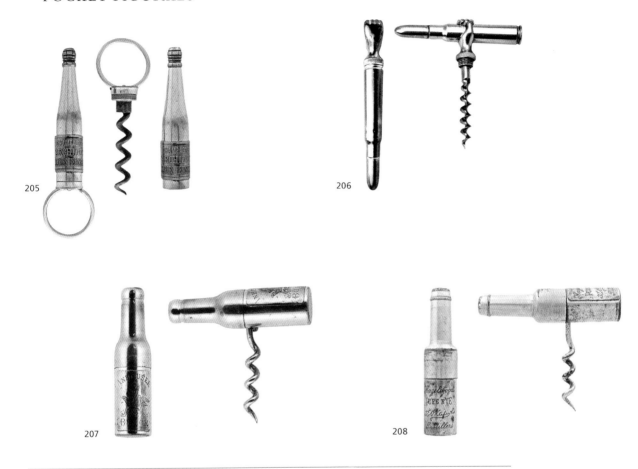

205

206

207

208

205   Pocket figural finger-pull corkscrew with threaded bottle case, brass cork detail and faux brass label stamped "CHAMPAGNE 'ARCHDUC' CHARLES HEIDSIECK", tapered helical worm, c. 1900. Worn nickel-plated brass and steel, 3.75" closed. Made in France.

206   Sheath and worm corkscrew with 9mm Mannlicher bullet handle and a smooth shaft topped by a threaded hand-shaped ringmount catching the bullet mid-flight when assembled, bladed center worm, Pfeffer & Weber patent, 1898. Nickel-plated brass, 3.25" closed, 4" assembled for use. Made in Germany.

207   Bottle handle folding figural corkscrew with copper faux label engraved "Anheuser Busch" and logo, "Williamson Co. Patented June 1, '97 Newark, NJ" stamped on bottom, pivoting helical worm, 1897. Worn nickel-plated brass, engraved brass and nickel-plated steel, 2.75" closed, 2.5" assembled for use. Made in USA.

208   Folding figural bottle handle corkscrew with brass faux label engraved "HAZELWOOD PURE RYE T.E. O'KEEFE DISTILLERS" and stamped on bottom "Williamson Co. Patented June 1, '97 Newark, NJ", pivoting helical worm, 1897. Worn nickel-plated brass, engraved brass and nickel-plated steel, 3" closed, 2.75" assembled for use. Made in USA.

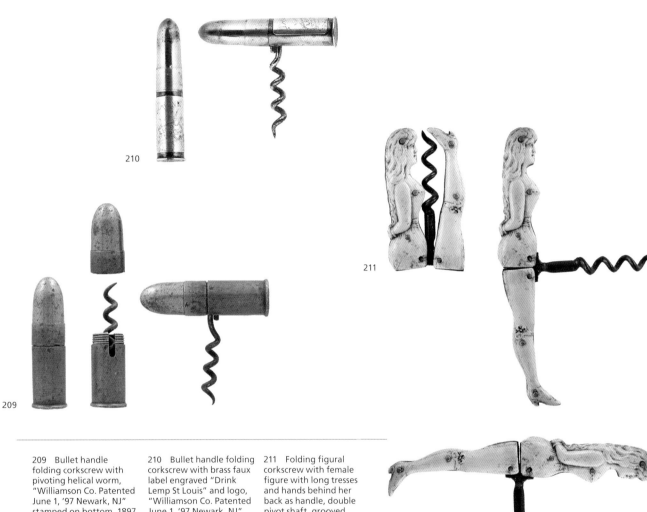

209   Bullet handle folding corkscrew with pivoting helical worm, "Williamson Co. Patented June 1, '97 Newark, NJ" stamped on bottom, 1897. Worn nickel-plated brass, engraved brass and nickel-plated steel, 2.75" closed, 2.5" assembled for use. Made in USA.

210   Bullet handle folding corkscrew with brass faux label engraved "Drink Lemp St Louis" and logo, "Williamson Co. Patented June 1, '97 Newark, NJ" stamped on bottom, pivoting helical worm, 1897. Worn nickel-plated brass, engraved brass and nickel-plated steel, 3" closed, 2.5" assembled for use. Made in USA.

211   Folding figural corkscrew with female figure with long tresses and hands behind her back as handle, double pivot shaft, grooved helical worm, c. 1890. Pressed Celluloid and steel, 2.5" folded, 5" by 3" assembled for use. Made in Germany.

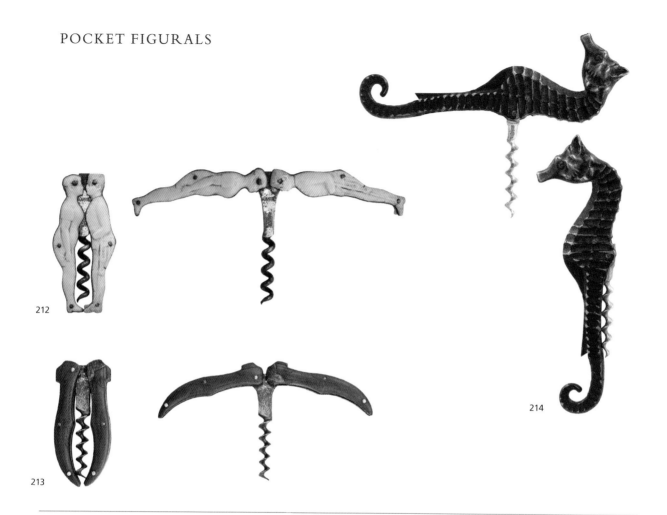

212

213

214

212 Folding facing couple corkscrew with soldier in uniform wearing sword and woman lifting her skirt as handle, double pivot shaft stamped "AMOR" on one side and "D.R.G.M. 105407"* on the other side, helical worm, Bewer patent, 1898. Pressed Celluloid, brass and steel, 2.75" closed, 5.75" by 2.75" assembled for use. Made in Germany.

213 Folding "Dandy" model corkscrew with Celluloid pair of shoes handle, double pivot shaft, bladed center worm, Steinfeld patent, 1897. Celluloid and steel, 2.5" closed, 2.5" assembled for use. Made in Germany.

214 Seahorse handle folding corkscrew with cap lifter tail, pivot shaft and center worm, c. 1950. Cast brass and steel, 5.5" closed, 4" assembled for use. Made in Germany.

215 (at right) Folding corkscrew with mother-of-pearl legs and stamped steel boot handles in half-open position, double pivot shaft stamped "D. Peres Germany", bladed center worm, 1894. Mother-of-pearl and steel, 2.75" from toe to hip. Made in Germany. (See other views on page 81.)

* D.R.G.M. stands for Deutsches Reichsgebrauchs-muster.

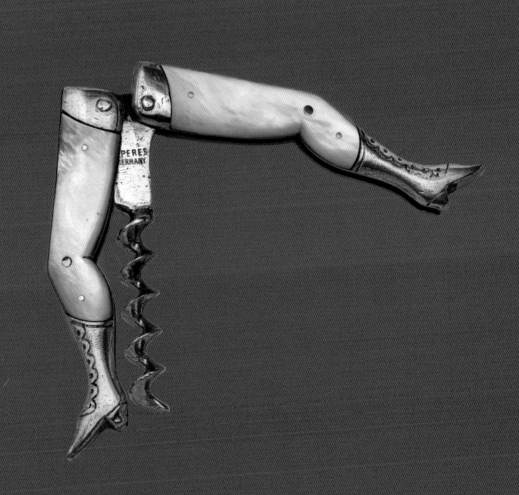

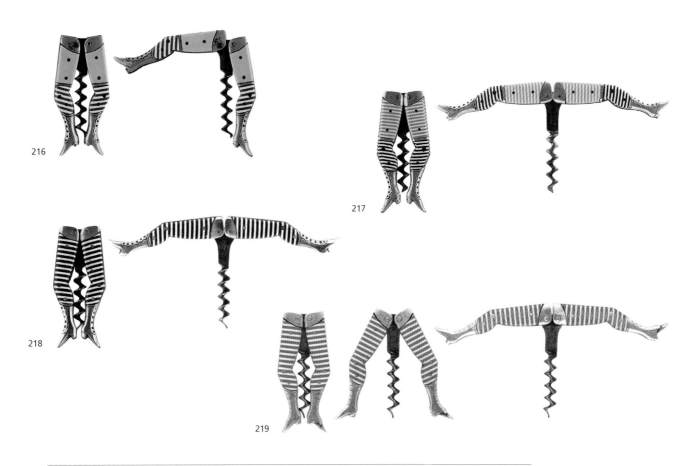

216 Folding corkscrew with blue and white striped Celluloid stockings, naked thighs and stamped steel boots as handle, double pivot shaft marked "Comfort S.R.D." (Severin R. Doescher, NYC importer) on one side and "Germany" on the other, bladed center worm, Steinfeld & Reimer patent, 1894. Celluloid and steel, 2.75" closed, 2.5" assembled for use. Made in Germany.

217 Folding corkscrew with two-tone striped Celluloid stockings and stamped steel boots as handle, double pivot shaft stamped "SRD" on arrow shaft (Severin R. Doescher, NYC importer) and "Germany", bladed center worm, Steinfeld & Reimer patent, 1894. Celluloid and steel, 2.75" closed, 2.5" assembled for use. Made in Germany.

218 Folding corkscrew with blue and white striped Celluloid stockings and stamped steel boots as handle, double pivot shaft stamped "Graef & Schmidt" on one side and "Germany" on the other, bladed center worm, Steinfeld & Reimer patent, 1894. Celluloid and steel, 2.75" closed, 2.5" assembled for use. Made in Germany.

219 Folding corkscrew with pink and white striped Celluloid stockings and stamped steel boots as handle, double pivot shaft stamped advertising "Val Blatz Brg Co. Made in Germany", bladed center worm, Steinfeld & Reimer patent, 1894. Celluloid and steel, 2.75" closed, 2.5" assembled for use. Made in Germany.

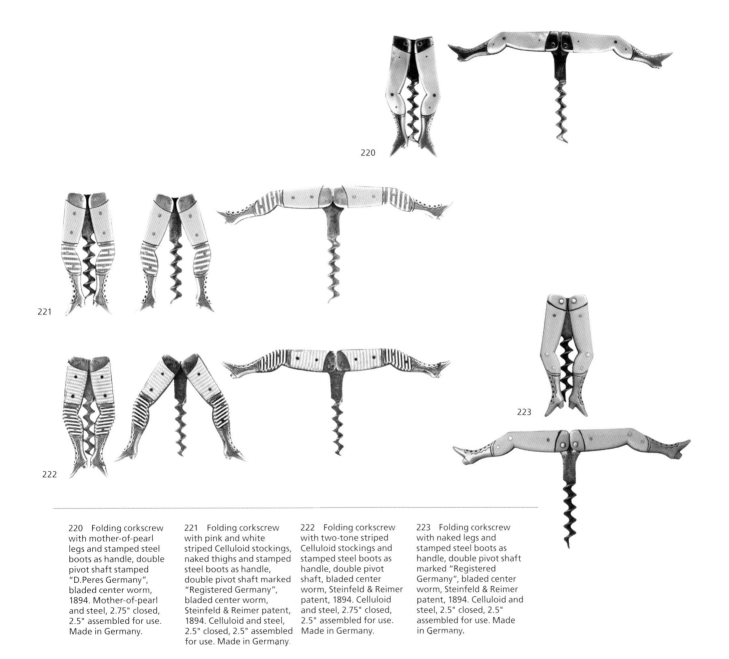

220 Folding corkscrew with mother-of-pearl legs and stamped steel boots as handle, double pivot shaft stamped "D.Peres Germany", bladed center worm, 1894. Mother-of-pearl and steel, 2.75" closed, 2.5" assembled for use. Made in Germany.

221 Folding corkscrew with pink and white striped Celluloid stockings, naked thighs and stamped steel boots as handle, double pivot shaft marked "Registered Germany", bladed center worm, Steinfeld & Reimer patent, 1894. Celluloid and steel, 2.5" closed, 2.5" assembled for use. Made in Germany.

222 Folding corkscrew with two-tone striped Celluloid stockings and stamped steel boots as handle, double pivot shaft, bladed center worm, Steinfeld & Reimer patent, 1894. Celluloid and steel, 2.75" closed, 2.5" assembled for use. Made in Germany.

223 Folding corkscrew with naked legs and stamped steel boots as handle, double pivot shaft marked "Registered Germany", bladed center worm, Steinfeld & Reimer patent, 1894. Celluloid and steel, 2.5" closed, 2.5" assembled for use. Made in Germany.

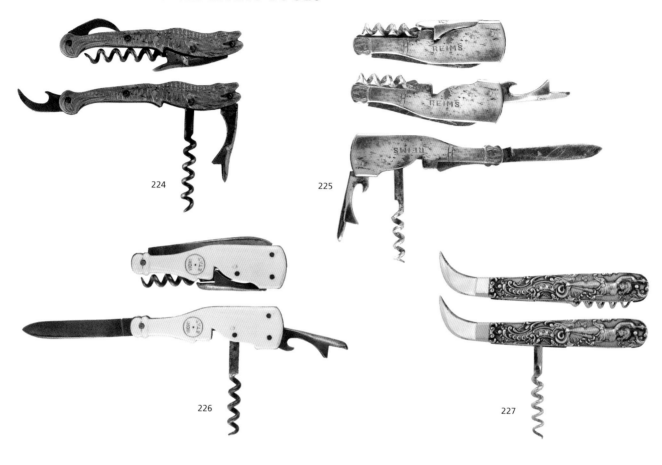

224

225

226

227

224   Folding corkscrew with Celluloid and iridescent paint alligator handle, wire cutter and footed lever stamped "Germany" below four-leaf clover logo on one side and "W.H.MORLE[Y] & SONS" (US importer) on the other, rectangular pivot shaft and helical worm, c. 1890. Pressed Celluloid

with paint and nickel-plated steel, 4.25" closed, 3" assembled for use. Made in Germany.

225   Folding multi-tool corkscrew with nickel-plated steel bottle handle marked "REIMS" on one side, "CHAMPAGNE HENRI ABELE" on the other, knife blade and a cap-lifter/lever which locks the worm stamped

"Made in FRANCE" with "A S" in oval logo, rectangular pivot shaft, squared helical worm, c. 1900. Nickel and steel, 3.5" closed, 3" assembled for use. Made in France.

226   Folding multi-tool corkscrew (with knife blade and cap-lifter/lever that is lock for worm), ivory Celluloid and steel bottle handle advertising

"VICHY ETAT" in circle logo on one side, rectangular pivot shaft and helical worm, c. 1890. Celluloid and steel, 3.75" closed, 3.25" assembled for use. Made in France.

227   Folding corkscrew with cast silver multi-tool handle depicting a nubile nude raising a glass while holding a sinuous grapevine and standing on

elaborate volute, stamped "STERLING" on reverse, stamped "Hudson Knife Co. GERMANY" on foil cutter collar, rectangular pivoting shaft, tapered helical worm, c. 1890. Sterling silver and steel, 5" closed, 2.75" assembled for use. Made in USA.

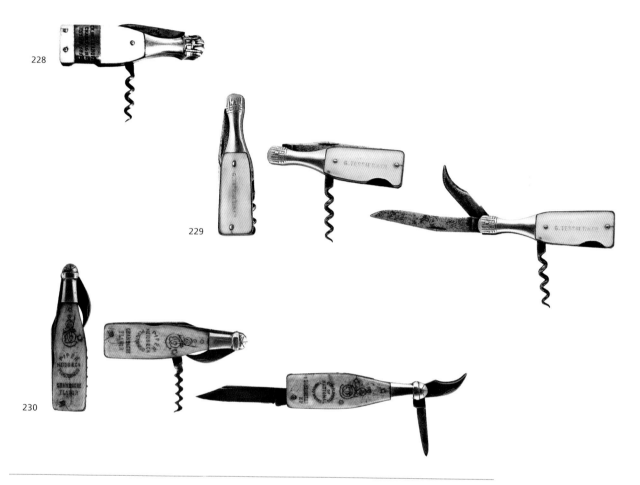

228   Folding multi-tool corkscrew with Champagne bottle shaped handle marked with inset label "Ch. De Cazanove Champagne est. 1811", carbon steel master blade and hawkbill foil cutter marked "Sauzedde Biat", pivot shaft, helical worm, c. 1890. Ivory, silver and steel, 3.5" closed, 3" assembled for use. Made in France.

229   Folding multi-tool corkscrew (knife blade and foil cutter) with ivory and steel Champagne bottle handle advertising "G. Tessier & Cie" on both sides, pivot shaft, tapered helical worm, c. 1890. Ivory and steel, 3.25" closed, 2.25" assembled for use. Made in France.

230   Folding multi-tool corkscrew (two knife blades and foil cutter) with bone and steel Champagne bottle handle advertising "Piper Heidsieck Plug Tobacco Champagne Flavor" on one side, "Compliments of National Tobacco Works Louisville, Ky." on the other, pivot shaft, tapered helical worm, Korn patent, c. 1890. Bone and steel, 3.25" closed, 2.25" assembled for use. Made in USA.

POCKET FIGURAL
MULTI-TOOLS

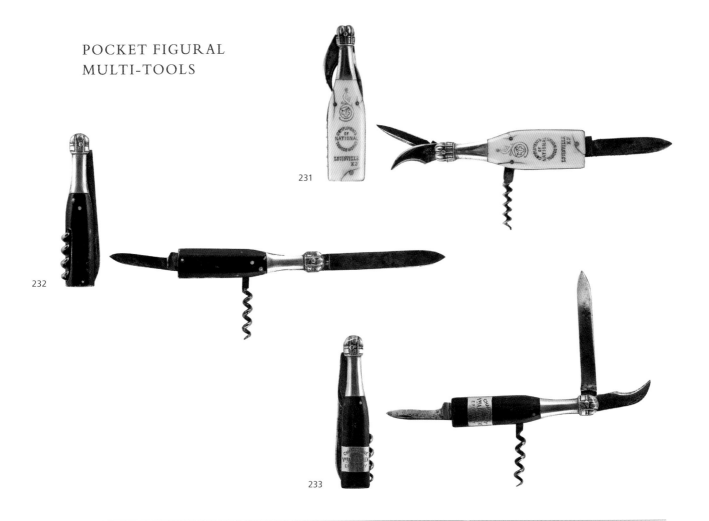

231

232

233

231 Folding multi-tool corkscrew (two knife blades and foil cutter) with Ivorine and steel Champagne bottle handle advertising "Piper Heidsieck Plug Tobacco Champagne Flavor" on one side, "Compliments of National Tobacco Works Louisville, Ky." on the other, pivot shaft, center worm, Korn patent, c. 1900. Ivory and steel, 3.25" closed, 2.75" assembled for use. Made in USA.

232 Folding multi-tool corkscrew (two knife blades, maker's mark and "12" on larger blade) with horn and nickel-plated steel Champagne bottle handle, pivot shaft, helical worm, c. 1885. Horn, nickel-plated steel and steel, 3.25" closed, 2.75" assembled for use. Made in France.

233 Folding multi-tool corkscrew (two knife blades and wire cutter blade) with horn and nickel-plated steel Champagne bottle handle marked "Champagne Vve. A. Devaux Epernay", pivot shaft, tapered helical worm, c. 1885. Horn, nickel-plated steel and steel, 3.25" closed, 2.5" assembled for use. Made in France.

234 Folding multi-tool corkscrew (wire cutter blade and knife blade stamped "92" in oval) with horn and nickel-plated steel Champagne bottle handle marked in faux label "AMY FRERES, SAUMUR", pivot shaft, tapered helical worm, 1885. Horn, nickel-plated steel and steel, 3.25" closed, 2.5" assembled for use. Made in France.

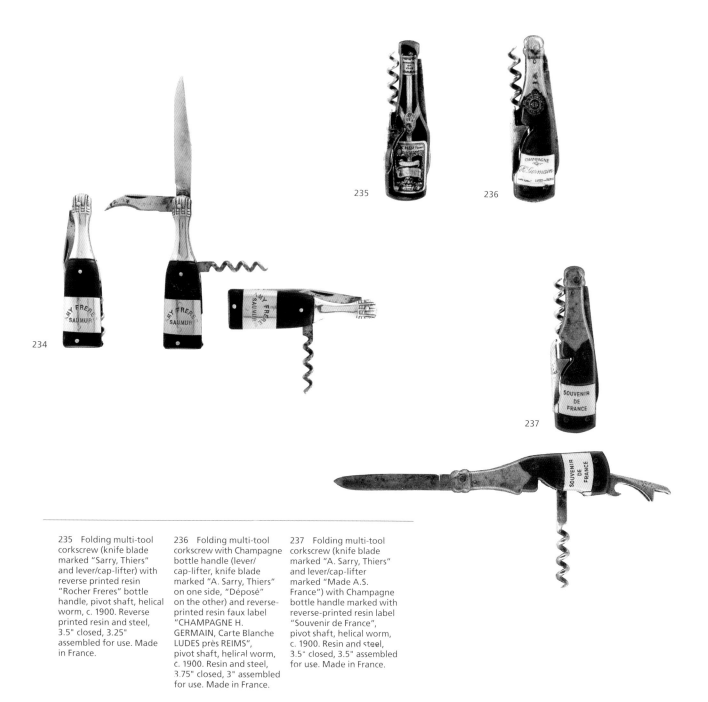

235 Folding multi-tool corkscrew (knife blade marked "Sarry, Thiers" and lever/cap-lifter) with reverse printed resin "Rocher Freres" bottle handle, pivot shaft, helical worm, c. 1900. Reverse printed resin and steel, 3.5" closed, 3.25" assembled for use. Made in France.

236 Folding multi-tool corkscrew with Champagne bottle handle (lever/cap-lifter, knife blade marked "A. Sarry, Thiers" on one side, "Déposé" on the other) and reverse-printed resin faux label "CHAMPAGNE H. GERMAIN, Carte Blanche LUDES près REIMS", pivot shaft, helical worm, c. 1900. Resin and steel, 3.75" closed, 3" assembled for use. Made in France.

237 Folding multi-tool corkscrew (knife blade marked "A. Sarry, Thiers" and lever/cap-lifter marked "Made A.S. France") with Champagne bottle handle marked with reverse-printed resin label "Souvenir de France", pivot shaft, helical worm, c. 1900. Resin and steel, 3.5" closed, 3.5" assembled for use. Made in France.

POCKET FIGURAL MULTI-TOOLS

238

239

240

238 Folding multi-tool corkscrew (two knife blades) with mother-of-pearl and steel Champagne bottle handle, pivot shaft stamped "J. D." between crossed swords, bladed center worm, c. 1890. Mother-of-pearl and steel, 3.5" closed. Made in Germany.

239 Folding multi-tool corkscrew (with two knife blades, marked "ROBt. KLASS OHLIGS SOLINGEN" with two storks on tang of large blade), "AUG. KAPSREITER SCHARDING SOLINGEN" on tang of small blade), silver and horn bottle shaped handle, pivot shaft, center worm, c. 1900. Silver and steel, 3.5" closed, 2" assembled for use. Made in Germany.

240 Folding multi-tool corkscrew (knife blade and cap-lifter/lever that is lock for worm) with nickel-plated steel bottle handle stamped "LE VIGNERON RESTAURANT REIMS", rectangular pivot shaft, squared helical worm, c. 1900. Nickel and steel, 3.5" closed, 3.25" assembled for use. Made in France.

241 Folding multi-tool corkscrew (with knife blade and hawkbill foil cutter, blade marked "S.L." on tang), nickel-plated bottle handle marked "CHAMPAGNE" on both sides, pivot shaft, tapered helical worm, c. 1900. Nickel and steel, 3.25" closed, 2.5" assembled for use. Made in France.

242 Folding corkscrew with female leg and ankle-strapped ballet slipper as handle, rectangular pivoting shaft, lever/cap-lifter stamped "THE DETROIT PATD. JULY 1894", center worm. Nickel-plated steel, 4.25" closed, 3.25" assembled for use. Made in USA.

241

242

243

243 Folding figural
corkscrew with lever and
wire cutter and a mermaid
with long tresses, scales
and hands at her breast
as the handle, pivot shaft
stamped "Germany"
below leaf logo, helical
worm, c. 1890. Pressed
Celluloid with paint and
steel, 4.25" closed,
4" assembled for use.
Made in Germany.

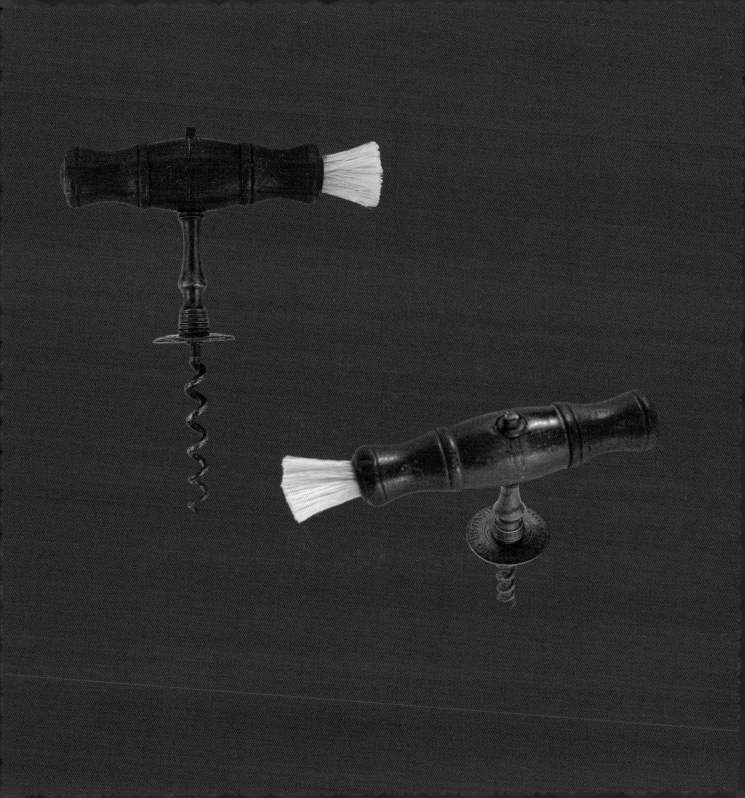

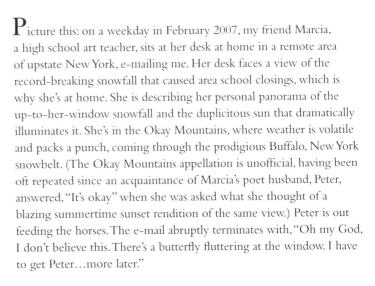

5 The Better Mousetrap: Deus Ex Machina
FINESSE AIDS THE PULL

244 (at left and above) Reverend Samuel Henshall's 1795 patented straight pull corkscrew with turned rosewood handle and a brush for clearing the bottle top of debris before drawing the cork. The handle is secured to a threaded balustered shaft with a steel fitting and a hole for ring atop, tapered helical worm with a domed button is marked "OBSTANDO PROMOVES – SOHO PATENT" which means "by standing firm, one moves forward." Henshall's patent was the first English patent for a corkscrew, 1795. Wood, vegetal fiber and steel, 5.75" high. Made in England.

Picture this: on a weekday in February 2007, my friend Marcia, a high school art teacher, sits at her desk at home in a remote area of upstate New York, e-mailing me. Her desk faces a view of the record-breaking snowfall that caused area school closings, which is why she's at home. She is describing her personal panorama of the up-to-her-window snowfall and the duplicitous sun that dramatically illuminates it. She's in the Okay Mountains, where weather is volatile and packs a punch, coming through the prodigious Buffalo, New York snowbelt. (The Okay Mountains appellation is unofficial, having been oft repeated since an acquaintance of Marcia's poet husband, Peter, answered, "It's okay" when she was asked what she thought of a blazing summertime sunset rendition of the same view.) Peter is out feeding the horses. The e-mail abruptly terminates with, "Oh my God, I don't believe this. There's a butterfly fluttering at the window. I have to get Peter…more later."

In her follow-up e-mail she told me that the caramel-colored butterfly was a newly emerged Harris' Checkerspot, certainly misguided in its response to the sunshine's booby trap, a doomed awakening. Double doomed. Before Marcia was able to get to her door, the unfortunate *Chlosyne harrisii* was devoured by a local cat on the hunt. The cat acted on a window of opportunity, albeit improbable and went on to the next feline issue. That's the nature of the beast.

The Checkerspot caterpillar, genetically destined to hibernate, had picked a place in propitious relationship to the sun, and destiny unfolded. This specific butterfly had survived the vicissitudes of the larval and then the pupal stages, averting death by starvation, desiccation and parasites. It made it through the snowstorm that closed all the schools in that sector of the state. Yet its checkerspotted camouflage didn't even have a trial run.

The taking of the Checkerspot and its swift, throwaway end may be likened to the unceremonious uncorking and crude swilling of a well-kept, aged Grands Échezeaux by a teenaged babysitter.

The chain of circumstance leading to the dramatic demise of the butterfly could not have been plotted or imagined before it happened. It could never have been predicted, nor could the blazing humdinger of a century of invention of corkscrew patents, the sparkling ingenuity of which can be credited to the corkscrew innovations shown in this chapter. Their inventors were unconventional reasoners, synthesizers of information from arcane angles. Each of these corkscrews materialized in the mind of a risk taker; an ingenious tool is not just the sum of its parts. We can literally observe ingenious tweaks accrue to the next innovation.

Mechanical corkscrews, by a small addition to basic corkscrew anatomy, finesse the pull. This enabling bit needn't move independently of the handle, shaft or worm. It simply has to be there. Although basic corkscrews had been in use since the early 1700s, the first corkscrew patent, issued to Samuel Henshall in 1795, was for a button he added on the shaft of a basic T corkscrew. When the worm penetrated the cork to the level of the button, it turned the cork in the bottle neck, breaking its crusted hold and enabling easier drawing of the cork. This plain small disk was a big idea, leading directly to patents for concave buttons, serrated buttons, grooved buttons, toothed buttons and daisy buttons.

During the nineteenth and early twentieth centuries, patents abounded in France, England, Germany and the United States. Corkscrew inventiveness exploded in a wild array of improbable devices, resolving the cork barrier. Unanticipated contrivances yielded spring barrels, split barrels and slide rings, bells and

245

closed frames, open frames, coffee cranks, threaded shafts and fly nuts, rack and pinion devices, complex single and double levers, two-part levers, concertinas and lazy tongs. This cacophony of "improved versions" was the result of singular sidewise envisionings of an old problem in a new way. Some are rare, others are not, but taken as a whole, this galaxy of desirable, novel and prized objects inhabits the past tense. Many were truly iconoclastic conceptions in their moment. Others nabbed an idea and tweaked it in an innovative way that aided function; the conception of some others seems remote and bewildering.

245 Mechanical corkscrew with figural open frame of two standing children, decorative cast silver handle, spring-assisted steel shank, short smooth shaft, bladed center worm, Thüringen manufacturer, c. 1910. Silver and steel, 6.5" high. Made in Germany.

246 Basic T corkscrew with a turned wood handle with brass collared foil cutter knife tip on one end and brush on the other, turned steel shaft with serrated button secured by steel pin running through the handle to steel loop fitting atop, tapered helical worm, Henshall 1795 patent, 1850s. Wood, animal fiber and steel, 6" high. Made in England.

247 Basic T corkscrew with turned bone handle with checker ends and a turned nickel-plated steel shaft with a grooved cork-grip button secured through the handle by peening over washer, center worm, 1890. Nickel-plated steel and horn, 5.25" high. Made in England.

STRAIGHT PULL BASIC T WITH BUTTON

Each of the corkscrews on the following pages has a brush on the handle for clearing the cork and the bottle cap of debris before drawing the cork; and each has a Henshall button.

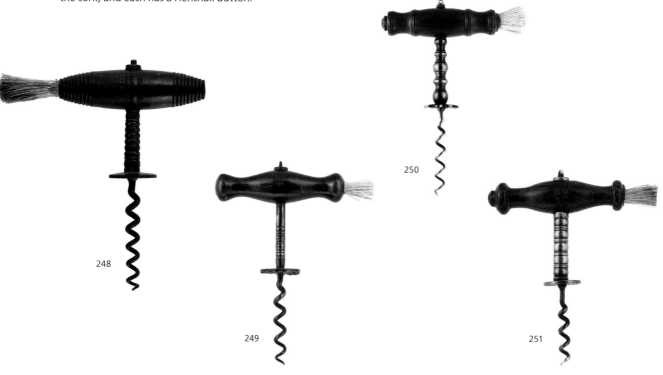

248

249

250

251

248 Basic T corkscrew with brush-tipped turned wood handle secured to a threaded turned steel shaft and button with a steel fitting and hole for ring atop, tapered helical worm, early nineteenth century. Wood, animal fiber and steel, 6.5" high. Made in England.

249 Basic T corkscrew with brush-tipped turned wood handle and a turned steel shaft with serrated button secured by a steel pin running through handle to a steel loop fitting atop, tapered helical worm, 1876. Wood, vegetal fiber and steel, 5.75" high. Made in England.

250 Basic T corkscrew with brush-tipped turned wood handle secured to a threaded turned steel shaft with daisy button and steel fitting for loop atop, tapered helical worm, early nineteenth century. Wood, vegetal fiber and steel, 5.5" high. Made in England.

251 Basic T corkscrew with brush-tipped turned wood handle and a turned steel shaft with serrated button secured by a steel pin running through the handle to a steel loop fitting atop, helical worm, c. 1870. Wood, vegetal fiber and steel, 5.5" high. Made in England.

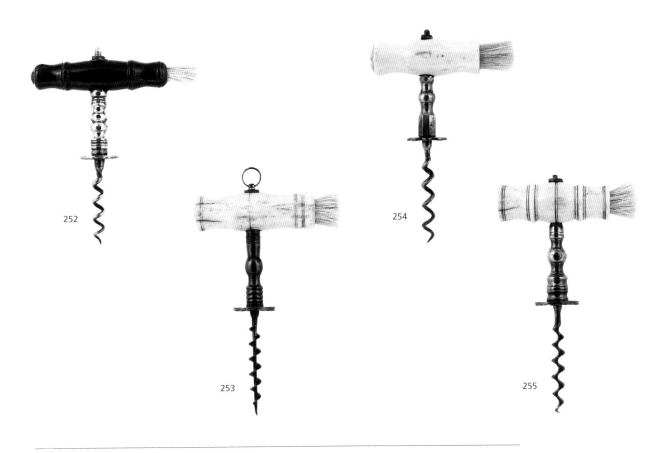

252

254

253

255

252 Basic T corkscrew with brush-tipped turned wood handle and a turned nickel-plated steel shaft with serrated cork grip button secured by a steel pin running through the handle to a steel loop fitting atop, tapered helical worm, c. 1860. Wood, vegetal fiber and nickel-plated steel, 5.5" high. Made in England.

253 Basic T corkscrew with brush-tipped turned bone handle and a cut steel shaft with serrated cork grip button secured by a steel pin running through the handle to a steel loop fitting and loop atop, Archimedean worm, 1830–50. Wood, vegetal fiber and steel, 7" high Made in England.

254 Basic T corkscrew with brush-tipped turned bone handle and a cut steel shaft with concave daisy button secured by a steel pin running through the handle to a steel loop fitting atop, tapered helical worm, 1850–70. Wood, animal fiber and steel, 6" high. Made in England.

255 Basic T corkscrew with brush-tipped turned bone handle and a turned steel shaft with serrated cork grip button secured by a steel pin running through the handle to a steel loop fitting atop, center worm, 1850–70. Wood, vegetal fiber and steel, 6.75" high. Made in England.

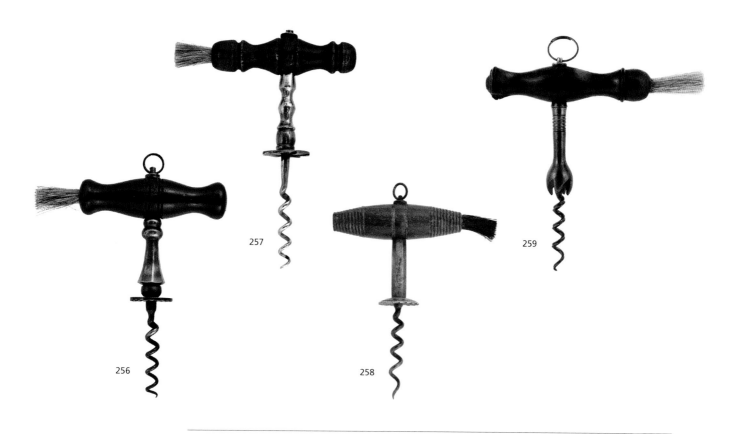

257

256

258

259

256   Basic T corkscrew with brush-tipped turned wood handle and a turned steel shaft with flared ribs and a serrated button secured by a steel pin running through the handle to a steel loop fitting and ring atop, tapered helical worm, 1850–70. Wood, vegetal fiber and steel, 6" high. Made in England.

257   Basic T corkscrew with brush-tipped turned wood handle and a turned steel shaft with wedged cork grip button secured by a steel pin running through the handle to a steel loop fitting atop, tapered helical worm, c. 1870. Wood, vegetal fiber and steel, 5.75" high. Made in England.

258   Basic T corkscrew with brush-tipped turned wood handle and a hexagonal steel shaft with wedged brass cork grip button secured by a steel pin running through the handle to a steel loop fitting atop with hanging ring, tapered helical worm, c. 1830. Wood, brass, animal fiber and steel, 5.25" high. Made in England.

259   Basic T corkscrew with brush-tipped turned wood handle and a turned steel tear drop shaft with dogtooth corkgrip secured by a steel pin running through the handle to a steel loop fitting and loop atop, tapered grooved helical worm, 1880. Wood, animal fiber and steel, 6.75" high. Made in England.

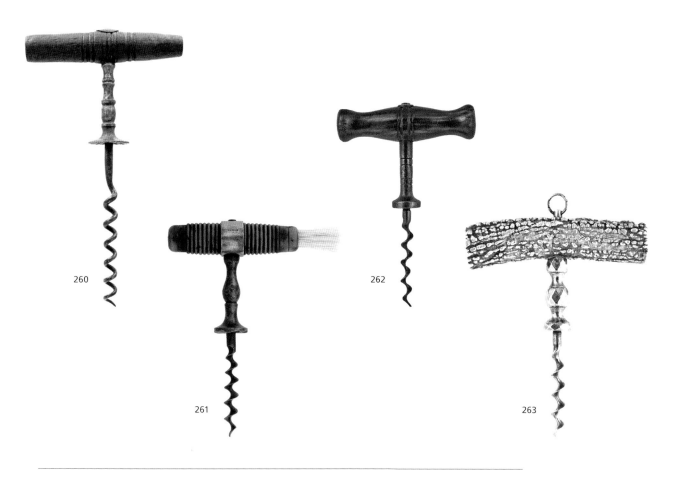

260   Basic T corkscrew
with turned wood handle
and a turned brass shaft
with grooved daisy button
secured by a brass pin
running through the
handle to a peened copper
fitting atop, steel tapered
helical worm, c. 1830.
Wood, brass, copper and
steel, 6.75" high. Made
in England.

261   Basic T corkscrew
with brush-tipped turned
wood handle and a turned
steel shaft with serrated
cork grip button secured
by a steel pin running
through the handle to
a steel fitting atop, nickel-
plated brass band around
the midsection of the
handle stamped "L.B. Paris
Déposé" (Le Boulanger,
maker), center worm,
c. 1890. Wood, nickel-

plated brass, vegetal fiber
and steel, 5.25" high.
Made in France.

262   Basic T corkscrew
with turned wood handle
and a turned steel shaft
with plain button secured
by a steel pin running
through the handle to a
steel loop fitting atop,
center speed worm,
1880–90. Wood and steel,
5" high. Made in England.

263   Basic T corkscrew
with silver on stag-horn
handle and a cut and
turned steel shaft with
plain button secured
through the handle
with loop atop, bladed
center worm, Thiery and
Croselmire patent, 1886.
Silver, horn and steel,
6" high. Made in USA.

264 Mechanical beehive corkscrew with painted turned wood handle attached by an end to end internal rod to a smooth shaft and loosely coiled spring barrel. A slideable pin with central peg penetrates the shaft perpendicularly, locking the sliding barrel into position for cork drawing. Removing the pin from the shaft hole allows the barrel to be moved up to the handle for easy cork removal, Sommers patent, center worm, 1895. Wood and steel, 5.5" high. Made in Germany.

265 Mechanical beehive corkscrew with printed, simple turned wood handle attached by an end to end internal rod to a smooth shaft and loosely coiled spring barrel. A slideable pin with central peg penetrates the shaft perpendicularly, locking the sliding barrel into position for cork drawing. Removing the pin from the shaft hole allows the barrel to be moved up to the handle for easy cork removal, Sommers patent, center worm, 1895. Wood and steel, 5.5" high. Made in Germany.

266 Mechanical beehive corkscrew with contoured steel handle attached to a threaded steel shaft supporting a loosely coiled steel spring barrel and triple-wing flynut. When spun clockwise, the flynut compresses the barrel and draws the cork, center worm, 1876. Steel, 6" high. Made in France.

267 Mechanical beehive corkscrew with contoured steel handle attached to a threaded steel shaft supporting a tightly coiled steel spring barrel and triple-wing flynut. Upon meeting the barrel, the flynut raises the shaft and draws the cork, center worm, 1876. Steel, 6" high. Made in France.

268 Mechanical beehive corkscrew with printed, simple turned wood handle attached to a smooth steel shaft with a peg supporting a loosely coiled steel spring barrel. Turning the barrel clockwise will raise it toward the handle, allowing access to free the cork from the center worm, Kürschner patent, 1914. Steel, 6" high. Made in Germany.

269 Mechanical beehive corkscrew with turned wood handle attached by an end to end internal rod to a smooth shaft. The shaft is penetrated by protruding pegs which engage the slideable lock, holding the coiled spring barrel in position for drawing of the cork. Disengaging the lock from the pegs allows the barrel to be moved toward the handle to facilitate access to the drawn cork for easy removal from the bladed center worm, Kürschner patent, 1898. Wood and steel, 6.25" high. Made in Germany.

270 Mechanical corkscrew with wood dowel handle connected to a fixed conical spring-assisted smooth shaft which runs through and stabilizes an open frame. With the frame placed on the bottle lip, the handle is rotated, penetrating the cork while compressing the spring. The open frame enables easy removal of the cork from the bladed center worm, Dunisch & Schöler patent, c. 1883. Steel with traces of silver paint and wood, 6" high. Made in Germany.

271 Mechanical corkscrew with painted turned wood handle connected to a spring-assisted smooth shaft and decorative edged steel bell with cap-lifter stamped "Caplifter Germany". With the bell placed on the bottle lip, the handle and center worm are rotated to penetrate the cork compressing the spring, aiding cork extraction, c. 1930. Wood, paint and steel, 5" high. Made in Germany.

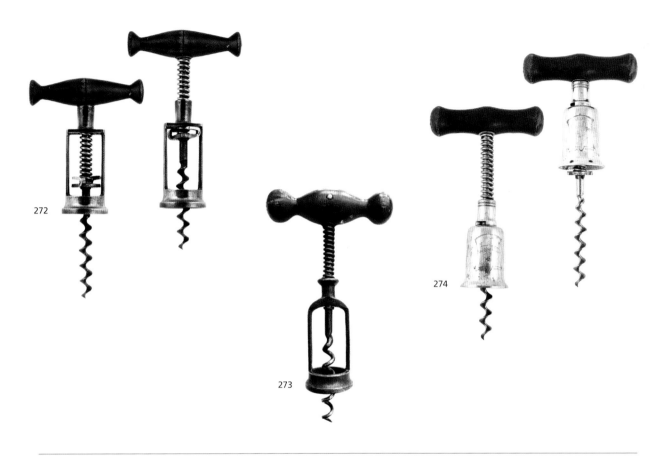

272

273

274

272   Mechanical open-frame corkscrew with turned wood handle connected to a fixed spring-assisted smooth shaft with a steel stop stamped "D.R.G.M."* With the frame placed on the bottle lip, the handle is rotated to penetrate the cork while the fixed stop compresses the spring, aiding in cork extraction. The sliding open frame enables easy cork removal

from the bladed center worm, Usbeck patent, 1902. Steel and wood, 6.5" high. Made in Germany.

273   Mechanical open-frame corkscrew with turned wood handle connected to fixed spring-assisted shank running through an open frame to a smooth shaft and helical worm. With the frame placed on the bottle lip, the handle is rotated

to penetrate the cork causing the fixed stop to compress the spring, aiding cork extraction. The open frame enables easy removal of the cork from the worm, after Dunisch & Scholer patent, c. 1883. Steel and wood, 6.75" high. Made in Germany.

274   Mechanical corkscrew with turned painted wood handle connected to a spring-

assisted smooth shaft and steel locking bell stamped "Neue HERKULES, D.R.G.M."* With the bell placed on the bottle lip, the handle is rotated to penetrate the cork causing the crossbar locking hooks on the shaft to engage the stop and release slot, immobilizing the bell. Continued rotation compress the spring and the sliding bell enables

easy cork removal from the center worm, Usbeck patent, c. 1933. Wood, paint and steel. 6.75" high. Made in Germany.

275   (at right) (See caption 277 on following page for description.)

* D.R.G.M. stands for Deutsches Reichsgebrauchs-muster.

SPLIT BARRELS & SLIDE RINGS

Each of the corkscrews on this spread has a split barrel with a locking ring that engages to create pressure on the bottle neck while drawing the cork. Raising the locking ring splits the barrel for ease in cork removal.

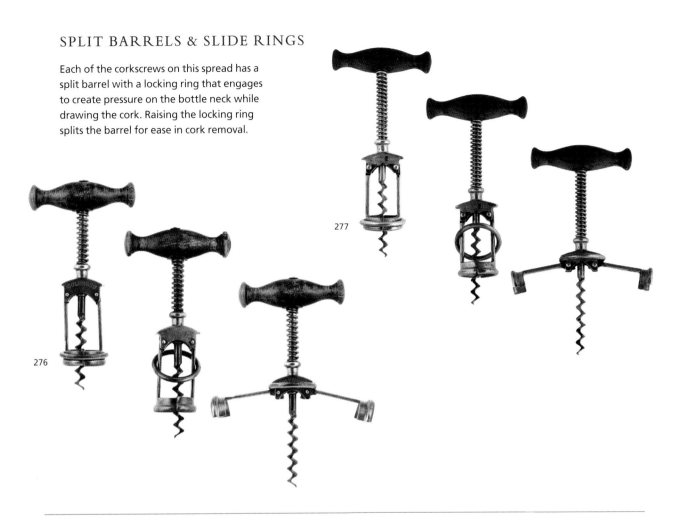

276 Mechanical corkscrew with simple turned wood handle attached to a coiled spring shaft by a long steel pin through the length of the handle tip to tip. Becker patent split barrel with slideable locking ring, stamped "Columbus D. R. Patent 70879"* on top, long center worm, 1893. Wood and nickel- plated steel, 7" high. Made in Germany.

277 Mechanical corkscrew with simple turned wood handle attached to a coiled spring shaft by a long steel pin through the length of the handle tip to tip, split barrel with slideable locking ring, stamped at top "B. Altman & Co. M. I. Germany", long center worm, Becker patent, 1893. Wood and nickel-plated steel, 7" high. Made in Germany. (See also page 99.)

278 Mechanical corkscrew with simple turned wood handle attached to a coiled spring shaft by a long steel pin through the length of the handle tip to tip, split barrel with slideable

locking ring stamped on side "Germany", long center worm, Becker patent, 1893. Wood and steel, 7" high. Made in Germany.

279 Mechanical T corkscrew with cast steel handle, ball bearings enclosed where shank passes through the Becker patent split barrel, stamped "SAXONY" on

top, to a smooth shaft. The ball bearings ease handle rotation in building pressure at the bottle neck on which the barrel rests to draw the cork, slideable locking ring, long bladed center worm, Usbeck patent, 1909. Steel, 6.25" high. Made in Germany.

278

279

280   Mechanical
corkscrew with simple
turned wood handle
attached to a coiled
spring shaft by a long
steel pin run through
the length of the handle,
split barrel stamped on
top "Columbus D. R.
Patent 70879",* slideable
locking ring, long center
worm, Becker patent,
1893. Wood and nickel-
plated steel, 6" high.
Made in Germany.

* **D.R.** stands for
Deutsche Reich.

280

BELLS & CLOSED FRAMES

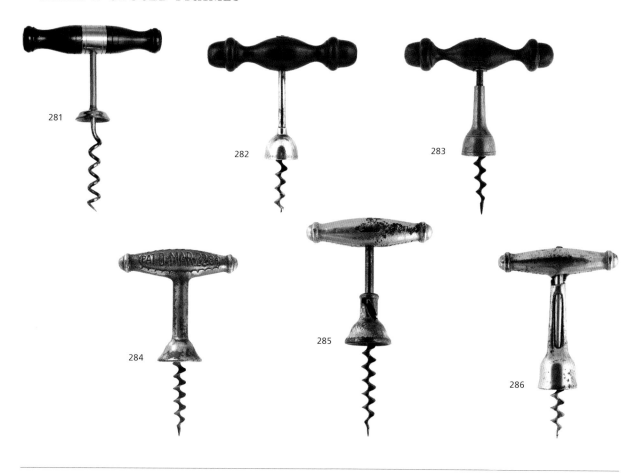

281

282

283

284

285

286

281   Basic T corkscrew with turned wood handle and steel band, stamped "PATENT APPLIED FOR", attached to a smooth steel shaft with short steel bell, helical worm, c. 1885. Steel and wood, 5.25" high. Made in USA.

282   Basic T corkscrew with acorn-tipped turned wood handle attached by peened shaft end through a brass washer to the smooth steel shaft supporting a short fixed brass bell stamped "Magic Cork Screw. Pat. May 12, 1883". As the worm is turned, the pressure of the bell on the bottle rim breaks the seal and raises the cork slightly to ease the pull, Bennit patent, bladed center worm, 1883. Brass, wood and steel, 5" high. Made in USA.

283   Basic T mechanical corkscrew with acorn tipped shaped wood handle attached by peened shaft end through brass washers to the smooth steel shaft and attached brass sliding funnel-shaped bell. As the worm is turned, the pressure of the bell on the bottle rim breaks the seal, partially raising the cork and easing the pull, Griswold patent, bladed center worm, 1884. Brass, wood and steel, 5" high. Made in USA.

284   Basic T mechanical corkscrew with cast steel combined nickel-plated acorn tipped steel handle and elongated diagonal slotted locking bell. The handle is attached to a smooth steel shaft within and is marked, in scalloped brackets, "T. CURLEY. TROY. N.Y" on one side and "PAT'D MAR. 22. 84" on the other, bladed center worm, 1884. Steel, 5.25" high. Made in USA.

285   Basic T mechanical all steel corkscrew with acorn tipped handle attached to smooth steel shaft and locking bell secured by two pins. The handle is marked, "T. Curley. Troy, N.Y." on underside, "Pat. 84" on topside bracketing the peened shaft end, bladed center worm, 1884. Nickel-plated steel, 6" high. Made in USA.

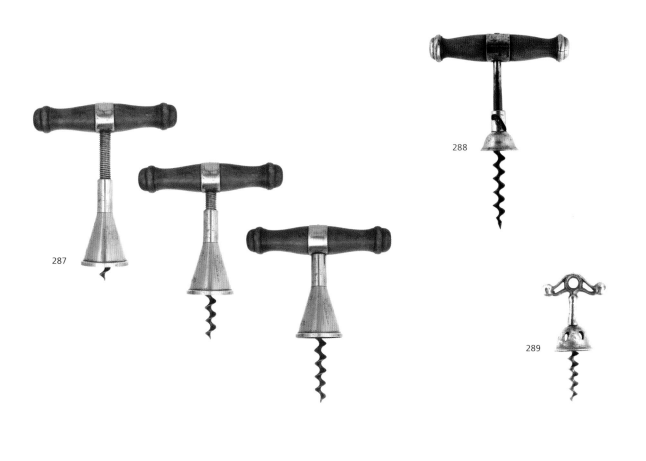

287

288

289

286 Basic T mechanical all steel corkscrew with acorn tipped locking handle marked, "T. Curley Pat'd" on top bracketing peened shaft end and "Troy, N.Y." on underside. The smooth steel shaft runs through an elongated vertically slotted locking bell to a bladed center worm. With the bell resting on the bottle neck, the handle is turned clockwise until the bell

and handle meet and lock; continued rotation draws the cork upward and into the bell, 1884. Nickel-plated steel, 5.25" high. Made in USA.

287 Basic T mechanical self-puller corkscrew with acorn tipped turned wood handle attached by brass band to a threaded shank and threaded funnel-shaped bell, stamped "Pat. June. 12, '83." With the bell in the raised

position, the worm is screwed into the cork until the bell rests on the bottle lip. Continued rotation of the handle engages the threaded shank, drawing the cork upward into the bell, Strait patent, bladed center worm, 1883. Brass, wood and steel, 5" high. Made in USA.

288 Basic T mechanical corkscrew with nickel-plated acorn tipped turned wood handle

attached by a peened end through a center band, stamped "Pat. Apr 22, 84 T. Curley. Troy, N.Y." to a tapered smooth steel shaft with two pins attaching the nickel-plated brass bell, bladed center worm, 1884. Nickel-plated brass, wood and steel, 5.5" high. Made in USA.

289 Mechanical self-puller Viktoria corkscrew with shanked mustache handle attached to a

short smooth shaft and perforated bell. The handle is turned until the worm penetrates the cork and the bell collar rests on the bottle lip, continued turning exerts pressure drawing the cork up and partially out of the bottle, bladed center worm, Müller patent, 1892. Steel, 4.25" high. Made in Germany.

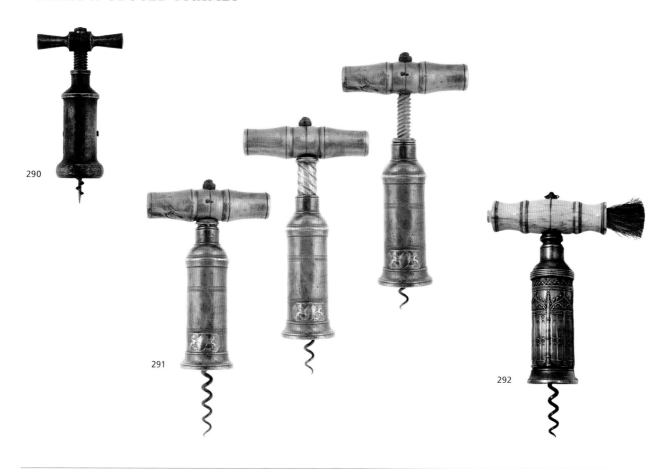

290

291

292

290   Mechanical barrel corkscrew with flared cruciform steel handle and closed frame with two vertical slots for sliding cross brace on threaded shank, short tapered shaft, Archimedean worm, c. 1875. Steel, 6.25" high. Made in Italy.

291   Mechanical closed-frame corkscrew with turned wood handle attached through the center to a threaded steel shaft by loop fitting atop.

A counterthreaded brass shank telescopes into a bronze barrel with maker's plate depicting an oval shield marked "Patent", flanked by rampant lion and unicorn, tapered helical worm, Thomason patent, 1802. Wood, brass, bronze and steel, 10" fully extended, 7.25" closed. Made in England.

292   Mechanical closed frame corkscrew with brush-tipped turned ivory handle attached through

the center to a threaded steel shaft by loop fitting atop. A telescoping counterthreaded brass shank nests into a bronze barrel decorated with encircling Gothic church doors. With the barrel resting on the bottle lip, the Thomason patent enables the penetration, drawing, extraction and removal of the cork from the worm (without handling the cork) in a continuous counterclockwise then clockwise

motion, tapered helical worm, 1802. Ivory, brass and steel, 9.5" fully extended, 8" closed. Made in England.

293   (at right) Mechanical closed-frame corkscrew with turned whalebone handle attached by peened end of threaded steel shaft. A counter-threaded brass shank telescopes into a bronze barrel with "Dowler" maker's plate depicting an oval "Patent" shield

flanked by recumbent lion and unicorn. With the barrel resting on the bottle lip, the Thomason patent enables the penetration, drawing, extraction and removal of the cork from the worm (without handling the cork) in one continuous counterclockwise then clockwise motion, center worm, 1802. Whalebone, brass, bronze and steel, 9.75" fully extended, 7.5" closed. Made in England.

OPEN FRAMES

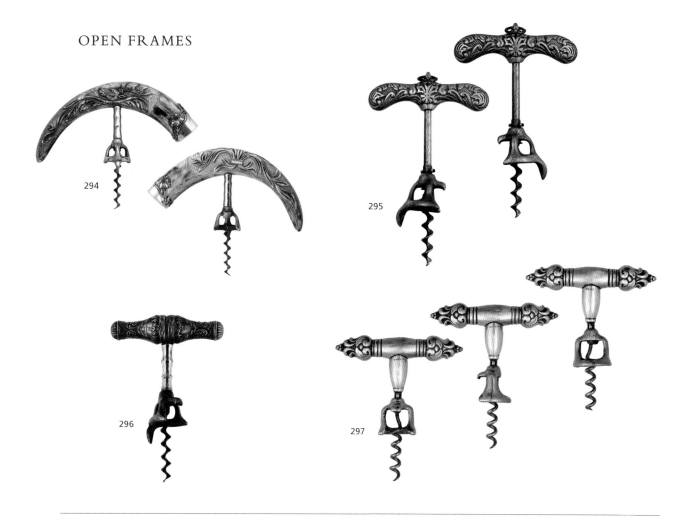

294

295

296

297

294 Mechanical self-puller corkscrew with carved tusk handle (featuring stag head with leafy surround on one side, decorative foliage on the other and a silver floral theme end cap, stamped "Sterling") attached to a shaft with nickel-plated brass sheath and steel Walker Collar open bell which incorporates both a prong cap-lifter and talon wire breaker. The handle is rotated until the worm penetrates the cork and the open bell collar rests on the bottle lip, continued turning exerts pressure drawing the cork up and partially out of the bottle, center worm, 1900. Tusk, silver, nickel-plated brass, and steel, 4.25" high, 7.75" long. Made in USA.

295 Mechanical self-puller corkscrew with ornate steel handle, hanging ring atop, attached to a smooth shaft with nickel-plated steel Walker Collar held in place by a Cotter pin, center worm, Walker patent, c. 1897. Steel and nickel-plated steel, 6.25" high. Made in USA.

296 Mechanical self-puller corkscrew with decorative silver covered wood core handle (stamped "F & B"inside pennant above "Sterling 1489") attached to smooth shaft with nickel-plated brass sheath and steel Walker Collar open bell which incorporates both a prong cap-lifter and talon wire breaker. The handle is turned until the worm penetrates the cork and the open bell collar rests on the bottle lip, continued turning exerts pressure drawing the cork up and partially out of the bottle, center worm, 1900. Silver, nickel-plated brass and steel, 5.5" high. Made in USA.

297 Mechanical self-puller corkscrew with ornate silver handle attached to smooth shaft with silver cover (stamped with the International Silver Company hallmark and "Sterling" on one side and "NX35" on the other) and nickel-plated steel Walker Collar open bell incorporating a prong

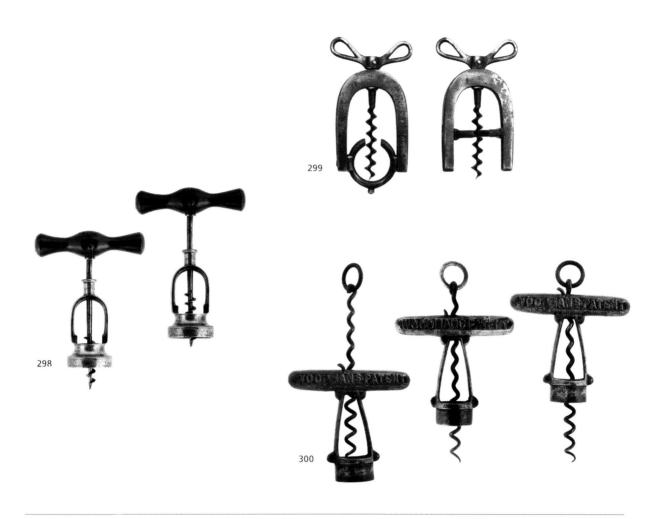

cap-lifter and talon wire breaker, helical worm, Walker patent, c. 1900. Nickel-plated steel and sterling silver, 4.75" high. Made in USA.

298   Mechanical T corkscrew with turned wood handle pinned through center to smooth steel shaft fitted through an open brass frame, Archimedean worm, 1880s. Wood, brass and steel, 5.25" high. Made in Italy.

299   Mechanical self-puller folding corkscrew with steel open wing handle pinned to a shaft which passes through an arched open frame stamped "ANDREE" and "D.R.G.M. 118056"*. The open frame is constructed with a sliding ring that rests on the bottle neck; as the wings are rotated, the cork is penetrated and the ring slides toward the handle. Held fast by the

narrowing arch, continued rotation of the handle withdraws the cork, bladed center worm, neck ring pivots to fold flat for pocket portability, Everts patent, 1899. Nickel-plated steel, 4.25" high. Made in Germany.

300   Mechanical T corkscrew with cast brass spurred handle (marked "WOODMAN'S PATENT" on one side and "PATd

JAN.Y 6. 1886" on the other) attached through mid-section to a steeply pitched twisted wire shaft terminating in a looped ring on one end and a tapered helical worm on the other. The ring end manually locks to the handle spur, securing the cast steel conical frame for cork rotation and penetration. The loop is manually disengaged from the spur and

continued rotation of the handle extracts the cork, Woodman patent, 1886. Brass and steel, 6" high. Made in USA.

* D.R.G.M. stands for Deutsches Reichsgebrauchs-muster.

OPEN FRAMES

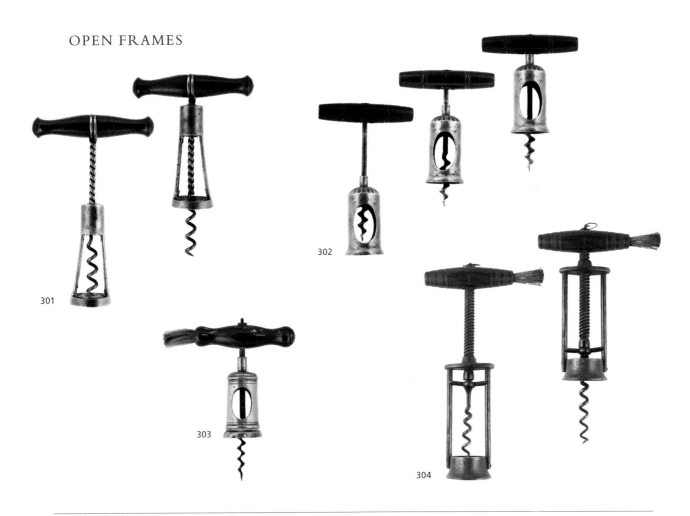

301

302

303

304

---

301 Mechanical T "power cone" corkscrew with turned wood handle attached around the mid-section to a single twisted wire shaft and worm fitted through a cast steel open frame, the top section of which is threaded to match the twisted wire shaft. When the frame rests on the bottle lip and the handle is turned, the worm penetrates the cork and extracts it. The openings in the frame enable the grasping of the cork to turn it off the worm, helical worm, Clough patent, Williamson manufacture, 1876. Wood and steel, 6.25" high. Made in USA.

302 Mechanical T long bell corkscrew with turned wood handle attached through the center to a smooth steel shaft by a square fitting below and a brass washer and peened rod atop. The shaft is fitted through a brass open frame, stamped "CHINNOCK'S PATENT May 27, 1862". When the handle is turned and the worm penetrates the cork, the bell resting on the bottle lip exerts pressure, extracting the cork. The openings in the bell cap enable the grasping of the cork to turn it off the worm, bladed center worm, 1862. Wood, brass and steel, 5" high. Made in USA.

303 Mechanical T corkscrew with brush-tipped turned wood handle attached through the center to a smooth steel shaft fitted through a brass open frame with a fitting for a loop atop. The bell cap rests on the bottle neck, exerting pressure to extract the cork when the handle is turned. The openings in the bell cap enable the grasping of the cork to turn it off the worm, bladed center worm, Chinnock patent, 1862. Wood, vegetal fiber, brass and steel, 5.5" high. Made in USA.

304 Mechanical corkscrew with brush-tipped turned wood handle connected to a smooth tapered steel shaft through the center of a threaded steel shank and bolted atop. The open frame guides a sliding crosspiece along the shank,

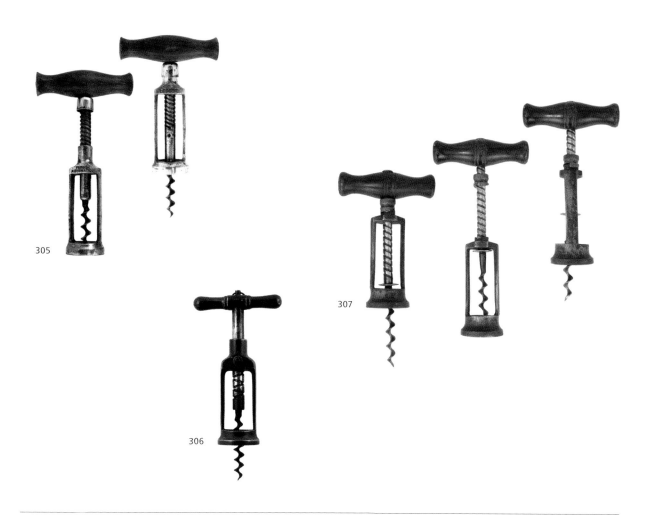

305

307

306

keeping the cork centered. With the open frame resting on the bottle lip, rotating the handle turns the worm to penetrate the cork, thereby building force to draw the cork, based on John Coney's model, tapered helical worm, c. 1854. Steel, wood and fiber, 7.5" high. Made in England.

305   Mechanical double action corkscrew with a turned wood handle attached to a threaded steel shank supporting an open frame, stamped "Perfect Automatique" on one side and "Déposé" on the other. With the frame resting on the bottle lip, the worm penetrates the cork and, when fully inserted, an internal spring-loaded clutch disengages the worm allowing cork extraction by a continuous clockwise rotation of the handle, smooth shaft, center worm, A.H. Kunz patent, 1932. Steel, 6.25" high. Made in Germany.

306   Mechanical "Perpetual" model corkscrew with cast steel handle attached to a short smooth shaft with a loop atop and an open steel frame by a crisscross grooved steel shank and guide pin. When frame rests on bottle neck and handle is turned, the cork is penetrated and removed as the cross threads reverse the direction of the continuous motion, bladed center worm, Demmler patent, 1884. Steel, 6.5" high. Made in Germany.

307   Mechanical corkscrew with turned rosewood handle and threaded brass shank supporting an open frame and clutch, stamped "THE KING" on one side and "PATENT 6064" on the other. When fully inserted, continuous clockwise rotation of the handle engages the clutch with the frame, thereby extracting the cork, smooth shaft, bladed center worm, Sunderland patent, manufactured by John Coney & Co. and John Cox, 1904. Steel with traces of bronzing, brass and wood, 6.75" high. Made in England.

308

309

310

311

312

308 Mechanical corkscrew with cast steel rod handle and an open frame terminating in a flared neck, through which a threaded steel shank runs to a smooth shaft. A handle locking sleeve stabilizes and releases the shank, center worm, Ehrhardt patent, 1891. Steel, 5.75" high. Made in Germany.

309 Mechanical T corkscrew with cast steel flared handle, smooth shaft and open nickel-plated brass frame stamped "SOLON D.R.G.M. No.152004".* Ball bearings, enclosed where the shank passes through the frame, ease the handle rotation required to build necessary pressure at the bottle neck for cork extraction, center worm, Scharff "Solon" patent (first model), 1901. Nickel-plated brass and steel, 5.25" high. Made in Germany.

310 Mechanical T corkscrew with cast steel handle stamped "Registered 13186" and smooth steel shaft fitted through an open frame stamped "The Surprise". With the frame resting on the bottle neck, continued rotation of the long center worm exerts pressure to withdraw the cork, Willetts patent, 1884. Nickel-plated steel, 5.25" high. Made in England.

311 Mechanical T corkscrew with steel handle stamped "Foreign" at center, smooth shaft and conical open frame with serrated ring atop. Ball bearings enclosed where the shank passes through the open frame ease the rotation required to build necessary pressure at the bottle neck for cork extraction, long bladed center worm, Usbeck patent, 1909. Steel, 5" high. Made in Germany.

312 Mechanical T corkscrew with cap-lifter handle (marked "DRGM MONOPOL UNIVERSAL GERMANY"* within

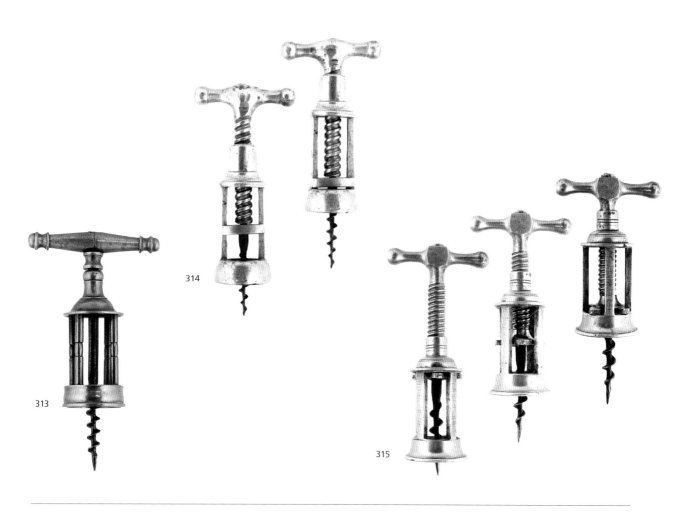

313

314

315

a filigree grape design), a smooth shaft and an open nickel-plated steel frame. Ball bearings exposed where the shank passes through the open frame ease handle rotation required to build pressure at the bottle neck to draw the cork, center worm, Usbeck patent (second model), 1909. Steel, 6" high. Made in Germany.

313   Mechanical corkscrew with turned brass handle peened to a long smooth brass shaft which serves as the axis of a four column open frame. The cage rests on the bottle lip while the handle is turned, penetrating the cork and building force to extract, Archimedean worm, c. 1880. Brass and steel, 7" high. Made in Italy.

314   Mechanical corkscrew with ball-tipped brass handle and threaded brass shank (cast in one piece) connected to a smooth tapered steel shaft, peened atop and running through the center of the hollow shank. A sliding brass crossbar tracks down the brass open frame stabilizing the shank and worm as rotation of the handle

builds force to draw the cork, Archimedean worm, c. 1880. Brass and steel, 6.75" high. Made in Italy.

315   Mechanical corkscrew with round tipped brass handle and threaded brass shank (cast in one piece) connected to a smooth tapered steel shaft, bolted atop and running through the center of the hollow shank. A sliding

brass crosspiece tracks down the brass open frame stabilizing the shank and worm as continued rotation of the handle builds force to draw the cork, Archimedean worm, c. 1880. Brass and steel, 6.75" high. Made in Italy.

* D.R.G.M. and DRGM stand for Deutsches Reichsgebrauchsmuster.

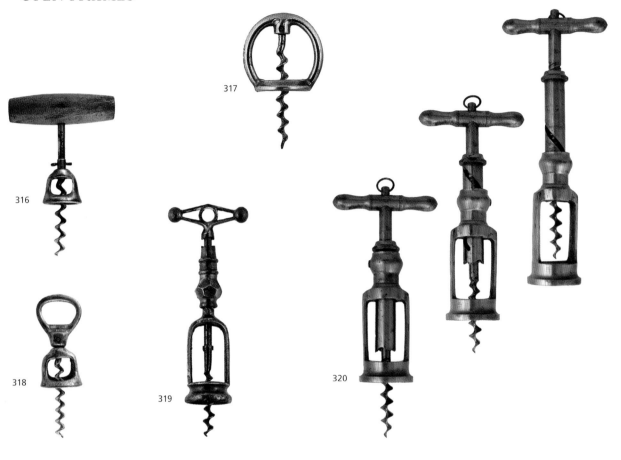

316 Mechanical self-puller corkscrew with wood handle attached to smooth shaft stamped "WILLIAMSON" through which a steel open bell is pinned. The handle is turned until worm penetrates cork and the collar rests on the bottle lip. Continued turning exerts pressure drawing the cork up and into the open bell, center worm, Williamson patent, 1897. Wood and steel, 4.5" high. Made in USA.

317 Fixed self-puller corkscrew with smooth shaft pinned to the top of an open frame constructed to rest on the bottle neck and function as an integrated handle, exerting pressure to withdraw the cork as it is rotated, bladed center worm, Genot & Günther patent, 1900. Nickel-plated steel, 3.75" high. Made in France.

318 Mechanical self-puller corkscrew, or "Power Corkscrew," with nickel-plated steel cap-lifter handle pinned through a smooth shaft above a short open frame. The bladed center worm is rotated into the cork until the open frame comes to rest on the bottle neck; continued rotation exerts the necessary force for extraction, Williamson patent, 1930-40. Nickel-plated steel, 4" high. Made in USA.

319 Mechanical T corkscrew with applied steel ball-tipped Perille handle with faceted locking threaded shank and frame, stamped "Diamant JP Paris", through which the threaded steel shaft passes, center worm, Perille patent, 1887. Steel, 7" high. Made in France.

321

322

320 Mechanical corkscrew, called the "Mauser," with hanging ring atop a turned steel handle attached to a threaded steel shank supporting an open frame and surrounded by a slotted jacket. With the frame resting on the bottle neck and the shank in the extended position, clockwise rotation of the handle penetrates

the cork and locks; continued rotation raises the jacket and withdraws the cork, smooth shaft, center worm, Louis Kummer patent, 1904. Steel, 7" high compressed. Made in Germany.

321 Mechanical corkscrew, called the "Mauser," with turned wood handle and an applied half crab-piece

collar pinned to a steel shank supporting an open frame (stamped "RGM") and surrounded by a slotted jacket with reciprocal crab-piece atop. With the frame resting on the bottle neck, clockwise rotation of the handle penetrates the cork and engages the locking crab-piece; continued rotation raises the jacket and withdraws the cork,

center worm, Louis Kummer patent, 1904. Steel and wood, 7" compressed. Made in Germany.

322 Mechanical "Mauser" model corkscrew with hanging ring atop a cast steel handle attached to a smooth shaft by a threaded steel shank, marked "GERMANY",

supporting an open frame. While turning the handle continuously clockwise, a four point cork grip, or "Austosser," at the end of a slotted hollow jacket holds the cork fast and allows for automatic extraction, center worm, Kummer patent, c. 1915. Nickel-plated steel, 7.5" compressed. Made in Germany.

OPEN FRAMES

323

324

325

323 Mechanical corkscrew with nickel-plated brass capped turned blond buffalo horn handle attached to a threaded steel shank and a nickel-plated brass open frame and with a sliding crosspiece marked "L'EXCELSIOR A.G. Bte SGDG PARIS",* smooth shaft, bladed center worm, Guichard patent,

1880. Buffalo horn and nickel-plated steel, 6.75" high. Made in France.

324 Mechanical corkscrew with perforated steel handle attached to a threaded steel shank supporting an open frame. The handle is turned, worm penetrating the cork, until the frame rests on the bottle lip; a

contoured flynut, turned clockwise, performs a "double action," drawing the cork, smooth crimped shaft, center worm, 1875. Steel, 7" high. Made in France.

325 Mechanical corkscrew with nickel-plated brass capped turned ebony handle attached to a threaded

steel shank and a nickel-plated brass open frame and with a sliding crosspiece marked "L'Excelsior A.G. Bte SGDG Made in France",* smooth shaft, bladed center worm, Guichard patent, 1880. Nickel-plated brass, steel and wood, 6.75" high. Made in France.

* Bte SGDG stands for Breveté Sans Garantie Du Gouvernement.

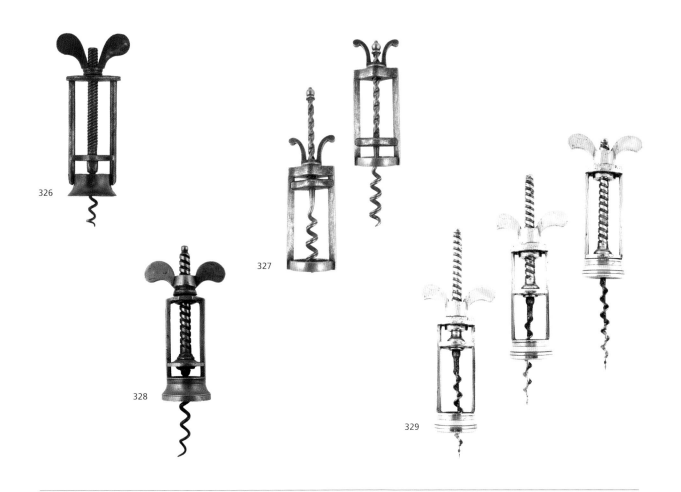

326   Mechanical open
frame corkscrew with
wingnut handle on
a threaded steel shank
which is the axis for an
open frame with sliding
cross brace. With the
worm lowered, the frame
is turned until the collar
rests on the bottle lip;
the handle may then be
rotated clockwise, raising
the cork, short tapered
shaft, tapered helical

worm, c. 1820. Steel,
6" high. Made in England.

327   Hand-forged open
frame mechanical
corkscrew with wingnut
handle on a threaded steel
shank which is the axis for
an open frame and sliding
crossbar. With the worm
lowered, the frame is
turned until the collar
rests on the bottle lip;
the handle may then be

rotated clockwise, raising
the cork, smooth shaft,
grooved helical worm,
c. 1800. Steel, 5.75" high.
Made in France.

328   Mechanical "Farrow
& Jackson" type corkscrew
with a brass wingnut
handle on a threaded
brass shank which is the
axis for an open frame and
sliding circular slide. With
the worm lowered, the

frame is turned until the
collar rests on the bottle
lip; the handle may then
be rotated clockwise,
raising the cork, short
tapered shaft, wide-pitch
tapered helical worm,
c. 1850. Brass and steel,
6.5" high. Made in England.

329   Mechanical "Farrow
& Jackson" type corkscrew
with wingnut handle on a
threaded shank which is

the axis for an open frame
and circular slide. With the
worm lowered, the frame
is turned until the collar
rests on the bottle lip; the
handle may then be
rotated clockwise, raising
the cork, short shaft,
Archimedean worm,
c. 1855. Nickel-plated
steel, 7.25" high. Made
in England.

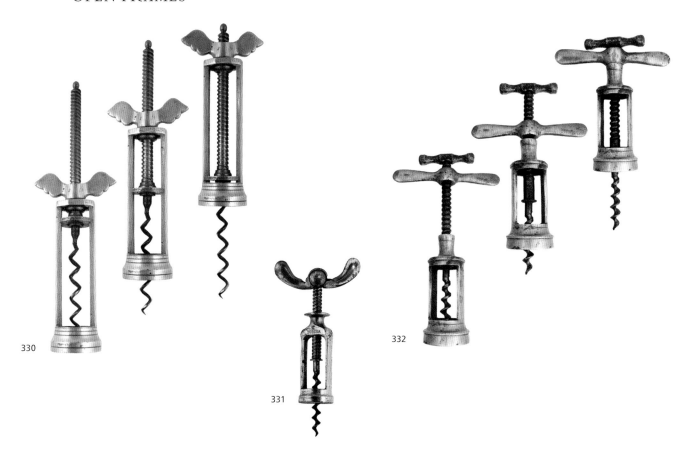

330

331

332

330 Mechanical "Farrow & Jackson" type corkscrew with winged brass wingnut handle on a threaded brass shank which is the axis for an open frame and circular slide. With the worm lowered, the frame is turned until the collar rests on the bottle lip; the handle may then be rotated clockwise, raising the cork, short tapered shaft, wide-pitch triangular helical worm, c. 1850. Brass and steel, 8.5" high. Made in England.

331 Mechanical T corkscrew with nickel-plated steel locking handles that rotate around a threaded steel shank fitted through an open frame stamped "Bodega". The locked handle is rotated with the frame resting on the bottle neck, penetrating the cork; the handle unlocks when it meets the frame and continued rotation raises the cork, smooth shaft, center worm, Scharff patent, 1899. Nickel-plated steel and steel, 6" high. Made in Germany.

332 Mechanical open-frame corkscrew with steel handle attached to a threaded steel shank supporting an oversized brass flynut (nicknamed "helicopter") and an open brass frame. When the frame rests upon the bottle lip and the worm has penetrated the cork, clockwise rotation of the flynut draws the cork, performing "double action," smooth shaft, bladed center worm, c. 1880. Brass and steel, 6.5" high. Made in Italy.

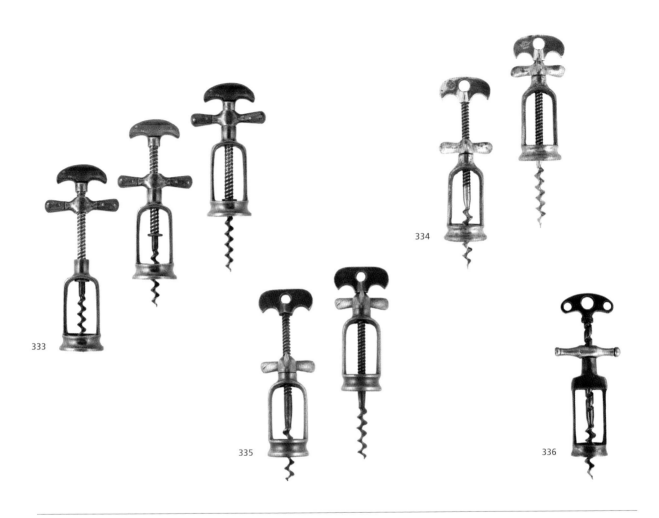

333

334

335

336

333 Mechanical corkscrew with crescent steel and horn panel handle attached to a threaded steel shank supporting a horn panel steel flynut and open frame. When the frame rests upon the bottle lip and the worm has penetrated the cork, clockwise rotation of the flynut draws the cork, performing "double action," smooth shaft, center worm, Monopol maker, c. 1875. Steel, 6.25" high. Made in Germany.

334 Mechanical corkscrew with perforated steel handle (stamped "J. PERILLE Déposé PARIS" on one side, JP logo in serrated circle on the other) attached to a threaded steel shank supporting a three-armed flynut and open frame. When the frame rests upon the bottle lip and the worm has penetrated the cork, clockwise rotation of the flynut draws the cork, performing "double action," smooth shaft, bladed center worm, 1876. Steel, 6.5" high. Made in France.

335 Mechanical corkscrew with perforated steel handle attached to a threaded steel shank supporting a three-armed brass flynut and open frame. When the frame rests upon the bottle lip and the worm has penetrated the cork, clockwise rotation of the flynut draws the cork, performing "double action," smooth shaft, center worm, 1876. Steel and brass, 6.5" high. Made in France.

336 Mechanical corkscrew with perforated steel handle attached to a ribbon threaded steel shank that supports a ball-tipped brass flynut and open frame, stamped "BF Déposé Le Francais". When the frame rests upon the bottle lip and the worm has penetrated the cork, clockwise rotation of the flynut draws the cork, performing "double action," smooth tapered shaft, center worm, 1875. Steel and brass, 6.25" high. Made in France.

337

337 Mechanical corkscrew with foliate handle, fitted locking sleeve and a threaded steel shank running through a baroque open frame; rotating the sleeve sets or releases the lock. A locked handle turns the worm, penetrating the cork; releasing the lock and rotating the handle down the threaded shank exerts pressure between the frame and bottle lip, extracting the cork, smooth shaft with small button, bladed center worm, Thüringen version, rolling ring type, Ehrhardt patent 1891 (purchased by Reissmann, c. 1900, silver-plated by Gorham). Steel, 5.5" high. Made in Germany and USA.

338 Mechanical corkscrew with ball-tipped foliate handle, fitted locking sleeve and a threaded steel shank running through a baroque open frame with two grotesque faces and two fantasy dolphins; rotating the sleeve sets or releases the lock. A locked handle turns the worm, penetrating the cork; releasing the lock and rotating the handle down the threaded shank exerts pressure between the frame and bottle lip extracting the cork, smooth shaft with small button, bladed center worm, Thüringen version, rolling ring type, Reissmann patent, 1891. Nickel-plated brass and steel, 5.5" high. Made in Germany.

339 (on facing page) Mechanical corkscrew with an Egyptian revival handle, fitted figural locking sleeve and a threaded steel shank running through a baroque open frame featuring demon heads and classical female figures; rotating the sleeve sets or releases the lock. A locked handle turns the worm, penetrating the cork; releasing the lock and rotating the handle down the threaded shank exerts pressure between the frame and bottle lip, extracting the cork, Thüringen version, short smooth shaft with small button, bladed center worm, Ehrhardt patent 1891 (purchased by Reissmann, c. 1900). Nickel-plated steel, 7.5" high. Made in Germany.

338

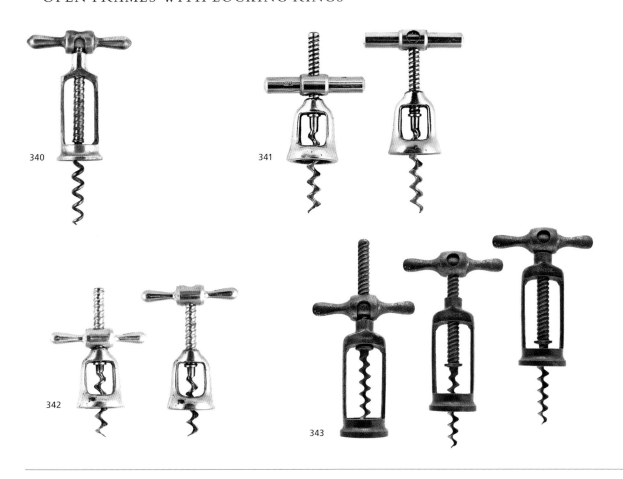

340

341

342

343

340 Mechanical corkscrew with shaped handle, fitted locking sleeve and threaded steel shank running through an open frame stamped "R. Murphy Boston". Rotating the sleeve locks or unlocks it; a locked handle turns the worm, penetrating the cork; releasing the lock and rotating the handle down the threaded shank exerts pressure between the frame and bottle lip, extracting the cork. Smooth shaft with small button, bladed center worm, 1900. Steel, 5.75" high. Made in USA.

341 Mechanical corkscrew with smooth rod handle, fitted locking sleeve and threaded steel shank running through an open frame. Rotating the sleeve locks or unlocks it; a locked handle turns the worm, penetrating the cork; releasing the lock and rotating the handle down the threaded shank exerts pressure between the frame and bottle lip, extracting the cork. Smooth shaft, bladed center worm, Williamson patent, c. 1940. Nickel-plated steel, 5.25" high. Made in USA.

342 Mechanical "Burgundy" model corkscrew with shaped nickel-plated brass handle, fitted locking sleeve and threaded nickel-plated brass shank running through an open frame. Rotating the sleeve locks or unlocks it; a locked handle turns the worm, penetrating the cork; releasing the lock and rotating the handle down the threaded shank exerts pressure between the frame and bottle lip, extracting the cork. Smooth shaft, bladed center worm, Williamson patent, 1946. Nickel-plated brass and nickel-plated steel, 4.5" high. Made in USA.

343 Mechanical corkscrew with shaped locking handle and threaded steel shank running through an open frame stamped

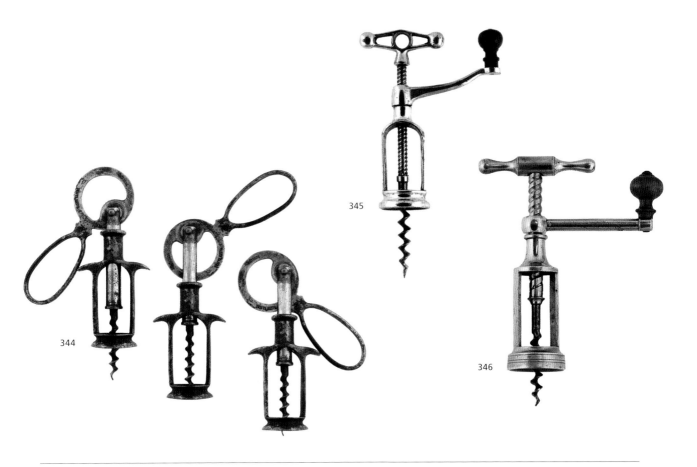

"E. Weck Germany". Rotating the sleeve locks or unlocks it; a locked handle turns the worm, penetrating the cork; releasing the lock and rotating the handle down the threaded shank exerts pressure between the frame and bottle lip, extracting the cork. Smooth shaft with small button, bladed center worm, Ehrhardt patent, 1891. Steel, 5.5" high. Made in Germany.

344 Mechanical corkscrew with steel loop handle stamped "Ultra Rapide" and "Bte. S.G.D.G."* The frame is turned until the collar rests on the bottle lip, lifting the handle extracts the penetrated cork, Fernand François patent, 1902. Steel, 6" high. Made in France.

345 Mechanical "Manivelle" crank model corkscrew with applied steel ball-tipped Perille handle fixed to a threaded steel shank which is the axis for an an open frame and coffee grinder arm with turned black wood knob. With the frame resting on the bottle lip and the shank extended, the handle is turned to penetrate the cork; the crank handle is then turned for extraction, performing "double action." Tapered shaft, bladed center worm,

Perille patent, 1910–20. Wood, nickel-plated steel and steel, 7" high. Made in France.

346 Mechanical corkscrew with nickel-plated cast brass handle fixed to a threaded steel shank which is the axis for an open frame and coffee grinder arm with turned light wood knob. With the frame resting on the bottle lip and the shank extended, the handle is

turned to penetrate the cork; the crank handle is then turned for extraction, performing "double action." Smooth shaft, bladed center worm, 1910–20. Wood, nickel-plated brass and steel, 7" high. Made in Italy.

* Bte. S.G.D.G. stands for Breveté Sans Garantie Du Gouvernement.

THOMASON CORKSCREWS

Thomason's 1802 patent was the second corkscrew patent after Henshall's Button. In this innovation the handle is connected to the worm by a telescoping double-threaded shaft system within a closed frame. With the frame resting on the bottle lip, the handle, turned in a continuous counterclockwise then clockwise motion, makes the worm penetrate and extract the cork, then enables the removal of the cork from the worm.

347

347   Thomason III Variant mechanical closed frame corkscrew with bristle brush-tipped turned wood handle topped by a smaller brass handle attached through the center to a threaded steel shaft. A counterthreaded brass shank telescopes into a bronze barrel with a maker's plate showing an oval shield marked "THOMASON PATENT NE PLUS ULTRA" topped by the lion of Britannia

standing on a crown and flanked by a rising lion and a rising unicorn, all atop a festoon marked "DIEU ET MON DROIT". Tapered helical worm, Thomason patent, 1802. Wood, brass, bronze, fiber and steel, 7" high. Made in England.

348   (at right) Mechanical closed frame corkscrew, Thomason V serpent variant, with recumbent lion and unicorn handle

topped by the English imperial crown. A threaded steel shaft and telescoping, counter-threaded brass shank nest into a silver-on-bronze barrel topped by a coiled snake handle (with intricate scaling and jaws closed on a bristle brush) passing through the grooved neck of the barrel. Barrel is engraved in elaborate script "to [P, T or] J Baillie" with a timeworn boar, the

clan's mascot, on front and "from G Ross" on back. Below the script, the maker's plate is comprised of a lion and unicorn rampant on an imperial crown, and stamped with "THOMASONS Patent NE PLUS ULTRA DIEU ET MON DROIT", tapered helical worm, Thomason patent, c. 1830. Silver, animal fiber and steel, 10" fully extended, 8" closed. Made in England.

KINGS SCREWS

A Kings Screw has a top handle that is connected to the worm by a threaded shaft and rack jacket within a closed barrel or columned frame to penetrate the cork. Extraction of the cork is accomplished by turning clockwise the added feature of a second smaller, side handle which activates a rack and pinion system to raise the cork out of the bottle.

350

349

349   Kings Screw, with hanging loop fitting atop brush-tipped turned bone handle attached through the center to a threaded steel shank within a brass rack jacket and closed copper barrel stamped "TT". Turned bone side handle raises the cork. Helical worm, smooth shaft, c. 1855. Copper, brass, bone and steel, 7" fully compressed. Made in England.

350   Kings Screw, with hanging loop atop a brush-tipped turned ivory handle attached thorough the center to a threaded steel shank within a steel rack jacket and closed turned bronze barrel frame bearing the maker's brass plate "Jos Rodgers & Sons Sheffield". Turned silver side handle raises the cork. Smooth shaft, tapered helical worm, c. 1860. Bronze, brass, silver, ivory, steel and vegetal fiber, 8.75" fully extended. Made in England.

351　Lund Kings Screw mechanical rack & pinion corkscrew with steel pinion handle and a brush-tip turned wood handle with a fitting for a hanging ring. The telescoping, counter-threaded steel shank and narrow steel rack nest into a brass barrel supporting a three-spring bottle grip stamped with a crown and "LUND'S PATENT 57 CORNHILL LONDON", smooth shaft, tapered helical worm, Lund patent, 1838. Wood, brass, steel and animal fiber, 7.75" high closed, 12" fully extended. Made in England.

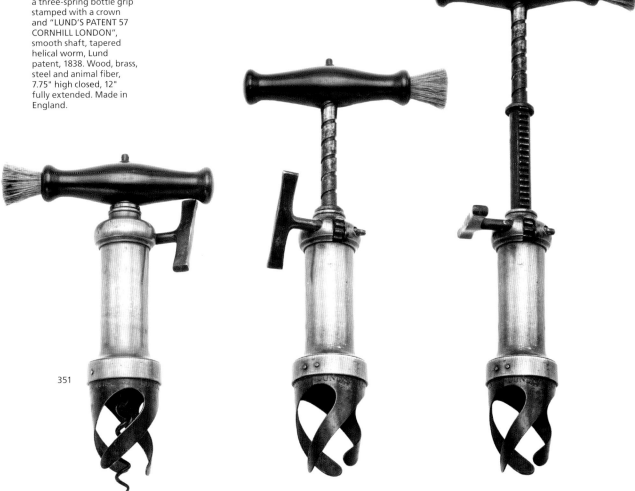

351

KINGS SCREWS

352

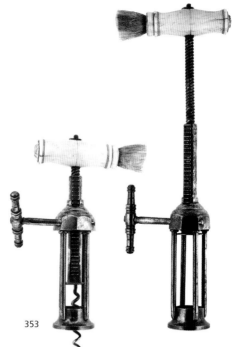

353

352   Kings Screw with brush-tipped turned bone handle, hanging loop atop, attached through the center to a threaded steel shank within a steel rack jacket and open four-post frame with octagonal cap, steel side handle, smooth shaft, tapered grooved helical worm, 1800–30. Bone, animal fiber and steel, 8" high fully compressed. Made in England.

353   Kings Screw with hanging loop atop a brush-tipped turned bone handle, which turns the threaded steel shaft within the steel rack shank (with slide) to penetrate the cork. The turned steel side handle rotates the steel pinion gear to elevate the cork within an octagonal topped open four-post frame, smooth shaft, tapered helical worm, 1800–30. Bone, animal fiber and steel, 9.5" fully compressed. Made in England.

RACK & PINION CORKSCREWS

Rack and pinion corkscrews have a two-part mechanical function, to penetrate and then to remove the cork. With the frame resting on the bottle lip, turning the top handle clockwise rotates the worm to penetrate the cork. Removal of the cork from the bottle neck is effected by turning the side handle, which activates two reciprocating parts, a circular pinion gear that engages a notched rack shank thereby converting a circular motion into into a vertical motion, lifting the cork out. The cork can be removed from the worm by holding it still while turning the top handle counterclockwise.

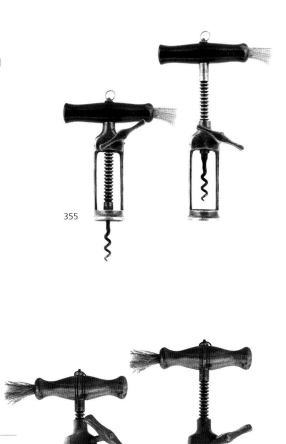

355

354

356

354 Rack and pinion corkscrew with brush-tipped turned rosewood handle with hanging loop atop. The collar of the rack shank is stamped "LUND'S PATENT LONDON RACK—", steel side handle, short smooth shaft with cork grip button, tapered helical worm, 1855. Steel with traces of bronzing on the frame, wood and vegetal fiber, 8" fully compressed. Made in England.

355 Rack and pinion corkscrew with brush-tipped turned wood handle to which the rack shank is connected through the middle with a brass washer and loop atop. The open brass frame, in which the rack shank and worm rotate, is stamped "London J D Patent.", steel side handle, short smooth shaft, tapered helical worm, c. 1860. Wood, vegetal fiber and steel, 7.5" fully compressed. Made in England.

356 Steel rack and pinion corkscrew with a brush-tipped turned wood handle and rack shank connecting through the middle to a loop atop. With the open steel frame resting on the bottle lip, turning the wood handle rotates the rack shank to penetrate the cork; the steel side handle controls a pinion gear, which engages the rack to elevate the cork, short smooth shaft, tapered helical worm, Lund patent, 1855. Wood, vegetal fiber and steel, 7" high. Made in England.

RACK & PINION CORKSCREWS

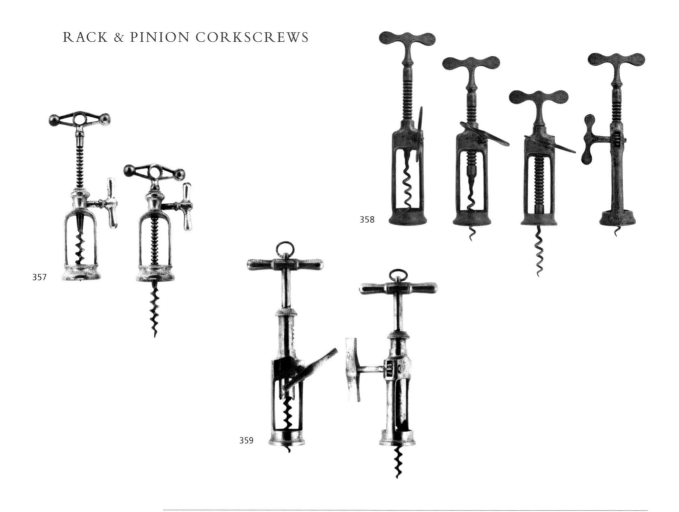

357

358

359

360

357 Steel rack and pinion corkscrew with ball-tipped Perille handle applied to the rack shank which passes through an open frame (stamped within a serrated circle "Déposé PARIS JP"), nickel-plated steel side handle, smooth tapered shaft, bladed center worm, Perille patent, 1876. Nickel-plated steel and steel, 6.5" high fully extended. Made in France.

358 Rack and pinion corkscrew with contoured steel handle to which the rack shank is connected through an open frame, contoured steel side handle, short tapered shaft, tapered helical worm, c. 1850. Steel with traces of bronzing on the frame and lower handle, 7.5" fully compressed. Made in England.

359 Nickel-plated steel rack and pinion corkscrew with turned steel handle, hanging loop and threaded steel shaft within a toothed cork gripper rack shank, nickel-plated steel side handle, smooth shaft, bladed center worm, Kummer maker, c. 1900. Nickel-plated steel and steel, 8" fully compressed. Made in Germany.

360 Nickel-plated steel Boué-Deveson rack and pinion corkscrew with ball-tipped handles and an open frame stamped with "JB" within a star and "Modèle Déposé, Made in France", smooth shaft, bladed center worm, c. 1930. Nickel-plated steel and steel, 6.5" high. Made in France.

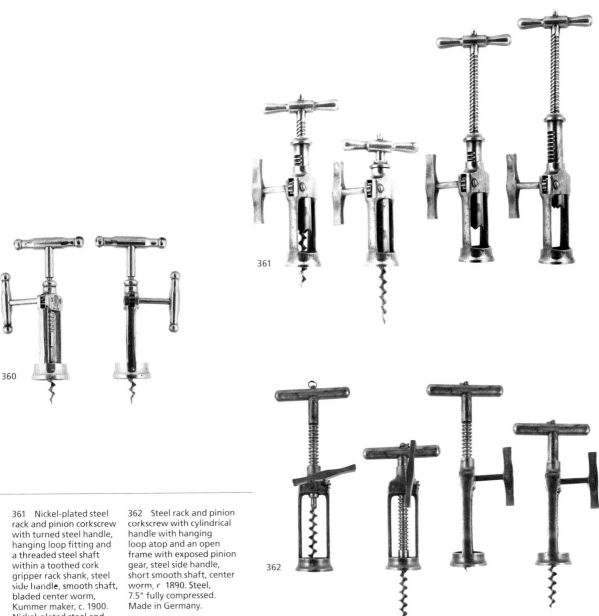

360

361

361 Nickel-plated steel rack and pinion corkscrew with turned steel handle, hanging loop fitting and a threaded steel shaft within a toothed cork gripper rack shank, steel side handle, smooth shaft, bladed center worm, Kummer maker, c. 1900. Nickel-plated steel and steel, 7.5" fully compressed. Made in Germany.

362 Steel rack and pinion corkscrew with cylindrical handle with hanging loop atop and an open frame with exposed pinion gear, steel side handle, short smooth shaft, center worm, c. 1890. Steel, 7.5" fully compressed. Made in Germany.

362

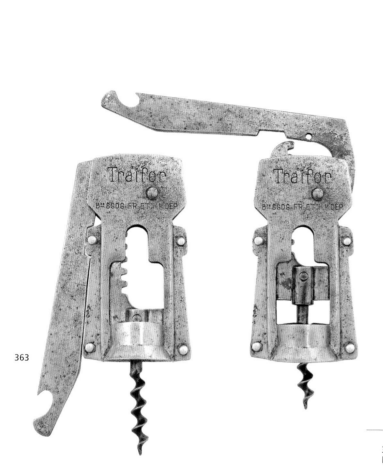

363

363 Mechanical single-lever type corkscrew with steel cap-lifter handle and open frame stamped "Bte. S.G.D.G. FR. ET M. M. DEP."* When the worm is turned to penetrate the cork and the frame rests on the bottle lip, the lever is raised for cork extraction, Traifor model (pun on *très fort* meaning "very strong"), smooth shaft, center worm, Grandfils patent, 1947. Steel, 6" closed. Made in France.

* Bte. S.G.D.G. FR. ET M. M. DEP stands for Sans Garantie Du Gouvernement, France et Etranger, Marque et Modèle Déposé.

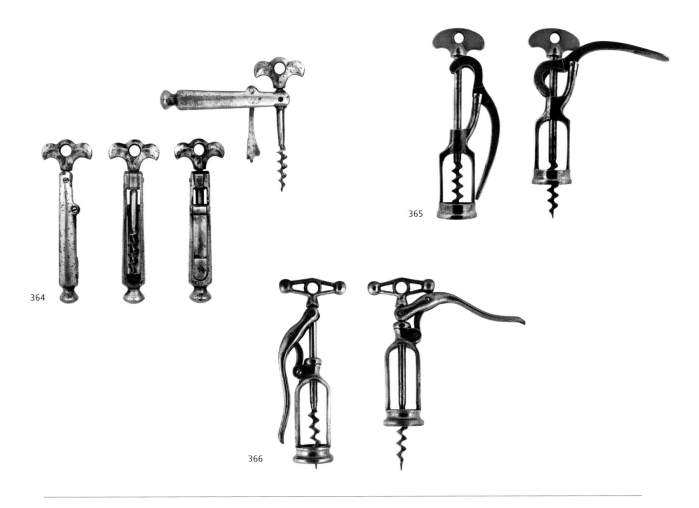

364

365

366

364 Single-lever mechanical corkscrew with a perforated lever handle and an inset pivoting foot stamped "JP". With the foot resting on the bottle neck and the handle perpendicular to the bottle, the worm is independently turned to penetrate the cork. The lever is then pressed downward to extract the cork, Levier model, pivoting tapering shaft, bladed center worm, Perille patent, c. 1884. Steel, 5" closed. Made in France.

365 Mechanical single lever corkscrew, known as "Le Rapide," with steel contoured handle and an open frame cast with a lever support arm and stamped "105". As the worm is turned to penetrate the cork, the lever raises to its apex; the lever is then lowered to extract the cork, based on the Gooch (American patent), long smooth shaft, center worm, 1870. Steel, 6.75". Made in France.

366 Mechanical single-lever corkscrew with steel applied ball-tipped Perille handle and an open frame with short lever raising arm stamped "Paris JHP Déposé Le Presto". As the worm is turned to penetrate the cork, the lever raises to its apex; the lever is then lowered, extracting the cork, long smooth tapering shaft, center worm, Perille patent, 1897. This model was reissued in the 1930s as "Le Presto" (later issued as Presto, then as Lesto). Steel, 6.5" high. Made in France.

ONE MECHANICAL LEVER (A LEG UP)

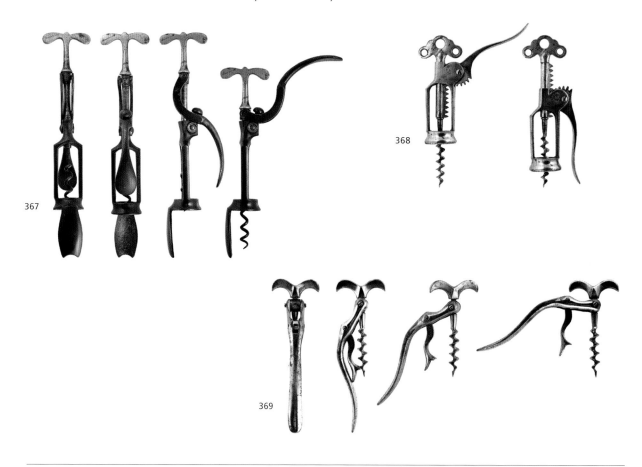

367

368

369

367 Mechanical single-lever corkscrew with wings and peak steel handle stamped "DRAKE & CO NY", a pivoting lever arm attached to the shank and a cast steel open frame and cam with brass hardware. With lever handle down and the frame resting on the bottle lip, the worm is turned to penetrate the cork, raising the lever to its upright position.

Lowering the lever extracts the cork and again raising it brings the worm into the frame for efficient manual cork removal, Royal Club model, smooth shaft, tapered helical worm, based on the Hull patent, 1864–66. Brass and steel, 9.75" in lever down position. Made in England or possibly New York.

368 Mechanical single-lever "Le Parfait" corkscrew with perforated stamped steel handle, toothed lever meshed with a rack shank-jacket and an open frame imprinted "Bte. S.G.D.G. A. C., Paris".* With the frame resting on the bottle neck the worm is turned to penetrate the cork, raising the lever to its upright position; cork extraction is attained by

lowering the lever, tapered smooth shaft, bladed center worm, Rousseau patent, 1905. Steel, 6.5" closed. Made in France.

369 Single-lever mechanical corkscrew with eyebrow handle and pivoting foot stamped "Déposé JHP Paris" in a serrated circle. With the handle perpendicular to the bottle and the foot

resting on the neck, the worm is independently turned to penetrate the cork; cork extraction is achieved by lowering the lever, Subito model, tapering pivot shaft, bladed center worm, c. 1900. Steel, 6.5" closed. Made in France.

* Bte. S.G.D.G. stands for Breveté Sans Garantie Du Gouvernement.

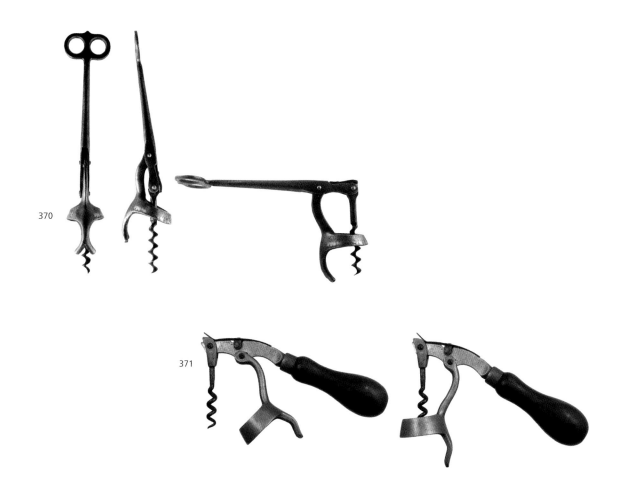

370 Single-lever
mechanical corkscrew
with spring-loaded lever
arm stamped "PAT'D SEP
3. 1878". With the handle
in the upright position
and the pivoting collar on
the bottle neck, the
forked foot centers and
stabilizes the also pivoting
cylindrical shaft and

worm; full rotation
penetrates the cork and
the lever arm may then
be lowered for extraction,
center worm, Tucker
patent, 1878. Steel,
9" fully extended, 3.5" in
lowered position. Made
in USA.

371 Collared single-lever
mechanical corkscrew with
a turned wood "pump
handle" lever arm marked
"PATD MAY 28, 1878"
and replaceable worm on
a pivoting spring-loaded
shank. With the lever
handle raised and the
collar resting on the bottle
neck, the worm is turned

to penetrate the cork;
lowering the lever toward
the bottle extracts the
cork, tapered smooth
shaft, tapering helical
worm, Sperry patent,
c. 1878. Brass, steel and
wood, 6.75" long, 4.25"
high. Made in USA.

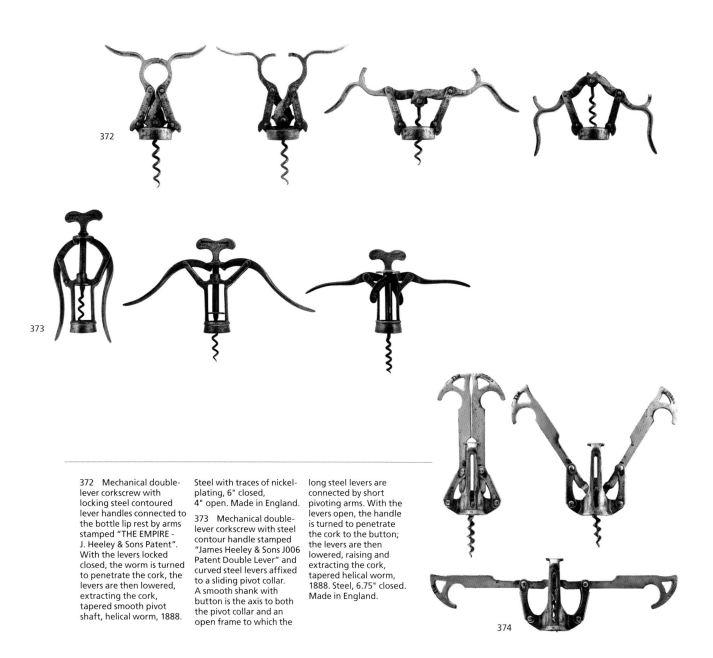

372 Mechanical double-lever corkscrew with locking steel contoured lever handles connected to the bottle lip rest by arms stamped "THE EMPIRE - J. Heeley & Sons Patent". With the levers locked closed, the worm is turned to penetrate the cork, the levers are then lowered, extracting the cork, tapered smooth pivot shaft, helical worm, 1888.

Steel with traces of nickel-plating, 6" closed, 4" open. Made in England.

373 Mechanical double-lever corkscrew with steel contour handle stamped "James Heeley & Sons J006 Patent Double Lever" and curved steel levers affixed to a sliding pivot collar. A smooth shank with button is the axis to both the pivot collar and an open frame to which the

long steel levers are connected by short pivoting arms. With the levers open, the handle is turned to penetrate the cork to the button; the levers are then lowered, raising and extracting the cork, tapered helical worm, 1888. Steel, 6.75" closed. Made in England.

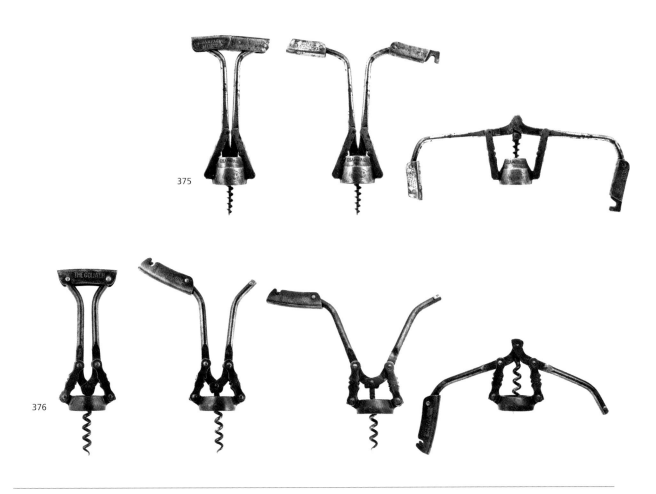

375

376

374 Mechanical double-lever corkscrew with steel slot-locking pivot lever handles, stamped "TYR Bte. S.G.D.G."* and connected to the bottle lip rest by short pivoting lever arms. With the levers locked closed, the worm is turned to penetrate the cork; the levers are then lowered for cork extraction, smooth pivot shaft, center worm, Baker patent, 1880. Steel, 7.25" closed. Made in France.

375 Mechanical double-lever corkscrew with two-part pivoting lever lock handle (stamped "A B CHAMPAGNE MOET ET CHANDON") and steel pivoting levers (stamped "tt") connected to the bottle lip rest (stamped in an oval logo "CHAMPAGNE MOET CHANDON") by decoratively cast steel pivoting lever arms — identifying this as the first model. With lever handle locked, the worm is turned until

the bottle lip rest is seated on the bottle; the levers are then unlocked and lowered, retracting the worm and extracting the cork. After returning the levers to locked position, the cork may be manually rotated off the worm, pivoting steel shaft, Archimedean worm, 1910–1940. Steel, 7.5" closed. Made in France.

376 Mechanical double-lever corkscrew with pivoting lever lock handle

stamped "THE GOLIATH Registered No.258915 Patent No. 24284/03 Made Abroad" and steel pivoting levers connected to a bottle lip rest by short stamped steel decorative pivoting lever arms, With the levers locked by the handle, the worm is turned to penetrate the cork until the frame rests on the bottle neck; the levers are then unlocked and lowered, retracting the worm and extracting

the cork. After returning the levers to locked position, the cork may be manually rotated off the worm, pivoting steel shaft, helical worm, Hausmann patent, 1903. Steel, 7" closed. Made in Germany, patented in England.

* Bte. S.G.D.G. stands for Breveté Sans Garantie Du Gouvernement.

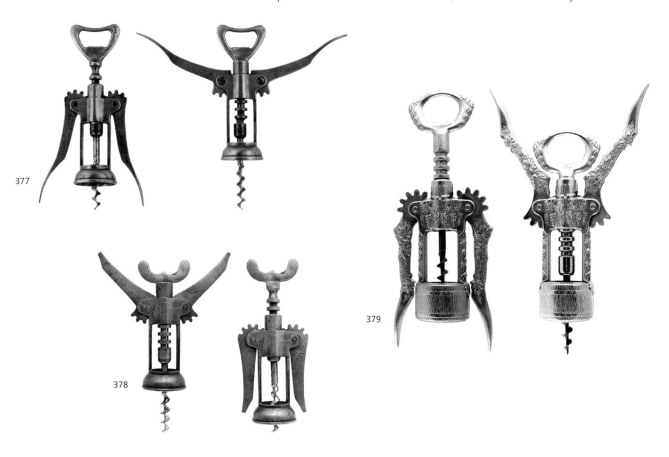

377

378

379

377 Mechanical double-lever corkscrew with cap-lifter handle stamped "Italy" and double pinion brass levers stamped "Castagna Verona Wines Bardolino-Chiaretto-Soave-Valpolicella". As the frame rests on the bottle neck and the handle turns the worm to penetrate the cork, the pinion shouldered levers reach their maximum raised position; lowering the levers extracts the cork, open brass frame, brass rack shank, smooth shaft, steel center worm, Rosati patent, 1930. Brass and steel, 6.25" closed. Made in Italy.

378 Mechanical double-lever corkscrew with brass wing-and-peak handle stamped "Made in Italy", and brass double pinion levers meshed to a rack shank within an open brass frame. As the frame rests on the bottle neck and the handle turns the worm to penetrate the cork, the pinion shouldered levers reach their maximum raised position; lowering the levers extracts the cork, smooth shaft, steel bladed center worm, Rosati patent, 1930. Brass and steel, 6" closed. Made in Italy.

379 Mechanical double-lever corkscrew with cap-lifter handle and rack shank, twin cast pinion levers and an open frame decoratively embellished with wine motifs: grapes, vines, leaves, tendrils and barrel. When the frame rests on the bottle neck and the worm is turned to penetrate the cork, the pinion shoulder levers reach their maximum raised position; lowering the levers extracts the cork, smooth shaft, steel Archimedean worm, Ghindini patent, 1973. Nickel-plated brass and steel, 7.5" closed. Made in Italy.

380 (at right) Mechanical double-lever corkscrew with hanging ring atop and dual cap-lifter shoulder lever handles; the pinions concealed in the pressed brass-plated steel open frame marked "Hootch Owl". With the levers up, the worm is turned to penetrate the cork; the levers are then lowered, raising and extracting the cork, square rack shaft, center worm, Smythe patent, 1936. Brass-plated steel and steel, 7" with levers up. Made in USA.

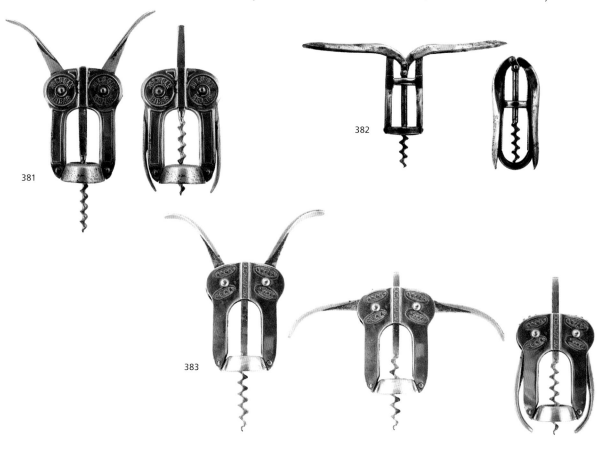

381

382

383

381 Mechanical double-lever corkscrew with twin lever handle shoulders and pinions concealed in the pressed nickel-plated steel open frame stamped "Jo-Lugan Eibar". With the levers up, the worm is turned to penetrate the cork; the levers are then lowered, raising and extracting the cork, square rack shaft, center worm, based on the

Smythe patent, 1935. Pressed nickel-plated steel and steel rivets, 8.5" with lever handles up. Made in Spain.

382 Mechanical double-lever corkscrew with steel pivoting lever handles stamped "Breveté Vogliotti Torino CARLO RUA & C TORINO Via Roma 42" and a cross-braced open-frame with folding bottle lip rest.

When the levers are raised and the bottle lip rest is opened, the worm is turned to penetrate the cork; the levers are then lowered, extracting the cork, smooth pivot shaft, center worm, Vogliotti patent, 1930. Steel, 4" closed, 4.75" open. Made in Italy or France.

383 Mechanical double-lever corkscrew with nickel-plated open frame

stamped "Magic LEVER CORK DRAWER PAT. APPD. FOR". With the levers raised, the worm is turned to penetrate the cork; the levers are then lowered, raising and extracting the cork, square shaft, center worm, 1938. Pressed nickel-plated steel and steel rivets, 8" with levers raised. Made in England.

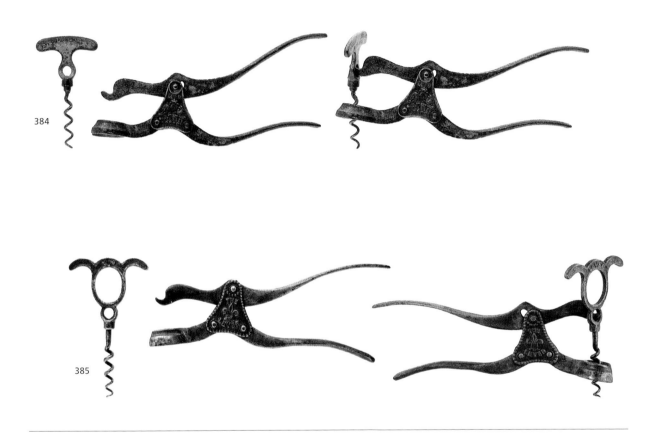

384 Paired-lever corkscrew with pivoting lever arms (hinged by cast steel badge depicting lion, shield and unicorn and marked "Lund Patentee, London -- Sold by The Patentee 24 Fleet Street & 57 Cornhill LONDON") and corkscrew with contoured perforated handle stamped "Lund Patentee and Maker 57 Cornhill & 24 Fleet Sts. LONDON". For extraction, the worm is inserted into the cork as a typical basic T (and may, if desired, be pulled manually). The split collar of the lower lever may then be fitted over the bottle lip and the hook passed into in the perforated corkscrew handle; pressing the lever handles toward each other with a firm grasp elevates the cork from the bottle, short smooth shaft, tapered helical worm, 1855. Steel with traces of copper paint, 8.5" long, 4" high. Made in England.

385 Paired-lever corkscrew with pivoting lever arms (hinged by triangular punchwork outlined badge marked "The Lever" with a fleur-de-lis) and corkscrew with eyebrow finger-pull applied handle, stamped "The Lever Signet", with perforated shank. For extraction, the worm is inserted into the cork as a typical three finger eyebrow (and may, if desired, be pulled manually). The split collar of the lower lever may then be fitted over the bottle lip and the hook passed into in the perforated shank; pressing the lever handles toward each other with a firm grasp elevates the cork from the bottle, tapered shaft, tapered helical worm, 1855. Steel with traces of copper paint, 8.5" long, 4.75" high. Made in England.

COMPOUND MECHANICAL LEVERS: CONCERTINAS & TONGS

Each of the concertinas and tongs operates as follows: with the compound levers compressed, the worm is turned to penetrate the cork. The cork is then extracted by the handle being drawn upward vertically, which raises the cork from the bottle. The cork may then be manually rotated off the worm.

386

387

386 Mechanical double compound-lever corkscrew, also called "Double Concertina," with wood bobbin handle attached by a rod running through the core from tip to tip to a series of scalloped, riveted compressible/extendable levers, each of which is stamped on the obverse "J.H.S. B." (James Heeley & Sons, Birmingham) or "Wier's Patent Double No. 4283", cross braces, pivoting bottle lip rest, flat arrowtail pivot shaft, helical worm, 1884. Steel with copper paint, 5" compressed, 8.75" extended. Made in England.

387 Mechanical compound-lever corkscrew, also called "Lady Concertina," with a pivoting steel finger grip handle riveted to a series of scalloped, riveted compressible/ extendable levers stamped "J.H.S. B." (James Heeley & Sons, Birmingham) and "Wier's Patent No. 4377", pivoting bottle lip rest, flat arrowtail pivot shaft, helical worm, 1884. Steel with copper paint, 5.5" compressed, 9" extended. Made in England.

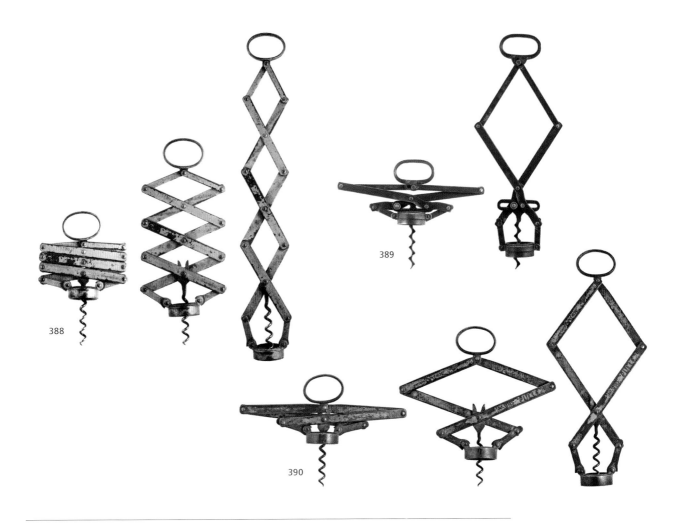

388 Mechanical compound-lever corkscrew with pivoting finger-pull handle attached by a rivet to equally sized compressible/extendable riveted levers stamped "PATENT Wier's Patent 12804 25 Septr 1884 Heeley & Sons Makers", pivoting bottle lip, arrowtail shaft, tapered helical worm, Heeley manufacturer,

Wier patent, 1884. Steel with copper paint, 5.5" compressed, 13.75" extended. Made in England.

389 Mechanical compound-lever corkscrew with two-finger pull handle attached by a rivet to unequally sized, riveted, compressible/ extendable levers stamped "H.D. Armstrong Patent",

braced pivoting bottle lip rest, slotted T shaft, center worm, 1903. Steel, 4.5" compressed, 10" extended. Made in England.

390 Mechanical compound-lever corkscrew with pivoting finger-pull handle attached by a rivet to unequally sized, riveted, compressible/ extendable levers stamped

"THE PULLEZI Heeley's 'ORIGINAL' Patent", and pivoting bottle lip rest brace, stamped "4507", Heeley manufacturer, arrowtail shaft, helical worm, based on Wier patent, 1885. Steel with copper paint, 4.75" compressed, 10" extended. Made in England.

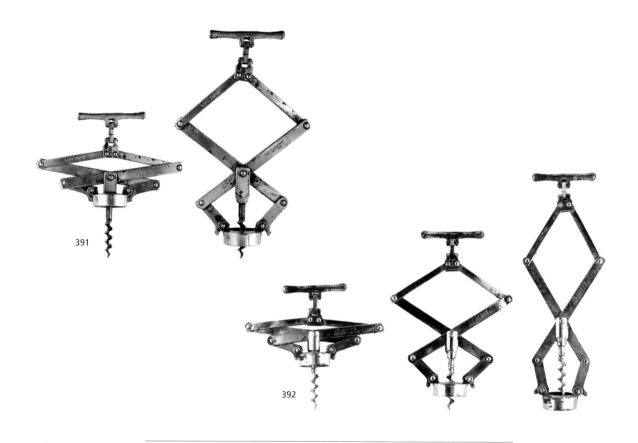

391

392

391 Mechanical compound-lever corkscrew with toggle bar handle attached by rivets to unequally sized, riveted, compressible/extendable levers stamped "PERFECT Breveté & Déposé", braced pivoting bottle lip rest, smooth shaft, center worm, based on Wier patent, c. 1885. Nickel-plated steel, 5.25" compressed, 8.5" extended. Made in France.

392 Mechanical compound-lever corkscrew with toggle bar handle attached by rivets to unequally sized, riveted, compressible/extendable levers stamped "PERFECT Breveté S.G.D.G.",* braced pivoting bottle lip rest, slotted shaft, center worm, based on Wier patent, c. 1910. Nickel-plated steel, 4.25" compressed, 8.75" extended. Made in France.

* S.G.D.G. stands for Sans Garantie Du Gouvernement.

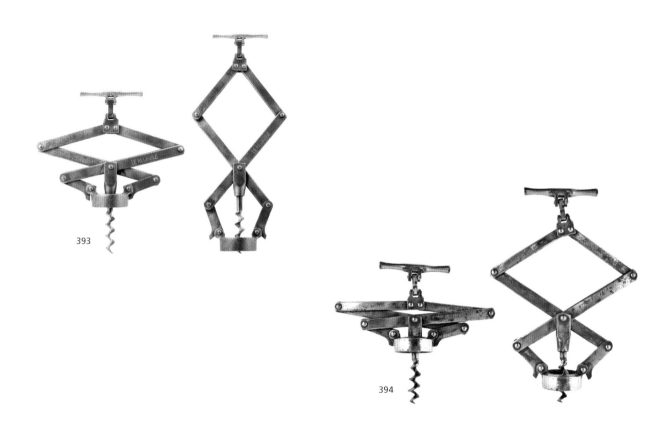

393 Mechanical compound-lever corkscrew with toggle bar handle attached by rivets to unequally sized, riveted, compressible/extendable levers stamped "LE RELIABLE", and steel braced pivoting bottle lip rest. "Le Reliable" is thought to be the transition model between "The Reliable" (American) and "Perfect" (French), smooth shaft, center worm, Wier patent,

c. 1885. Nickel-plated steel, 5.25" compressed, 8" extended. Made in USA, perhaps for the French market.

394 Mechanical compound-lever corkscrew with toggle bar handle attached by rivets to unequally sized, riveted, compressible/ extendable levers stamped "'THE RELIABLE' Pat. Nov. 10, 1885" (American patent), braced pivoting

bottle lip rest, slotted smooth shaft, center worm, based on Wier patent, 1885. Nickel-plated steel, 4.25" compressed, 8" extended. Made in France.

395

395 Mechanical compound lever corkscrew with oval, pivoting two-finger pull handle and riveted compressible/extendable levers ("LE TRIC TRAC" stamped on top lever, "DÉPOSÉ JP PARIS" stamped on second and "DÉPOSÉ PARIS" stamped on third), fixed bottle lip rest, pivoting arrowtail shaft, bladed helical worm, 1927. Steel with traces of nickel plating, 6.25" high compressed. Made in France.

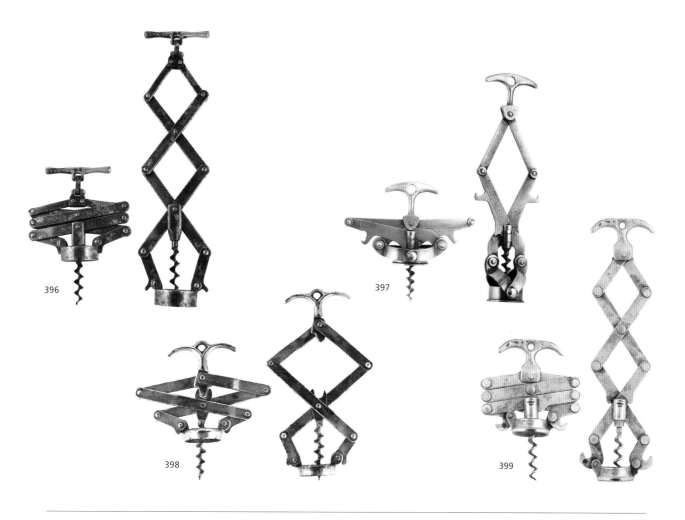

396 Mechanical compound-lever corkscrew with toggle bar handle attached by rivets to equally sized compressible/extendable riveted levers, stamped "Breveté & Déposé IDEAL PERFECT", braced bottle lip rest, rectangular shaft, bladed center worm, based on Wier patent, c. 1900. Steel with traces of nickel plating, 5" compressed, 10" extended. Made in France.

397 Mechanical compound-lever corkscrew with pivoting brass contour handle riveted to compound levers stamped "DEBOUCHTOUT Bte S.G.D.G. Marque et Modele Déposés France et Etranger";* cap-lifters are part of the two longest levers, pivot bottle lip rest, pinned smooth shaft, steep pitch bladed center worm, Bart patent, c. 1920. Steel and brass, 4.25" compressed, 8.25" extended. Made in France.

398 Mechanical compound-lever corkscrew with eyebrow handle, shank and braced pivoting cast bottle lip rest attached by rivet to unequally sized, riveted, compressible/extendable levers. When compressed the locking shank fastens to the worm shaft, slotted arrowtail shaft, center worm, based on Wier patent, 1920. Steel, 5" compressed, 7.75" extended. Made in France.

399 Mechanical compound-lever corkscrew with steel contour handle riveted to compound levers, cap-lifters are part of the two shortest levers, fixed bottle lip rest, pinned smooth brass shaft, center worm, c. 1920. Steel and brass, 5.25" compressed, 9.25" extended. Made in France.

* Bte S.G.D.G. stands for Breveté Sans Garantie Du Gouvernement.

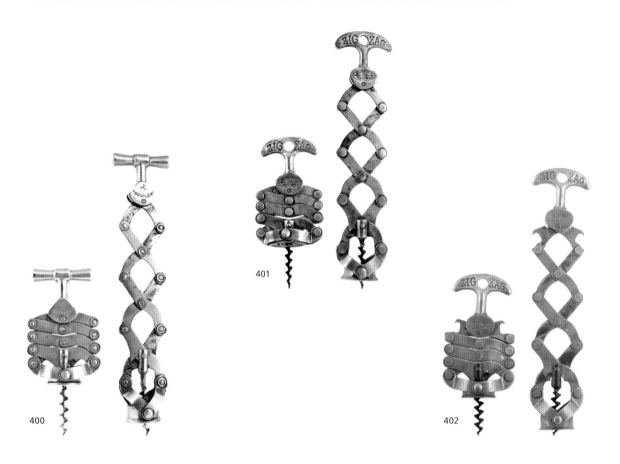

400

401

402

400 Mechanical compound-lever or concertina corkscrew with shaped T handle and plate, stamped "SOUPLEX PPP (Pierre Postel logo) Made in France", riveted to equally sized, sloped, compressible/extendable levers, pivoting bottle lip rest, spring-loaded top lever arms, pinned smooth shaft, steep pitch bladed center worm, after first Bart Patent, c. 1935.

Steel, 6" compressed, 11" extended. Made in France.

401 Mechanical compound-lever corkscrew with cast contour handle and spring-loaded oval base, stamped "ZIG ZAG" and "Breveté. S.G.D.G. Marque Déposée France et Étranger",* attached by a pin to a set of riveted compressible/extendable lever arms, pivoting bottle lip rest, pivot shaft, steep

pitch bladed center worm, Bart Patent, 1920. Steel, 6.25" compressed, 10" extended. Made in France.

402 Mechanical compound-lever corkscrew with cast contour handle and spring-loaded oval base, marked "ZIG ZAG" and "Bte. S.G.D.G. Fr. et Et. M. & M. DEP.",** attached by a pin to a set of riveted compressible/ extendable lever arms, stamped "Made in France",

cap-lifter epaulets on top levers, pivoting bottle lip rest, pivot shaft, steep pitch bladed center worm, Bart Patent, 1928. Steel, 6.25" compressed, 10.25" extended. Made in France.

403 Mechanical compound-lever corkscrew with a stamped steel eyebrow handle attached by a rivet to equally sized, curved, riveted compressible/extendable

levers, stamped "Made in France", pivoting bottle lip rest, pivot shaft, bladed center worm, c. 1920. Steel, 6.25" compressed, 9" extended. Made in France.

404 Mechanical compound-lever corkscrew with eyebrow handle and spring-loaded curved lever arms attached by peened rivet, stamped "KIS-PLY PARIS". The pull mechanism is riveted to

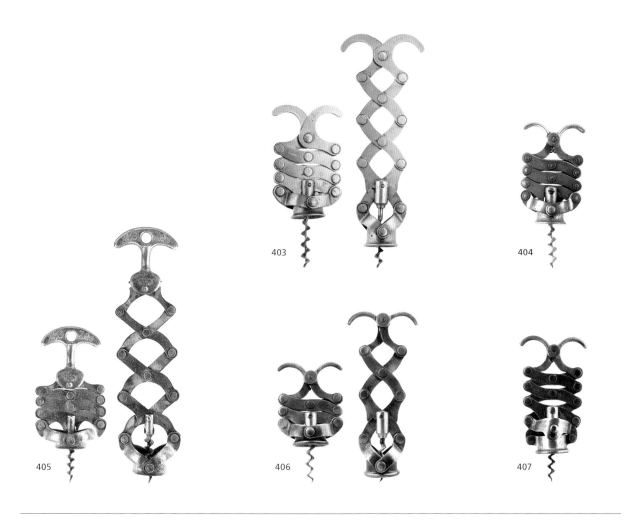

403

404

405

406

407

equally sized, sloped, riveted compressible/extendable levers stamped "Universal Cutlery Co. N.Y. France", pivoting bottle lip rest, pivot shaft, bladed center worm, Thomas patent, 1932. Steel, 5.5" compressed. Made in France.

405   Mechanical compound-lever corkscrew with cast contour handle and spring-loaded oval base, marked "ZIG ZAG"

and "42 Bte. S.G.D.G. Fr. et Et. M. & M. DEP.",** attached by a pin to a set of riveted compressible/extendable stamped steel lever arms. This lighter gauge, stamped steel Ziq Zaq corkscrew evidences WWII era metal shortages, pivoting bottle lip rest, pivot shaft, steep pitch bladed center worm, Bart Patent, 1942–46. Steel, 6" compressed, 10" extended. Made in France.

406   Mechanical compound-lever corkscrew with a riveted spring-loaded brass eyebrow lever handle stamped "KIS-PLY PARIS Breveté Déposé" attached to equally sized, curved, riveted, compressible/extendable levers, pivoting brass bottle lip rest, brass pivot shaft, bladed center worm, Thomas patent, 1931.

Steel, 4.5" compressed, 6.5" extended. Made in France.

407   Mechanical compound-lever corkscrew with riveted spring-loaded brass eyebrow handle stamped "KIS-PLY PARIS Breveté Déposé" attached to equally sized, curved, riveted, compressible/extendable levers, pivoting brass bottle lip rest, brass pivot shaft, bladed center worm, Thomas

patent, 1931. Brass and steel, 5.5" compressed. Made in France.

* S.G.D.G. stands for Sans Garantie Du Gouvernement.

** Bte. S.G.D.G. Fr. et Et. M. & M. DEP. stands for Breveté Sans Garantie Du Gouvernement, France et Étranger, Marque et Modèle Déposé.

6 *The In and Out of It*
BAR CORKSCREWS

In April 1973, I was in Paris with Ivan and our four-year-old son, Jesse. After visiting the studio of Erro, an artist whose paintings Ivan intended to exhibit at the OK Harris Gallery that year, we went to Chez René, a neighborhood bistro, for a late lunch. The restaurateur was a fan of Erro's work. After a fine repast of specialties that were not on the menu, he offered a round of a crystal-clear cordial that was poured from a bottle fitted with a pink hand-knit zippered coverall. Smitten by sumptuous food, starched white table linen, engaging conversation and copious libation, we enjoyed the brandy; it was a fitting close to our meal. Jesse, who had been quietly entertaining himself with toy cars and tableware obstacles, reached over and unzipped the bottle cover. "You drank that," he said pointing his finger. There was an elegantly preserved gray viper, tightly knotted at the bottom of the bottle with its open-mouthed head and bright eyes extending up and into the bottle's neck.

Apparently, French peasants from the Pyrenees know how to make good things from life's unavoidable afflictions. They are "can do" when it comes to subduing vipers with alcohol. Post-glacial generations of Basques have perfected viper liqueur. This is the recipe: Force a sugar cube into an empty, clear, uncapped wine bottle and place it on its side under your bed, in a dark corner of your barn or workshop or wherever you've previously seen a viper. Leave a cork within easy reach and be patient. Cork the bottle as soon as you discover that the viper has entered. While the snake is enthralled in a sugar high, pour in an inch of the nearest thing to pure high proof alcohol and quickly recork. Do this daily. As the regurgitated sugar, alcohol and venom marry, the snake's head gets closer to the top of the bottle in search of oxygen and revenge. Flavor-wise, something magical happens to the liquid and it remains clear. I have thought about who first figured this out while

408 (at left) Wall mounted rack and pinion cork lifter with 19th century corkscrew, "C F" with center anchor at top of mount is the maker's mark of Camion Frères. An independent corkscrew is rotated to penetrate the cork, with the pinion handle in raised position, the bottle is fitted into the neck rest below the rack and pinion mechanism with the handle of the corkscrew on the double hook, then the handle of the mechanism is lowered to raise the cork. Bronzed steel, brass, steel, 15" high, c. 1900. Made in France.

kicking stones along the banks of the Garonne River or in the mountains around Arthez-de-Béarn. It must have been someone who regarded the given conditions of life sidewise.

With analogous lateral thinking, applying the principle of putting the machine in the service of humankind, a spate of complex bar-top contraptions were invented to dispatch the cork and get the wine poured with industrial efficiency to thirsty customers at pubs, bistros and bars. In the late nineteenth century, large mechanical brass, cast iron and steel lever-handled corkscrews, C clamped or bolted to bar tops or behind the counter or on a wall, were developed for saloons, bars, clubs and restaurants that required speedy service of beverages to their clientele. Ardent imagining produced uncorking machines that swiftly and unceremoniously facilitated cork removal, often out of sight of the purchaser, frequently ejecting the cork from the worm into the trash bin (or onto the floor) in the same quick extracting motion or by moving the handle in reverse of the opening motion after the bottle had been released. The deed was done by bar or waitstaff, in circumstances that didn't require white gloves, sniffing the cork or any of the protocol of decorous wine service at the table.

Bar screws epitomize an era that was infatuated with the idea of machines as labor-saving devices. At the end of the nineteenth and beginning of the twentieth centuries, a variety of bar screws and wall-mounted corkscrews were patented in the U.K., the U.S. and France. Some are embellished with sinuous Art Nouveau foliage while others possess straightforward industrial presence. The idea that the muscle resided in the gadget and anyone could clamp the bottle and yank the tightest cork had its appeal. These devices were ingeniously engineered in a surprising variety of forms and a medley of motions from clamping, cranking, upward and downward extraction, levering and serial gear changes on the worm slide for cork drawing and ejection. Each bar screw is a muscular mechanism with imaginative reach and visual integrity that speaks volumes about other times when they were the fastest game in town.

409   Presto bar corkscrew, cast steel case marked "PRESTO", wall mounted, spring-loaded, speed worm. A single upward motion penetrates, extracts and frees the cork from the worm, Winterberger patent, 1934. Cast steel, 13" high. Made in USA.

410   Wall mounted rack and pinion bar screw with a spring-loaded, ball-topped handle (lowering extends the worm), large external gears, center speed worm, Barraud Lerenard, 1925. Painted cast iron, steel and brass, 12" in raised handle position. Made in France.

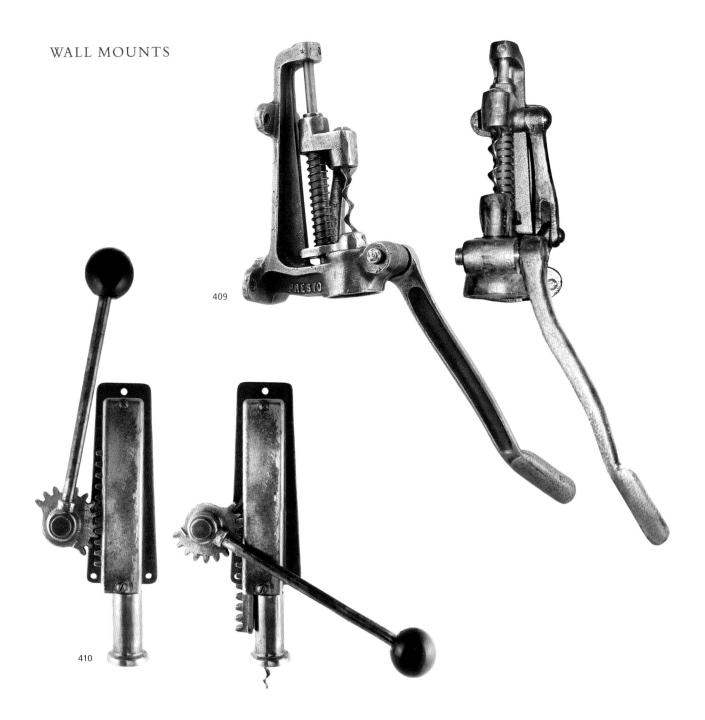

409

410

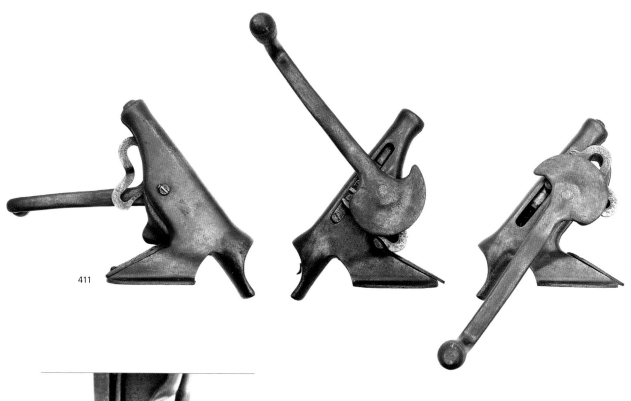

411

411 "Unique" screw-
mounted counter bar
screw with curved cam
and yoke mechanism
(also called "Quick and
Easy"), cast steel case
and case plate marked
"1898 UNIQUE American
Manufacture Pat'd in
America & Europe",
turned wood handle grip,
steel handle, closed
frame, smooth shaft,
speed worm, Walker

patent, 1898. With the
bottle neck inserted into
the closed frame and
the handle parallel to the
case plate and bar top,
the handle is pulled
upright and down to make
a 3/4 revolution around
the cam to penetrate and
draw the cork; reversing
the motion ejects the cork.
Steel and wood, 8" case,
12" with handle raised.
Made in USA.

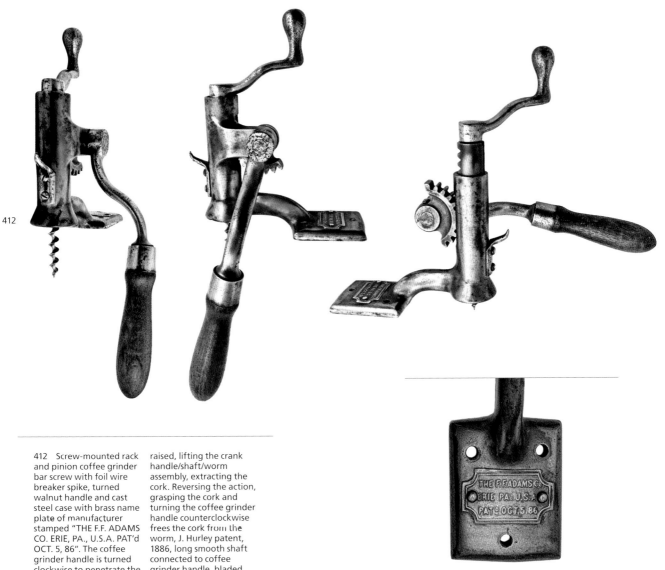

412 Screw-mounted rack and pinion coffee grinder bar screw with foil wire breaker spike, turned walnut handle and cast steel case with brass name plate of manufacturer stamped "THE F.F. ADAMS CO. ERIE, PA., U.S.A. PAT'd OCT. 5, 86". The coffee grinder handle is turned clockwise to penetrate the cork; the steel rack and pinion handle is then raised, lifting the crank handle/shaft/worm assembly, extracting the cork. Reversing the action, grasping the cork and turning the coffee grinder handle counterclockwise frees the cork from the worm, J. Hurley patent, 1886, long smooth shaft connected to coffee grinder handle, bladed center worm. Wood, brass and cast steel, 12" high.

COUNTER MOUNTS

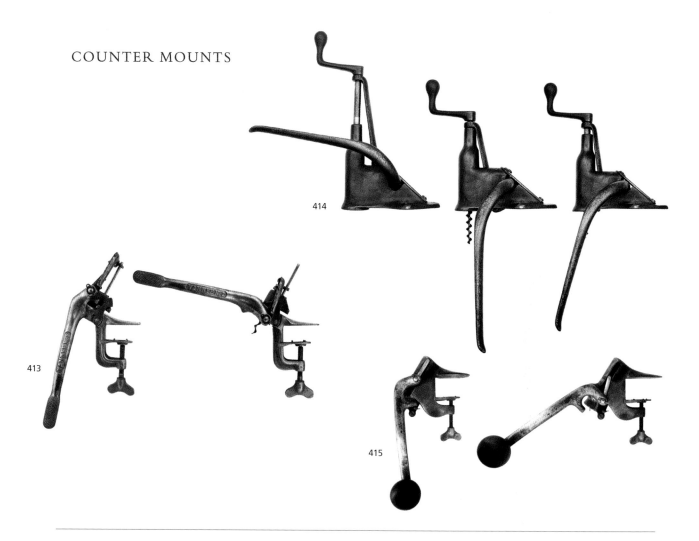

413   Yankee No. 2 bar screw marked "YANKEE No. 2" with patterned grip, bar mounting C-clamp, speed worm, Gilchrist patent, 1907. Beginning with the lever fully lowered, upward motion penetrates and extracts the cork; repeating the motion frees the cork from the worm. Cast steel with wood knob grip, 12" high. Made in USA.

414   Screw-mounted coffee grinder counter bar screw, cast steel case, long smooth shaft connected to coffee grinder handle, bladed center worm. With the beaver-tail lever raised, the coffee grinder handle is turned to penetrate the cork; the lever is then raised, extracting the cork. Holding the cork and turning the handle counterclockwise frees the cork from the worm, Walker patent, 1891. Cast steel, 14" high. Made in USA.

415   Midget mechanical bar screw with no markings, bar mounted by a C-clamp, wood knob handle on lever arm, speed worm, 1893. Beginning with the handle fully lowered, an upward handle motion penetrates the cork, the reverse downward motion expels the cork, freeing it from the worm. Steel with traces of nickel plating and wood knob handle grip, 10.5" high. Made in USA.

416   Heavy-duty bar mount corkscrew with steel scalloped C-clamp mount stamped "ACME", made by Samuel Mason, cast brass body and bottle neck frame, steel tap type pivoting double-lever handle with wood grip, long threaded shaft, speed center worm, Vaughan patent, 1887. With bottle neck inserted in the frame, the raised lever is firmly lowered and the worm penetrates the cork; raising the lever drawers the cork out of the bottle. The lever must be lowered again for manual cork removal. Wood, cast brass, steel, 21" high. Made in Ireland or England.

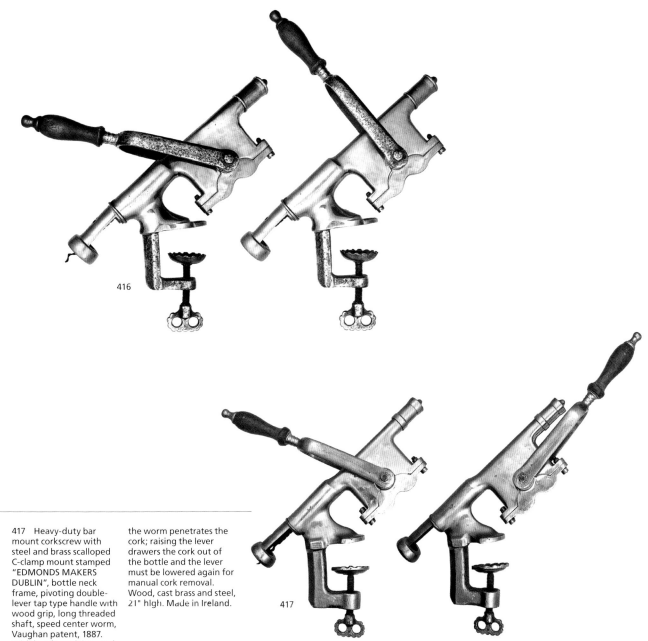

416

417 Heavy-duty bar mount corkscrew with steel and brass scalloped C-clamp mount stamped "EDMONDS MAKERS DUBLIN", bottle neck frame, pivoting double-lever tap type handle with wood grip, long threaded shaft, speed center worm, Vaughan patent, 1887. With bottle neck inserted in the frame, the raised lever is firmly lowered and the worm penetrates the cork; raising the lever drawers the cork out of the bottle and the lever must be lowered again for manual cork removal. Wood, cast brass and steel, 21" high. Made in Ireland.

417

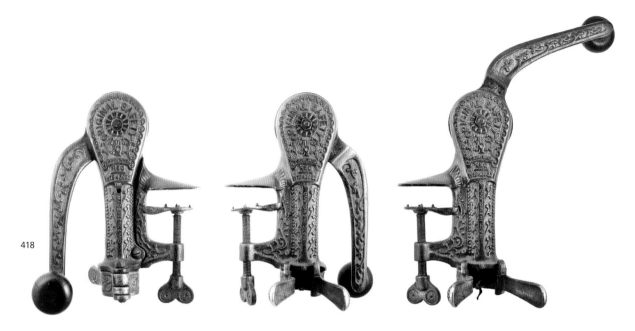

418

419

418   Original Safety mechanical bar screw with stylized floral design and trademark upraised hand on cast steel case marked "ORIGINAL SAFETY Trademark REG. No.543083 Made in England", bar mount C-clamp, bottle neck clamp, speed worm, Gilchrist patent, 1894. On one side there is a lubrication hole marked "Oil". Beginning with the handle fully raised, one continuous downward handle motion penetrates and extracts the cork; reversing the motion expels the cork from the worm. Cast steel with wood knob handle grip, 10.5" high. Made in England.

419   Champion mechanical bar screw with cast steel handle and wood grip, Art Nouveau floral design on the cast steel bar mounted C-clamp, bottle neck clamp and case (marked "CHAMPION. PAT. Sept. 7, 1897. BES. PAT. June 9, 1896" on both sides). Beginning with the handle fully raised and the bottle grasped in the neck clamp, one continuous downward motion penetrates and extracts the cork; reversing the motion frees the cork from the speed worm, Redlinger patent, case plate stamped "Made in USA". Cast steel with wood, 10" high. Made in USA.

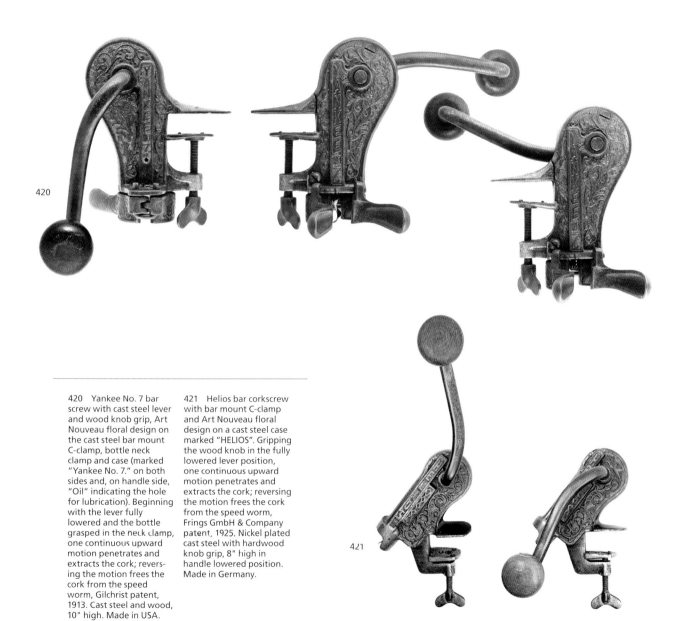

420 Yankee No. 7 bar screw with cast steel lever and wood knob grip, Art Nouveau floral design on the cast steel bar mount C-clamp, bottle neck clamp and case (marked "Yankee No. 7." on both sides and, on handle side, "Oil" indicating the hole for lubrication). Beginning with the lever fully lowered and the bottle grasped in the neck clamp, one continuous upward motion penetrates and extracts the cork; reversing the motion frees the cork from the speed worm, Gilchrist patent, 1913. Cast steel and wood, 10" high. Made in USA.

421 Helios bar corkscrew with bar mount C-clamp and Art Nouveau floral design on a cast steel case marked "HELIOS". Gripping the wood knob in the fully lowered lever position, one continuous upward motion penetrates and extracts the cork; reversing the motion frees the cork from the speed worm, Frings GmbH & Company patent, 1925. Nickel plated cast steel with hardwood knob grip, 8" high in handle lowered position. Made in Germany.

422

423

422 Hektor bar screw with original green paint with Art Nouveau floral design on cast steel case marked "HEKTOR" with "F 8" stamped below bar mount C-clamp, bottle neck support, speed worm, Frings GmbH & Company patent, 1925. Gripping the wood knob of the fully lowered lever, one continuous upward motion penetrates and extracts the cork;

reversing the motion frees the cork from the worm. Cast steel with wood knob grip, 9.5" in handle lowered position. Made in Germany.

423 "Champion" bar corkscrew, C-clamp counter mount with a black wook knob handle on a steel lever arm. Starting with the arm in raised position, downward motion extracts the cork; opposite motion ejects

the cork from the speed worm. Striped and blackened Art Deco case is marked "CHAMPION REG U.S. PAT OFF" and bottle neck clamp is marked "ARCADE MFG. CO. MADE IN U.S.A." Morton & Redlinger patents, 1896 and 1899, 1925–35 model. Nickel-plated steel, wood and paint, 9" high. Made in USA.

424   Daisy bar screw with Art Nouveau design on a cast steel case plate marked "The DAISY manf'd for Albert Pick & Co. Bar Supplies 100 to 209 Randolph St. Chicago, Ill. Pat. June 15, 1895", screw mounted, turned wood handle grip with nickel-plated brass collar, smooth shaft, speed worm, Morgan patent, c. 1895. Beginning with the handle fully back and the bottle grip forward, the upward and back again handle motion extracts the cork from the bottle; repeating the double motion with the bottle grip back in place, ejects the cork from the worm. Cast steel, brass and wood, 9.75" in handle raised position. Made in USA.

426

427

425

425 Mechanical corkscrew with a cast iron and turned wood handle ("HANDY" cast into lever arm), cast iron case with floral ornamentation and "PAT MAR 14 1903", and C-clamp counter mount. With the bottle neck inserted into the tube, raising the handle penetrates the cork. As the handle is lowered and the bottle withdrawn, the cork is extracted and ejected, speed worm, Tscherning patent, 1903. Cast iron and wood, 12" with handle lowered, 15.25" with handle fully extended. Made in USA.

426 New Era slant bar corkscrew with cast steel handle and Art Nouveau floral design on cast steel case marked "PAT JAN 15 1895 SEPT 7 1897 MAR 14 1898" on one side, "WILLIAMSONS" on the other side. Beginning with the handle down, upward motion penetrates the cork and activates the small levers on the worm slide. Lowering the handle again raises the slide and extracts the cork. Quickly repeating the double motion rearranges the small lever positions and ejects the cork from the worm, Morgan patents, bar mount C-clamp, smooth shaft, speed worm, manufactured by

the Arcade Mfg. Co., 1903. Nickel-plated cast iron, 10" high. Made in USA.

427 New Era vertical bar corkscrew with cast steel handle and Art Nouveau floral design on cast steel case marked "PAT JAN 15 1895 SEPT 7 1897 MAR 14 1898" on one side, "WILLIAMSONS" on the other side. Beginning with the handle down, upward motion penetrates the cork and activates the small levers on the worm slide. Lowering the handle again raises the slide and extracts the cork. Quickly repeating the double motion rearranges the small lever positions and ejects the cork from the

worm, manufactured by the Arcade Mfg. Co. this is a vertical version of the Phoenix 30 counter mount bar corkscrew, Morgan patents, bar mount C-clamp, smooth shaft, speed worm, 1903. Nickel-plated cast iron, 10" high. Made in USA.

428 Phoenix 100 wall mount bar corkscrew with painted turned wood handle grip, nickel plated brass collar and Art Nouveau floral design on cast steel case marked "PAT JAN 15 1895 SEP 7 1897 MAR 14 1898". Beginning with the large handle fully lowered, the bottle is pressed against the bottle neck rest and

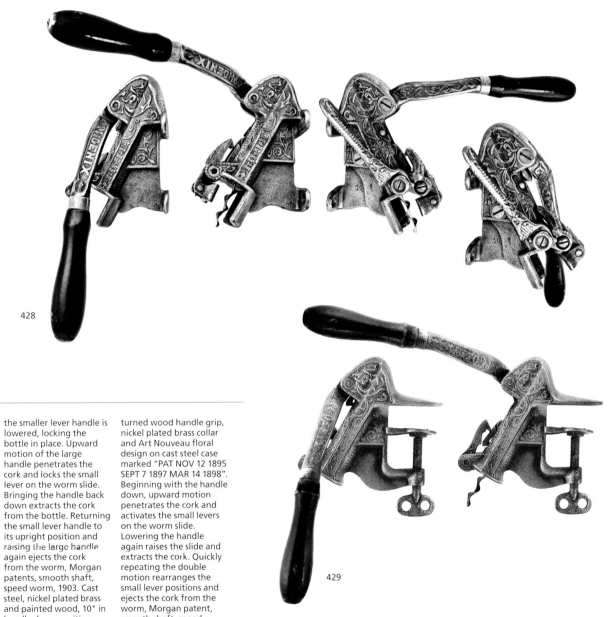

428

the smaller lever handle is lowered, locking the bottle in place. Upward motion of the large handle penetrates the cork and locks the small lever on the worm slide. Bringing the handle back down extracts the cork from the bottle. Returning the small lever handle to its upright position and raising the large handle again ejects the cork from the worm, Morgan patents, smooth shaft, speed worm, 1903. Cast steel, nickel plated brass and painted wood, 10" in handle down position. Made in USA.

429 Phoenix 30 bar mounted C-clamp corkscrew with painted turned wood handle grip, nickel plated brass collar and Art Nouveau floral design on cast steel case marked "PAT NOV 12 1895 SEPT 7 1897 MAR 14 1898". Beginning with the handle down, upward motion penetrates the cork and activates the small levers on the worm slide. Lowering the handle again raises the slide and extracts the cork. Quickly repeating the double motion rearranges the small lever positions and ejects the cork from the worm, Morgan patent, smooth shaft, speed worm, 1903. Cast steel, nickel plated brass and wood, 10" in handle down position. Made in USA.

429

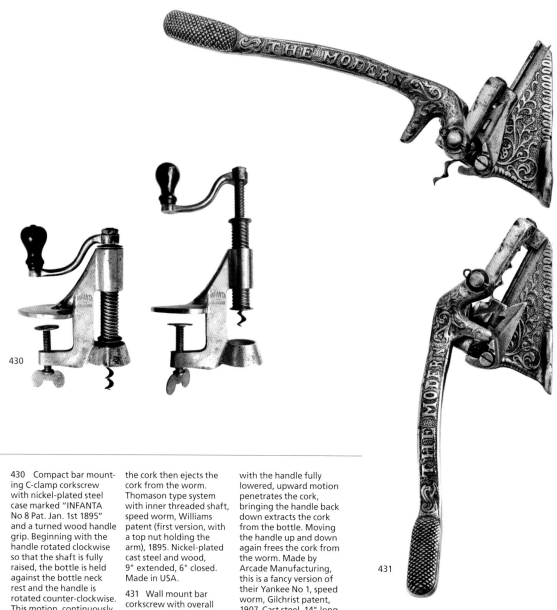

430

431

430   Compact bar mounting C-clamp corkscrew with nickel-plated steel case marked "INFANTA No 8 Pat. Jan. 1st 1895" and a turned wood handle grip. Beginning with the handle rotated clockwise so that the shaft is fully raised, the bottle is held against the bottle neck rest and the handle is rotated counter-clockwise. This motion, continuously applied, extends the inner threaded shaft, extracts

the cork then ejects the cork from the worm. Thomason type system with inner threaded shaft, speed worm, Williams patent (first version, with a top nut holding the arm), 1895. Nickel-plated cast steel and wood, 9" extended, 6" closed. Made in USA.

431   Wall mount bar corkscrew with overall floral pattern marked "THE MODERN" on cast steel handle. Beginning

with the handle fully lowered, upward motion penetrates the cork, bringing the handle back down extracts the cork from the bottle. Moving the handle up and down again frees the cork from the worm. Made by Arcade Manufacturing, this is a fancy version of their Yankee No 1, speed worm, Gilchrist patent, 1907. Cast steel, 14" long with handle raised. Made in USA.

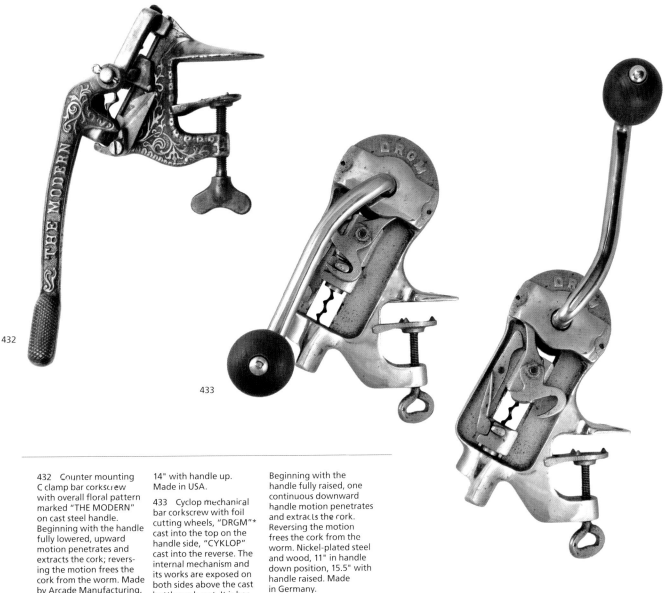

432

433

432 Counter mounting C clamp bar corkscrew with overall floral pattern marked "THE MODERN" on cast steel handle. Beginning with the handle fully lowered, upward motion penetrates and extracts the cork; reversing the motion frees the cork from the worm. Made by Arcade Manufacturing, this is a fancy version of their "Yankee No 2.," speed worm, Gilchrist patent, 1907. Cast steel, 12.5" with handle down, 14" with handle up. Made in USA.

433 Cyclop mechanical bar corkscrew with foil cutting wheels, "DRGM"* cast into the top on the handle side, "CYKLOP" cast into the reverse. The internal mechanism and its works are exposed on both sides above the cast bottle neck rest. It is bar mounted by a C-clamp, hardwood knob handle on lever arm, speed worm, Frings patent, 1925.

Beginning with the handle fully raised, one continuous downward handle motion penetrates and extracts the cork. Reversing the motion frees the cork from the worm. Nickel-plated steel and wood, 11" in handle down position, 15.5" with handle raised. Made in Germany.

* DRGM stands for Deutsches Reichsge-brauchsmuster.

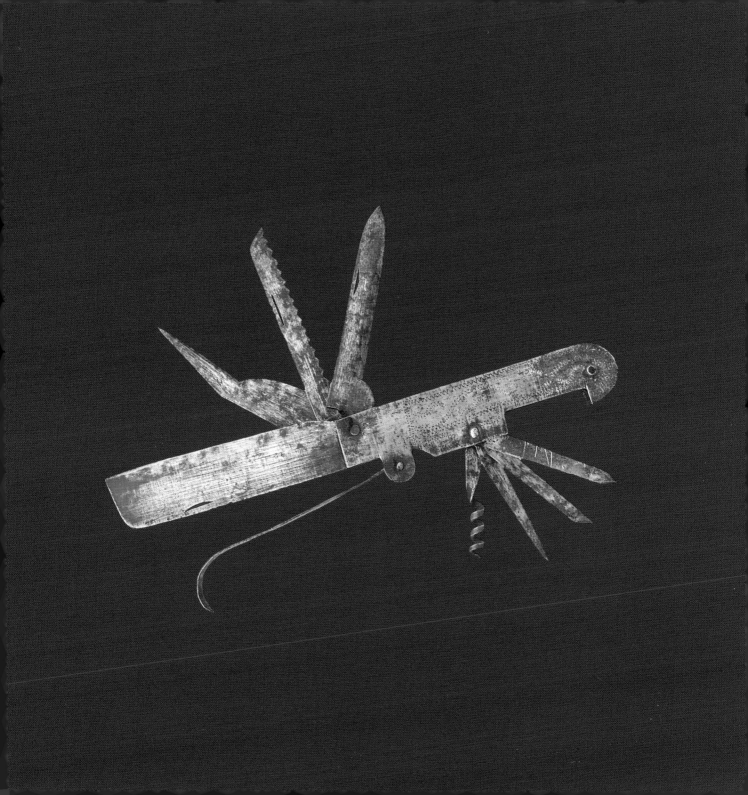

7 *The Turn of the Tune*
COMPOUND TOOLS WITH CORKSCREWS

The masterful engineering of the octagonal lantern of Ely Cathedral in England is its unique feature. Its timber structure supports four hundred tons of wood, lead and stained glass and admits glorious light to the nave and choir, seventy-two feet below. The fourteenth-century monk Alan of Walsingham conceived it, supervised its construction and is entombed in the floor below it. Eight sculptured limestone corbels support the lantern and they are carved with stone heads (including Walsingham's master mason and many churchy visages) that exemplify the excellence of the best medieval carving. The recorded history of a Saxon church at Ely began in 673. Between 1093 and 1189 the present Norman building was constructed, subsuming an earlier nunnery and churches on that location, although remnants are visible.

In comparable ways, and often on a smaller scale, innovative inventors subsume the useful parts of earlier designs into new concepts and mechanisms or find inspiration in the possibility of surpassing the ingenuity of predecessors. The evolution of corkscrews is a story of new insights built on old insights.

434   (at left and below) Revolutionary War officer's Travelers' Friend multi-blade tool with pinned pivoting implements folding into an engraved steel handle. Seen clockwise from the corkscrew is a hoof pick, straight razor, punch, saw, knife, fleam, beveled knife and sharp pick; the corkscrew has a grooved flat helical worm (also called grooved ribbon helix), 1774–75. Steel, 7.5" open, 4.25" closed. Made in France.

434

435

435   Revolutionary War medical officer's Travelers' Friend multi blade tool with pinned pivoting implements (four graduated fleams, pointed punch, bleeder, corkscrew with smooth, long flat pivot shaft and a short tapered helical worm, two curved blades and saw) folding into a steel handle with incised linear decoration and glyphs. Made in Colonial America, found in a military cache in Maine with articles that date this corkscrew previous to 1730. Steel, 3.75" long closed, 3.75" high worm opened, 6" diameter completely opened.

In 1982, we took a family road trip to see the astonishing architectural scale and remarkable craftsmanship of Ely Cathedral and the early churches of East Anglia. Our son, Jesse, was fourteen and Amie was two years old. Her surprising observations of worldly phenomena based on her experience were usually expressed in one terse sentence. One works with what one has. Perception depends on one's perspective. Looking directly up at the lantern at Ely Cathedral from her stroller, Amie asked, "Where's the octopus?"

Amie was referring to a painted papier-mâché octopus on the ceiling of an Italian restaurant in Coney Island, the best and highest ceiling that she had seen in her short life. What she had to work with was useful but limited, portable and adaptable. It was a sufficient referent to serve her purpose in an unexpected circumstance. Ely Cathedral is in England's fens country, in East Anglia in the U.K.; it's a far cry from Coney Island any way you look at it.

While traveling, one hopes that what one brings along—experience, knowledge, a sense of humor, medication, tools and comfortable shoes—will be of sufficient service to get through the rigors of travel, even if one has to make twists of use and crossovers of utility to encourage the tools to serve unanticipated functions. One hopes as well, that their ranges of adaptability and breadth of mutability will enable us to observe the wonders revealed.

436   Pivoting corkscrew in a pinned wine-colored plastic multi-tool handle (also containing a second slot with a pivoting four tine fork and a folding knife), rectangular pivot shaft, close-pitch helical worm, c. 1950. Plastic and steel, 3.5" in closed position, 2" assembled for use. Made in Russia.

436

Travelers' friends were unified portable, multifaceted tools, possessions that were useful in many circumstances. A worm was an essential part. This class of multi-tools was used in the eighteenth and nineteenth centuries and sported the small utensils and hardware that a traveler might need to prepare food, cutlery with which to eat, and tools to strike a spark, cut fruit and tinder, clean a horse's hoof, repair articles of clothing and horse gear. Travelers' friends were general- and specialized-use implements for demanding circumstances, all folding and slotting together for pocket portability.

Other pocketable compound tools were interchangeable blades and worms stored in a hollow handle for individual insertion into a universal shaft. These could be carried in a pocket, saddlebag or glove compartment. The essential tips were either stored in the handle or lost when a tip wasn't put back after use; consequently sets are often found with tools missing.

Folding multi-bladed sportsman's knives evolved in parallel to the development of multi-tooled folding bows, both typically containing a corkscrew and a selection from among a gimlet, awl, auger, leather punch, screwdriver, buttonhook, hoof pick, fleam, saw, chisel or screwdriver. Accommodations for smokers, hunters, gentlemen, ladies and Girl Guides were customized with specialty tools, all prototypes for the Swiss Army knife.

437 Corkscrew with multi-tool handle (pipe wrench, nail lifter and hammer square, scissors sharpener, knife sharpener, wire breaker, nippers, nutcracker, bolt holes, sliding can opener with adjustable stops which lock the pivoting corkscrew), maker's plate "H.NYLIN ERIE PA", "PAT 1909" (second version), wire pivot shaft and helical worm, 1909. Steel, 7.5" closed. Made in USA.

437

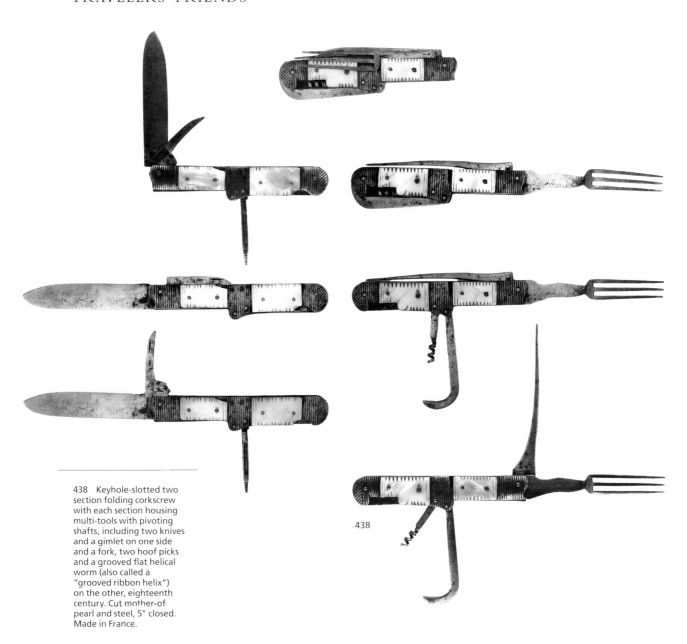

438   Keyhole-slotted two
section folding corkscrew
with each section housing
multi-tools with pivoting
shafts, including two knives
and a gimlet on one side
and a fork, two hoof picks
and a grooved flat helical
worm (also called a
"grooved ribbon helix")
on the other, eighteenth
century. Cut mother-of
pearl and steel, 5" closed.
Made in France.

438

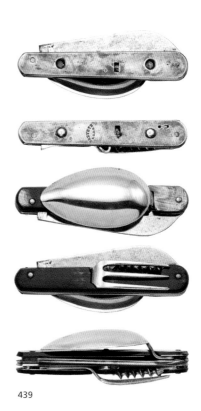

439

439 Spring-slotted, folding corkscrew, called a "French Hobo Knife," with buffalo horn handle and pivoting shaft multi tools including a sheepfoot knife marked "59 SAUVAGNAT", spoon, fork marked "59 SAUVAGNAT" and a grooved flat helical worm (also called grooved ribbon helix) marked "Breveté SGDG"* (patent mark) on one center liner, in original box, second half 19th century. Buffalo horn, brass, carbon steel and steel, 5" closed. Made in France.

* SGDG stands for Sans Garantie Du Gouvernement.

440   French campaign/travel set in black leather-clad hinged case with silver-plated beaker marked "A.Frenais" for Armand Frenais inside. The set holds a folding silver-plated fork and spoon, carbon steel knife, horn folding toothpick and snuff scoop and a cut steel peg & worm corkscrew, black horn scales on the flatware, Paris, c. 1870. Steel, silver, horn, and leather, 5.5" tall, 3.25" in diameter. Made in France.

441   Pivoting corkscrew in wood barrel handle, Engstrom and Segerstrom patents, that houses a folding knife with a pin locking mechanism within a brass sheath stamped "PATENT Segerstrom Eskilstuna Sweden", square pivot worm shaft; close pitch bladed center worm, c. 1905. Wood, brass and steel, 5" closed, 3" assembled for use. Made in Sweden.

442   Folding corkscrew with buffalo horn and steel multi-tool handle with cut-steel loop for hanging from belt and for pulling the cut-steel knife blade release pin, locking blade tang stamped "R 3 A. B.", square pivot worm shaft with cut steel ridges, close-pitch center worm, eighteenth century. Buffalo horn and steel, 5.5" closed, 2.75" assembled for use. Made in France.

443   Pivoting corkscrew and fork in an ivory and steel multi-tool handle, rectangular pivot shaft, close pitch center worm, nineteenth century. Ivory and steel, 3.5" closed. Made in Germany.

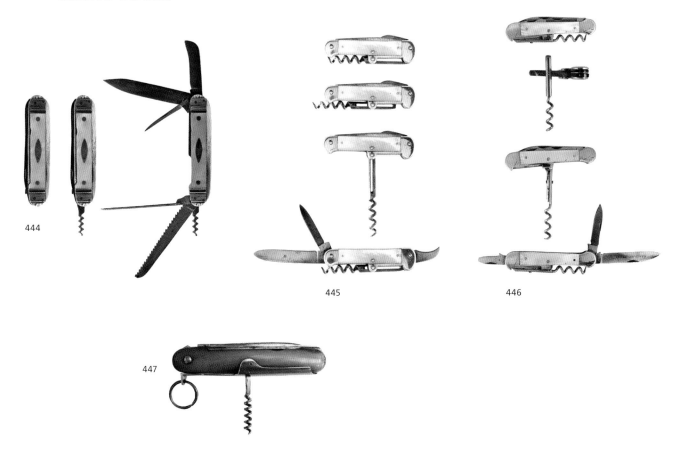

444

445

446

447

444   Folding corkscrew
with mother-of-pearl and
steel handle with cut
silver bolsters containing
multiple tools (saw, spike,
worm, quill sharpener
blade, pruning blade and
master blade and fire steel
stamped "A. BISSINGER"),
brass liners, pivoting
rectangular worm shaft,
close pitch center worm,
1890–1900. Mother-of-
pearl, brass, silver and
steel, 4" closed,

5" assembled for use.
Made in Germany.

445   Folding corkscrew,
multi-blade knife handle
with fiery mother-of-pearl
scales, nickel bolsters and
three blades including a
serrated hawkbill foil
cutter, all marked on the
tangs with "J.A.Henckels
Twinworks Solingen".
This corkscrew has a slide-
out slotted shaft and a
tapered, grooved helical

worm, Alfred Williams
1896 English patent and
Adolph Kastor 1897
US patent, c. 1900. Steel,
mother-of-pearl and
nickel, 3.25" closed,
3.5" assembled for use.
Made in Germany.

446   Folding corkscrew
with worm and multi-
blades (two blades and
one screwdriver) nested
in a nickel and mother-
of-pearl handle. The

corkscrew has a split shaft
that pivots and flips and
the master blade tang is
stamped "Sandvik Steel"
and "Ahlsrtom Eskilstuna
Sweden", helical worm,
G. Hammesfahr patent,
1903. Nickel, mother-of-
pearl and steel, 3.25"
assembled for use. Made
in Sweden.

447   Folding corkscrew
with blond buffalo horn
multi-tool sportsman knife

handle and mechanical
release in carry loop hardware. Locking blades
include a carbon steel
spear master blade
marked "Eloi" and bearing
Eloi Pernet trademark, a
saw with offset teeth,
screwdriver, can opener,
and spike blades, grooved
helix corkscrew recessed
in the back spring, c. 1930.
Steel and horn, 5.75"
closed. Made in France.

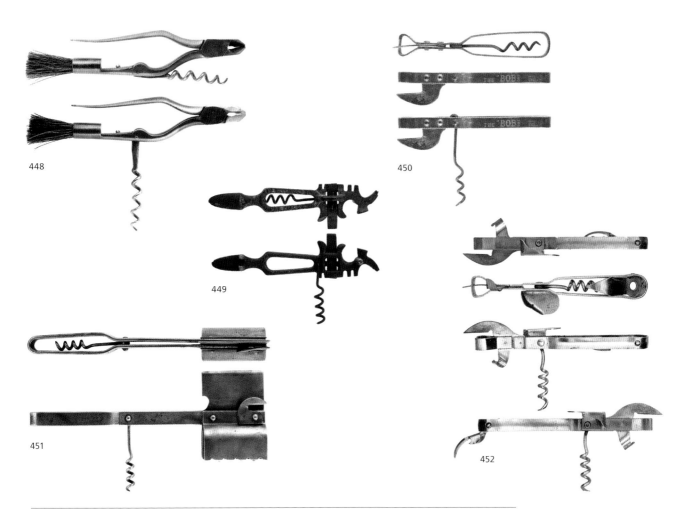

448   Wire nippers handle (for cutting the wire securing the cork stopper on Champagne bottles), brush tip and stop for tapered pivot shaft of grooved tapered helical worm on one handle and serrated ice breaker tip on other handle, c. 1880. Steel and animal bristle, 8" closed. Made in England.

449   Corkscrew as integral part of multi-tool steel handle showing "The Woodward Tool Pat. Aug. 24 '75", underside distinguished by tripod legs, pivot shaft, helical wire worm, 1875. Cast steel and steel wire, 5.5" closed, 2.75" assembled for use. Made in USA.

450   Nesting corkscrew in steel can opener handle stamped "The 'BOBs' Made in England", pivot shaft, helical worm, c. 1890. Steel, 5.25" closed 3.25" assembled for use. Made in England.

451   Corkscrew with multi-tool handle (can opener, cleaver, ice chopper/meat tenderizer), wire pivot shaft and helical worm, Clough patent, 1900–20. Steel, 8.5" closed. Made in USA.

452   Nesting corkscrew in steel can opener handle, blade stamped "Tool Steel Tempered", lid pry, can piercer and "THUMB GUARD" attachment, pivot shaft, graduated helical worm, c. 1920. Nickel-plated steel, 6.75" closed. Made in USA.

MULTI-TOOLS

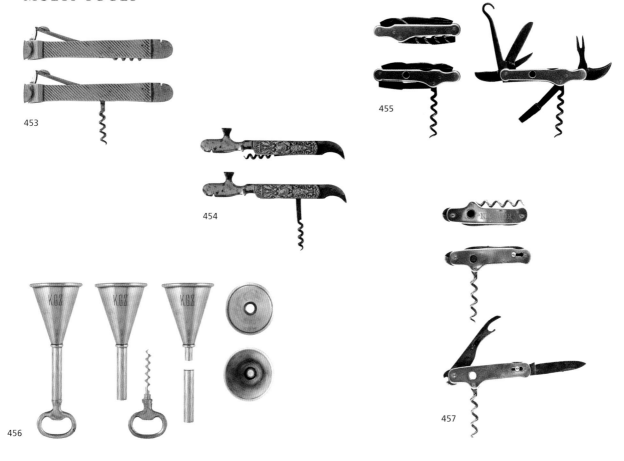

453   Folding multi-tool cigar box handler with silver cigar box tool consisting of pry, nail puller on one handle tip, spring-loaded cigar cutter on the other tip), square pivoting shaft, grooved helical worm, c. 1930. Sterling silver and steel, 6.25" closed, 3.25" assembled for use. Made in Germany.

454   Folding silver multi-tool cigar box handler (cigar box tool consisting of pry, nail puller and hammer to reset nail on one handle tip, foil cutter on the other tip), square pivoting shaft stamped "27 GERMANY I", grooved helical worm, c. 1880. Sterling silver and steel, 6.25" closed, 2.75" assembled for use. Made in USA, steel tools imported from Germany.

455   Multi-tool folding corkscrew with steel handle (hallmark at right side) containing pointed nail puller stamped "E. Draper & Co. Sheffield", foil cutter/ wire breaker stamped "CARTE BLANCHE", worm, carriage key, spring-loaded cigar cutter blade, button hook, knife blade and short blade, brass liners, pivoting square worm shaft, grooved helical worm,

1890–1900. Steel and brass, 3.5" closed, 3.25" assembled for use. Made in England.

456   Multi-tool corkscrew, cap-lifter, cup, and funnel in three sections. The cup, disengaged from the cap-lifter handle, worm and sheath, becomes a stemmed cup or jigger measure, rim stamped "STERLING 7309" with Blackinton hallmarks and engraved initials "K.G.Z."

Removal of the stem of the cup (which is also the sheath of the worm) transforms the cup into a funnel with a short internal stem for filling a flask. The corkscrew, when removed from the sheath, has a cap-lifter handle, smooth shaft and center worm, c. 1930. Sterling silver and nickel-plated brass, the worm in sheath is 3.5", the fully assembled multi-tool is 6" high. Made in England.

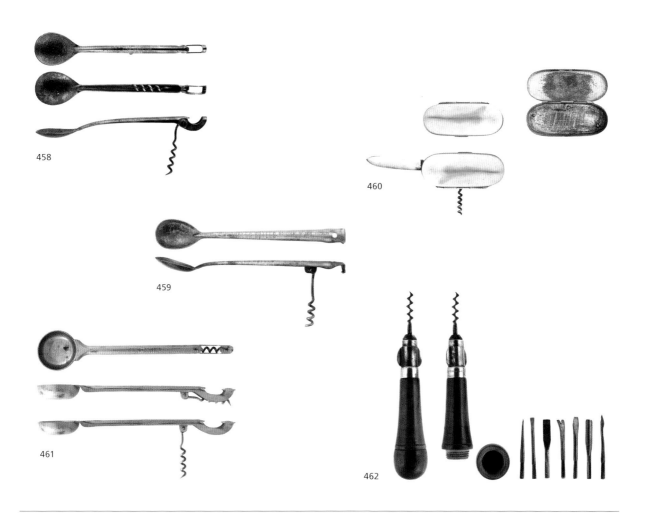

458

460

459

461

462

457 Multi-tool folding corkscrew with stamped steel handle advertising "NESTOR", knife blade stamped "John Watts Sheffield", spring-loaded cigar cutter blade/notched wire cutter/cap-lifter arm stamped "Watts's Patent Made in Sheffield England" with slot lock button, tapered grooved helical worm, pivoting square worm shaft, 1890–1900. Steel and brass, 3.5" closed, 3.25"

assembled for use. Made in England.

458 Folding corkscrew with cocktail spoon/cap-lifter handle advertising "LORRAINE HOTEL Broad Street at Ridge Ave. Philadelphia", pivot shaft, helical worm, c. 1920. Stamped steel, 7.25" closed. Made in USA.

459 Folding corkscrew with cocktail spoon/cap-lifter handle stamped "BINKLER HOTELS

Dispensers of True Southern Hospitality", pivot shaft, helical worm, Williamson patent, c. 1900. Stamped steel, 8" closed, 3.75" assembled for use. Made in USA.

460 Folding corkscrew, snuff box with hinged lid handle stamped "C.A.Eriksson & Co Eskilstuna Patent Sokt", and a blade and worm nested in the base, pivoting rectangular shaft,

helical worm, c. 1900. Nickel-plated brass, 3.5" close, 2.5" assembled for use. Made in Sweden.

461 Folding corkscrew with cocktail spoon/cap-lifter handle stamped "PRICE-PFISTER", pivot shaft, helical worm, c. 1930. Stamped steel, 8" closed, 2.25" assembled for use. Made in USA.

462 Multi-tool corkscrew set with worm, pick, small screwdriver, chisel, nail

puller, larger screwdriver, scorp and gimlet. Turned wood case handle with brass collar stamped "Patented Aug. 12, 1884", opens for tool storage, steel vise shank, square corkscrew shaft, 1884. Wood, brass and steel, 6" closed, 7.75" assembled for use. Made in USA.

463

464

465

466

463 Folding multi-tool corkscrew with flat stamped steel ruler/file handle, worm holder notch, cap-lifter and key chain hole, stamped "Patent 1680291 Designed by American Plate Glass Co. Bottle division, N.Y. Patent 1680291", smooth pivot shaft, helical worm in open position, Harding patent, 1928. Steel, 3" closed, 2.25" assembled for use. Made in USA.

464 Multi-tool handle corkscrew with hatchet, hammer stamped "WARRANTED FORGED STEEL", two wire clippers, wire nippers, pliers, pipe wrench, chisel/screwdriver, nail puller, worm and folding hawksbill foil cutter, rectangular pivot shaft and grooved helical worm, Bader patent, 1899. Steel, 5" closed, 7" assembled for use. Made in Germany.

465 Folding multi-tool stamped steel corkscrew showing worm holder notch, cap-lifter and key chain hole, stamped "GALLAGHER & BURTON" on one side and "GALLAGHER & BURTON, Inc. BALTO. MD. Fine Blended Whiskies Vaughn Chicago Made & Patent U.S.A." on the other, smooth pivot shaft, helical worm, Vaughn patent, 1916. Steel, 3" closed, 2.25" assembled for use. Made in USA.

466 Corkscrew with multi-tool handle, stamped "THE THOMAS MFG. CO. Dayton, O. U.S.A. Pat. Feb. 11, 1902" along cap-lifter tool; other tools include two lid pries, jar lid pliers, pivoting foil cutter, screwdriver and nail lifter, smooth pivot shaft and helical worm, Clark & Crume patent, 1902. Steel, 10.75" closed. Made in USA.

467 Corkscrew with multi-tool handle stamped "W C" in circular logo and "ABC" on arrow shaft (worm, hatchet, hammer, two wire clippers, wire nippers, pliers, pipe wrench, chisel/screwdriver, nail puller and fixed foil cutter), rectangular pivot shaft and grooved helical worm, Bader patent, 1899. Steel, 6.5" closed, 8.25" assembled for use. Made in Germany.

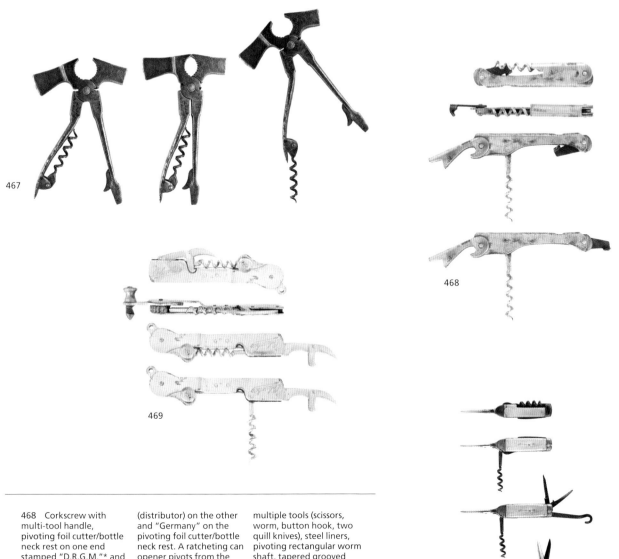

467

468

469

470

468   Corkscrew with multi-tool handle, pivoting foil cutter/bottle neck rest on one end stamped "D.R.G.M."* and a ratcheting can opener which pivots from the other, and smooth pivot shaft and helical worm, Kirchner patent, 1931. Steel, 4.25" closed. Made in Germany.

469   Corkscrew with multi-tool handle stamped "COLUMBUS" on one side, "Graef & Schmidt"

(distributor) on the other and "Germany" on the pivoting foil cutter/bottle neck rest. A ratcheting can opener pivots from the other handle end (with hole for hanging), smooth pivot shaft and helical worm, Steinfeld patent, c. 1900. Steel, 5" closed. Made in Germany.

470   Folding corkscrew with mother-of-pearl and steel pivoting scissors handle with cut silver bolsters, containing

multiple tools (scissors, worm, button hook, two quill knives), steel liners, pivoting rectangular worm shaft, tapered grooved helical worm, 1800–20. Mother-of-pearl, silver and steel, 3.75" closed, 2.25" assembled for use. Made in France.

* D.R.G.M. stands for Deutsches Reichsgebrauchsmuster.

MULTI-TOOLS

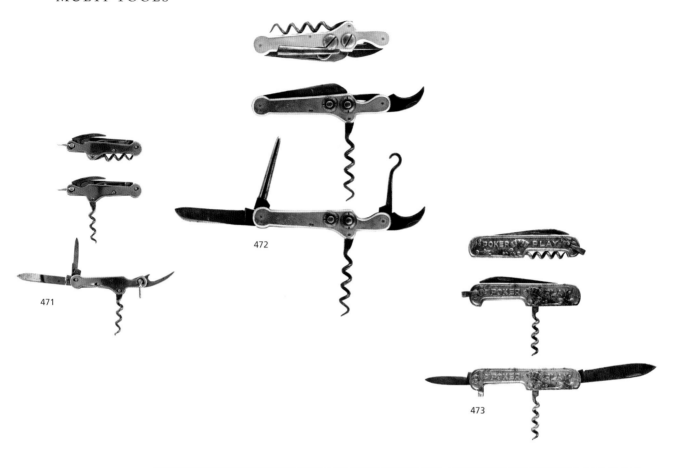

471

472

473

471 Folding corkscrew with steel handle and brass liners containing multiple tools, a master knife blade stamped "I*XL George Wostenholm Sheffield" on one side and "Oil the Joints" on the other side, a foil cutter blade/cap-lifter, a small blade stamped "I*XL George" and a

tapered grooved helical worm with a pivoting square worm shaft, 1890–1900. Steel and brass, 2.75" closed, 2" assembled for use. Made in England.

472 Folding corkscrew with steel handle fastened with firearm screws containing multiple tools each stamped

"MITCHELL Manchester" on its tang, serrated foil cutter/wire breaker, button hook, tapered grooved helical worm, knife blade and reamer, pivoting square worm shaft, 1890. Steel and brass, 4.25" closed, 3.5" assembled for use. Made in England.

473 Folding corkscrew with steel handle advertising "POKER PLAY" with a spread of five playing cards and pivot link, two blades and a worm are nested in the handle, pivoting rectangular worm shaft, helical worm, c. 1880. Steel, 3.75" closed, 2.25" assembled for use. Made in France.

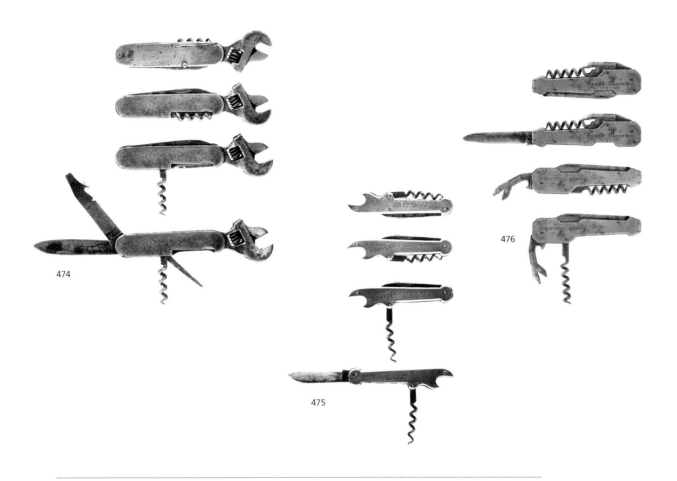

474   Multi-tool corkscrew with steel handle stamped "K.T.K. Breveté S.G.D.G."* The handle has a fixed adjustable wrench on one end and a pick, worm, knife blade (stamped "LA BECHE"), ruler, cap-lifter, file, screwdriver and wire cutter blade with peg assist (stamped "Déposé") nested inside, pivot shaft, grooved tapered helical worm, Soustre patent, 1930. Steel, 5.25" closed, 2.25" assembled for use. Made in France.

475   Folding corkscrew with a two-sided steel advertising cap-lifter handle stamped "Sss..ch..weppe..ssss" depicting a finger depressing a lever on a "Schweppes Soda Water" bottle on one side, and "Ask For Schweppes Table Waters, Cordials, etc." on the other, one blade and a worm are nested in the handle, pivoting rectangular worm shaft, tapered helical worm, c. 1910–20. Steel, 3.5" closed, 2.5" assembled for use. Made In England.

476   Folding multi-tool corkscrew with steel handle in the shape of an Art Deco bottle (also containing knife blade, cap-lifter/footed lever), rectangular pivot shaft, grooved helical worm, handle stamped "GRAND MARNIER liquor" on both sides, 1930. Steel, 3.75" closed, 3" assembled for use. Made in France.

* S.G.D.G. stands for Sans Garantie Du Gouvernement.

MULTI-TOOLS

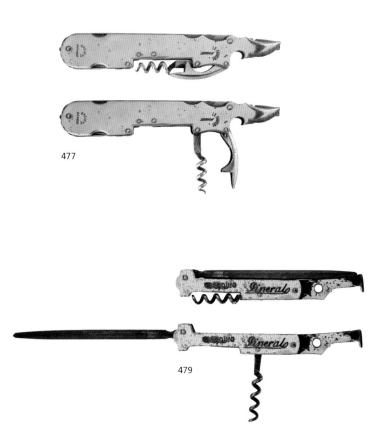

477

479

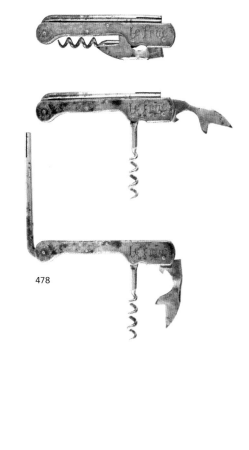

478

477   Folding corkscrew with steel handle stamped "LE FAVORI NOGENT, BREVETÉ DÉPOSÉ" and steel liners containing multiple tools, a master knife blade, a spike/punch, a long file with a slot for opening sardine cans, a serrated foil cutter, a footed bottle neck stand that also locks the helical worm into place, notched square pivoting shaft, 1930–50. Steel, 8" closed, 3" assembled for use. Made in France.

478   Folding multi-tool corkscrew with pivoting neckstand lever, foil cutter, cap-lifter and sardine can opener rod folded into handle stamped "Le Truc" and "BTE S.G.D.G. C.M. Paris",* pivot shaft, helical worm, Martinaud patent, 1919. Steel, 4.5" closed. Made in France.

479   Corkscrew with multi-tool handle advertising "OBSEQUIO PINERAL" with a tip protector and lid pry, pivoting sharpening steel and worm, squared pivot shaft, helical worm, Bewer patent, 1910. Steel, 6.25" closed, 3.25" assembled for use. Made in Germany for the South American market.

480   Folding hardwood bootjack impressed with the stamp "COURNET" in two places, brass hardware and a suede-lined bootjack opening secured with brass tacks. The case contains a number of equestrian tools including a folding multi-tool corkscrew, which is combined with a bootpuller and leather-punch handle, fluted grooved shaft, tapered helical worm, c. 1850. Steel, 6" closed, 5.5" assembled for use. Made in France.

* BTE S.G.D.G. stands for Breveté Sans Garantie Du Gouvernement.

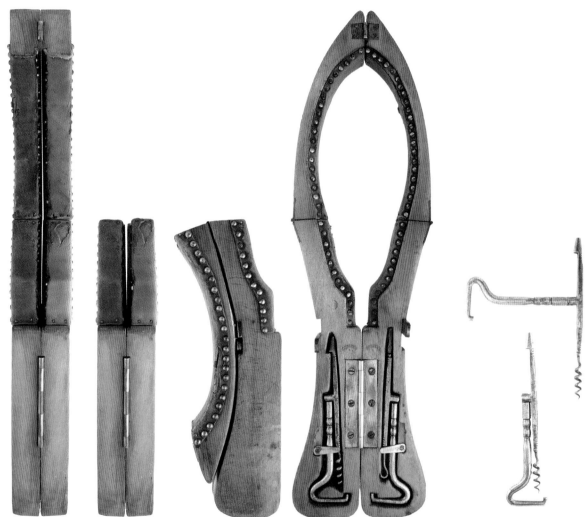

480

8 Putting the Screws On
SIDE ISSUES

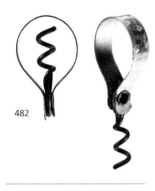

482

481 (at left) Group of miniature helical worm wire corkscrews with tag reading "Bunch of 25 corkscrews" sales tag and printed on reverse, "Don't swear. Use a corkscrew. Saves cork, time, temper. Keep one in every cork. C.T. Williamson Wire Novelty Co., Newark, N.J.", Clough patent, c. 1880. Steel wire, in graduated sizes 1"–2" high. Made in USA.

482 Miniature folding corkscrew, finger-pull handle with printed advertising on ring "LISTERINE", pinned wire shaft ending in a helical wire worm, Clough patent, c. 1884. Steel, 1.75" high open. Made in USA.

Wildlife abounds around our upstate New York farmhouse; animals frequently come close. We've seen woodchucks, rabbits and deer in the garden; skunks and possum on the porch; a wild array of birds in the berry bushes; foxes, coyotes, and recently black bear in the near field; hawks circling overhead until they dive for prey nearby; and nocturnal raccoons disassembling, with impunity, locked-down trash bins. On occasion, a creature comes indoors. I have had a grackle plummet through the chimney into the cold ashes in my potbelly stove, bats swoop through the breezeway, a fox at the kitchen screen door, a raccoon in the shed and field mice and a chipmunk in the living room. My response is guidance toward the great outdoors.

Not so in my New York City loft. I do not appreciate wildlife in my urban setting. Call it rodential profiling, but the city mouse and the country mouse do not receive equal treatment. In 1990 a mouse had the temerity to climb up to the fifth floor via vertical pipeways in the industrial building in which we live and had the further reckless confidence to stay. For weeks, this mouse climbed into closed kitchen drawers the back way and into our bulletproof nylon trash bin by gnawing a very small hole in the bottom, all the while making me very uneasy. I staged serial murderous showdowns running the gamut from cheese, cookie and peanut butter bait to gumdrops in a variety of mousetraps including spring-loaded neck breakers, vintage guillotines, tension-release garrotes, Mason jar impalers and glue traps—and the creature evaded them all. That's when ten year-old Amie spent her allowance on a hamster cage with a treadmill, wood chips and hamster food and named the mouse Chessman. She believed that Chessman should be cultivated for his/her IQ. Well, Chessman was too smart to enter the hamster

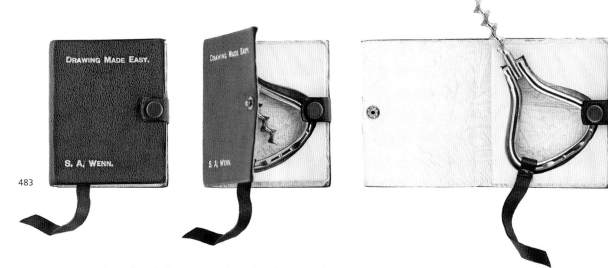

cage, spurning sybaritic luxury and shunning the wannabe pet-o-phile. We never found Chessman; the critter apparently left the way he/she came. Subsequently, Amie bought Mayonnaise, a white mouse with which she filled the void in the hamster cage.

I have always been fascinated by the ingenuity with which people have dedicated themselves to building a better mousetrap. I have a collection of original and creative antique mousetraps, each of which represents an ingenious attempt at capture, inspired by necessity. I employed some of them in my Get Chessman period.

Age-old solutions to the capture-the-mouse dilemma are almost as various as corkscrew forms dedicated to pull-the-cork difficulties, the main difference being that many mousetraps are homemade thingamajigs, and corkscrews, most requiring a precision steel worm, are manufactured affairs. Corkscrew and mousetrap inventors attempt to conceive a tool that will be user friendly and applicable to a variety of practical situations. In the last two centuries, many products besides wine were corked. The corkscrews in this chapter are tools that have been perfected with an attendant idea in mind, options that were created to address side issues to the central wine bottle cork removal application.

483 Folding cut steel bow corkscrew stamped "foreign" with faux leather bookmark pull, nested in open novelty snap-closure leather "book" stamped "'Drawing Made Easy.' by S. A. Wenn." Pinned cylinder shaft ending in handle pivot, bladed center worm, c. 1930. Nickel-plated steel, 4" open. Made in England.

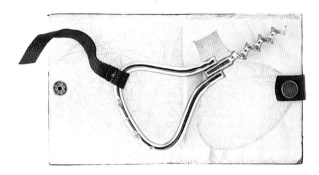

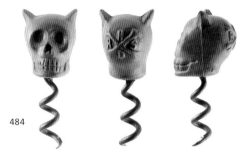

484

484 Poison bottle miniature corkscrew with horned grimacing skull on front, "RHSD" between crossed bones on back, sharp wire helical worm, c. 1880. Two-mold fired orange clay with sharply pointed horns to be clearly identified as containing poison in the dark among other medicine bottles, 1" high. Made in USA.

Besides wine, corks stoppered bottles of all sizes containing commodities and comestibles from ciders, beers, extracts, herbs, vinegars and oils to medicines, perfumes, chemicals and poisons. Some of these required miniature worms and vertical handles, others dictated handles of distinctive warning shapes that would be distinguishable by touch in the dark, to avoid poisoning oneself or others. Miniatures and *nécessaires* had been the universal household opener of corked bottles and jars in the kitchen, pantry, boudoir, dressing room and bathroom. They were the common denominator of perfume and cleansers, crossing all economic and product lines.

The sampling of clever novelty corkscrews indicates some flavors of humor in earlier times. Predictable gimcracks referring to male anatomy have not been illustrated here.

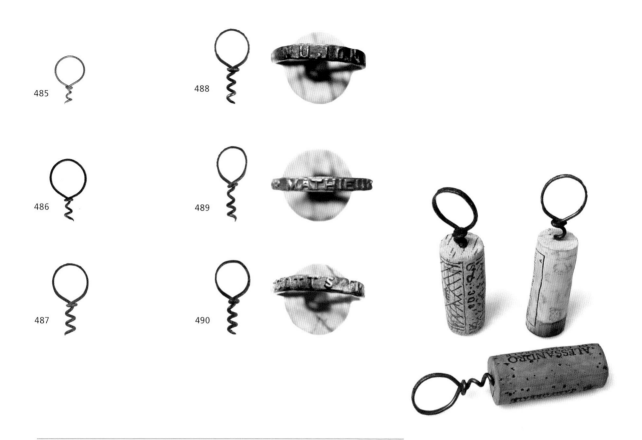

485   Miniature finger-pull corkscrew made from one wire, ring handle, twisted shaft with button, short helical worm, Clough patent, 1881. Steel wire, 1" high. Made in USA.

486   Miniature finger-pull corkscrew made from one wire, ring handle, twisted shaft with button, short helical worm, Clough patent, 1881. Steel wire, 1.25" high. Made in USA.

487   Miniature finger-pull corkscrew made from one wire, ring handle, twisted shaft with button, helical worm, Clough patent, 1881. Steel wire, 1.5" high. Made in USA.

488–490   Three miniature finger-pull corkscrews (each made from one wire) advertising ring handles stamped (A) "NUJOL", (B) "Sirop Matthieu's Syrup", (C) "Scott's Emulsion", twisted shafts with buttons, helical worms, Clough patent, 1881. Steel wire, 1.5" high. Made in USA.

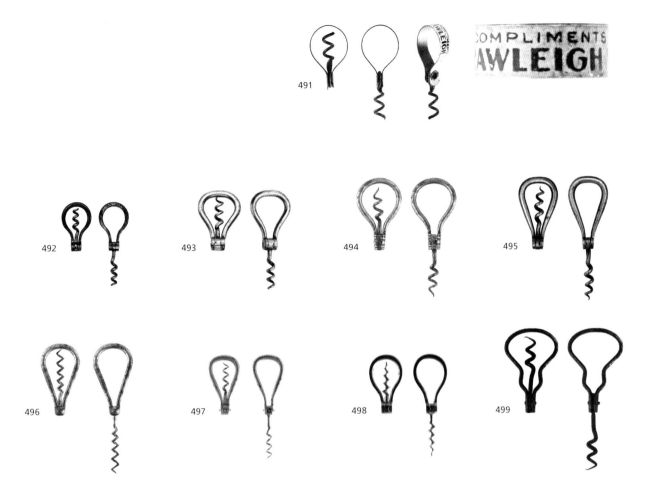

491 Miniature folding corkscrew with finger-pull handle, printed advertising on ring "Compliments The RAWLEIGH MAN Made in USA", pinned wire shaft ending in a helical wire worm, c. 1900. Steel, 2" open. Made in USA.

492 Miniature folding bow corkscrew with grooved locking hinge, locking pivot shaft, tapered helical worm, nineteenth century. Steel, 1" closed, 1.75" open. Made in England.

493 Miniature folding bow corkscrew with grooved locking hinge, locking pivot shaft, tapered helical worm, nineteenth century. Steel, 1.25" high. Made in England.

494 Miniature folding bow corkscrew with turned and grooved locking hinge, locking pivot shaft, tapered helical worm, early eighteenth century. Steel, 1.5" closed, 2.5" open. Made in England.

495 Miniature folding bow corkscrew with grooved locking hinge, locking pivot shaft, tapered helical worm, nineteenth century. Steel, 1.5" closed, 2.75" open. Made in England.

496 Miniature folding bow corkscrew with striated handle, pivot shaft, and reverse-tapered bladed helical worm, 1840. Steel with traces of nickel plating, 1.5" closed, 2.25" open. Made in England.

497 Miniature folding bow corkscrew with grooved locking hinge, locking pivot shaft, tapered helical worm, nineteenth century. Steel, 1.25" closed, 2" open. Made in England.

498 Miniature folding bow corkscrew with grooved locking hinge, locking pivot shaft, bladed tapered center worm, nineteenth century. Steel, 1.25" closed, 2.5" open. Made in England.

499 Miniature folding bow corkscrew with pear-shaped bow handle, pinned cylinder shaft ending in concave handle pivot, tapered helical worm, Havell patent, 1877. Steel, 1.75" closed, 3" open. Made in USA.

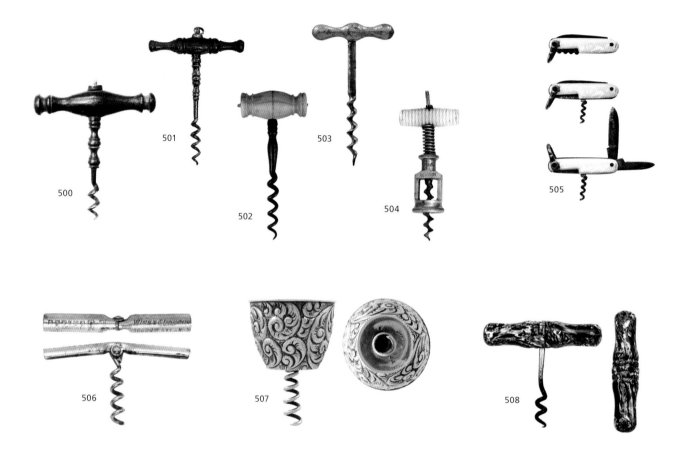

500   Basic T miniature corkscrew with a turned wood handle and a fitting for hanging loop atop, turned steel shaft, squared (sharpened) helical worm, c. 1840. Steel and wood, 2.5" high. Made in England.

501   Basic T miniature corkscrew with a turned wood handle, with fitting and hanging loop atop, turned steel shaft, squared (sharpened) helical worm, eighteenth century. Steel and wood, 2.5" high. Made in England.

502   Basic T miniature corkscrew with turned ivory handle secured to threaded turned steel shaft by peened top, tapered helical worm, c. 1870. Steel and ivory, 2.75" high. Made in England.

503   Basic T miniature corkscrew with turned nickel-plated brass handle with ball tips, tapered steel shaft, wide bladed center worm, c. 1890. Nickel-plated brass and steel, 2.5" high. Made in France.

504   Miniature mechanical corkscrew with a turned ivory handle with ring atop, connected to a fixed spring assisted smooth shaft, Hercules model, open frame stamped "GERMANY", bladed center worm, Usbeck patent, 1902. With the frame placed on the bottle lip, the handle is rotated until the worm penetrates the cork, which compresses the spring assist on the shaft, aiding in cork extraction. Steel and ivory, 2.75" high. Made in Germany.

505   Folding multi-tool corkscrew with Celluloid covered steel handle with hanging loop, two knife blades stamped "Vulcan Sheffield", rectangular pivot shaft, helical worm, c. 1930. Celluloid and steel, 1" high with worm extended, 1.5" closed. Made in England.

506   Folding corkscrew with clamping concave steel handles stamped "I. MERTZEL WINES & LIQUORS 1068-2nd AVE. N.Y.", pivoting wire shaft and helical worm, known as "The Dainty", Vaughan maker, c. 1919. Nickel-plated steel, 1.5" high. Made in USA.

NÉCESSAIRES

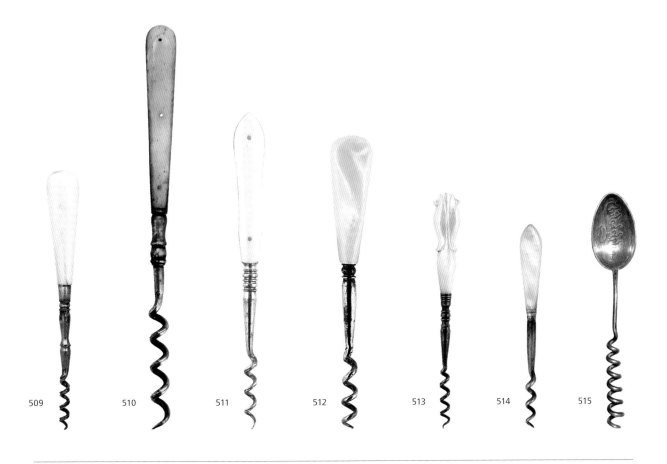

509   510   511   512   513   514   515

507   Miniature corkscrew with sterling silver repoussé cup handle with gilt interior, stamped "STERLING", "22" and hallmarked "Zeilin", reverse tapered helical worm peened and soldered to cup bottom, c. 1882. Silver, gold wash and steel, 2.25" assembled for use. Made in USA.

508   Roundlet corkscrew with two-part threaded Bakelite handle with a brass pivoting flange which opens, pivots and

reassembles to lock the flattened shaft and the tapered helical worm into a square notch, its functional place at right angles to the handle, c. 1920. Bakelite, brass, steel, 2.25" closed, 2" assembled for use. Made in USA.

509   Nécessaire, or ladies' corkscrew, with a round-ended handle, turned shaft and helical worm, c. 1850. Nickel-plated steel and ivory, 4.5" high. Made in England.

510   Nécessaire or, ladies' corkscrew, with pinned ivory sides on steel handle, turned nickel-plated steel shaft and tapered grooved helical worm, c. 1850. Nickel-plated steel and ivory, 7" high. Made in France.

511   Nécessaire, or ladies' corkscrew, with a steel handle with pinned ivory scales, turned nickel-plated steel shaft and tapered grooved helical worm, c. 1850. Nickel-plated steel and

ivory, 5.5" high. Made in England.

512   Nécessaire, or ladies' corkscrew, with a tapered, turned shaft and helical worm, c. 1880. Nickel-plated steel and mother-of-pearl, 5.25" high. Made in England.

513   Nécessaire, or ladies' corkscrew, with a carved handle, turned shaft and helical worm, c. 1860. Nickel-plated steel and mother-of-pearl, 4.25" high. Made in England.

514   Nécessaire, or ladies' corkscrew, with a mitre-shaped handle, turned shaft and helical worm, c. 1860. Nickel-plated steel and mother-of-pearl, 3.75" high. Made in England.

515   Nécessaire, or ladies' corkscrew, with a Philadelphia souvenir spoon handle, smooth shaft and helical worm, c. 1880. Silver, 4.25" high. Made in USA.

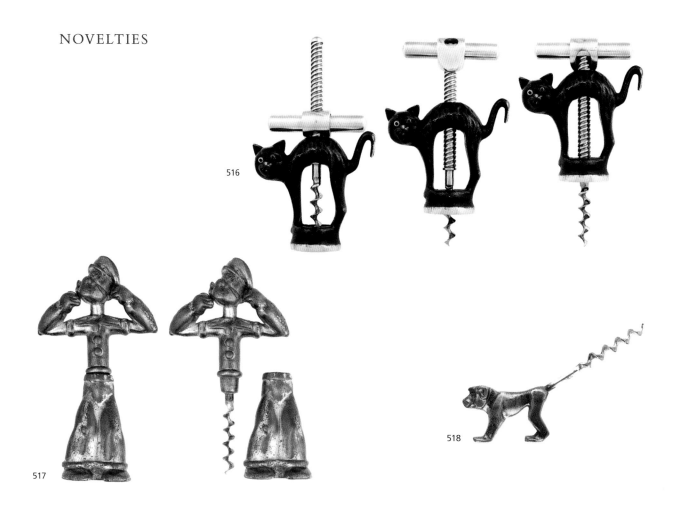

516

517

518

516 Mechanical novelty corkscrew with patinated brass black cat with glass eyes, open frame, smooth brass rod handle, with fitted sleeve lock and release hole at center, threaded brass shank, smooth steel shaft, bladed center worm, Ehrhardt patent, c. 1950. Locked "roll over" handle turns the worm to penetrate the cork; opening the lock and turning the rod handle exerts pressure on the frame to raise the cork. Brass, glass and steel, 5.25" high. Made in Germany.

517 Two-part novelty corkscrew of Popeye in the round. The top section with Popeye flexing his muscles is the handle and torso shank, smooth shaft and center worm. Popeye's lower half from belt to shoes provides the weighted housing into which the worm and shaft set to stand, stamped "Bulls Copyright Pat." under the shoes, 1937. Nickel-plated pewter, 5.5" assembled. Made in Sweden.

518 Cast steel monkey figural pull corkscrew, cylinder shaft, bladed center worm, c. 1925. Nickel-plated steel, 4.25" from nose to tail. Made in Sweden.

519 (at right) Novelty corkscrew of a character-ization of Prohibition with "OLD SNIFTER" cast into the base, nested worm behind figure pivots open by turning his head. The figure's hands rest on the cap-lifter umbrella handle which is stamped on the back side "Made in USA. PAT'D. NEGBAUR, N.Y.", smooth pivoting shaft, helical worm, Schuchardt patent, 1935. Nickel-plated steel and pot metal, 5.5" closed. Made in USA.

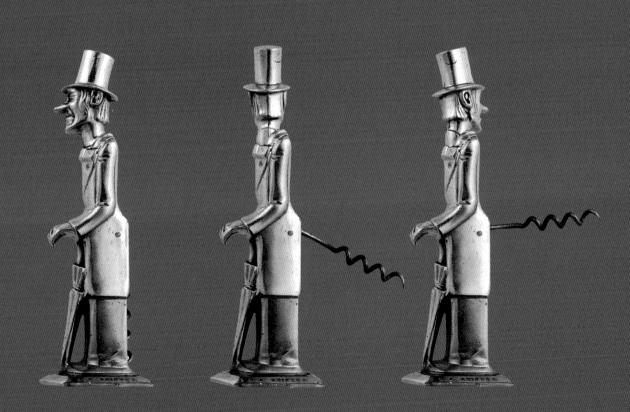

521

520

522

520   Two-part novelty corkscrew patented the year Prohibition ended, in the form of a two-faced figure with a jigger hat, stamped "8-16-32 U.S.A. WB Mfg." (Weidlich Bros. Mfg. Co.) in the open mouth cap-lifter. One side features a souse clutching a filled glass and the other side sports an angry, self-righteous temperance figure with a raised, scolding finger. The temperance side of the jigger hat has the souvenir logo of the 1933 Century of Progress, Chicago World's Fair. The legs of both figures end in a cocktail spoon. The figure houses the cylinder shaft and helical worm, Flauder patent, 1932. Silver-plated base metal, 10.75" assembled. Made in USA.

521   Little Brown Jug two-part novelty corkscrew. The top section is a steel cap-lifter handle, smooth shaft, helical worm. The cast rum jug with handle bottom section is marked "LITTLE BROWN JUG" on front, "Sterling, 23" stamped on rim, with Blackinton trademark, c. 1930. Sterling silver, 3.75" assembled. Made in USA.

522   Riding boot in the round two-part novelty corkscrew with silver-plated steel cap-lifter handle, smooth shaft and helical worm top section. The riding boot bottom section is stamped on the heel "Sterling, 738, Patent Applied For" with Blackinton trademark, c. 1930. Sterling silver, 3.75" assembled. Made in USA.

523

523   Four-part novelty
corkscrew of the corpse of
Prohibition, in the round.
The case is the original
novelty coffin box labeled
"BORN 1919/DIED _____"
on the outside, "Patent
App'd for/Copyright 1932"
on the inside of the casket
lid. The upper section
top hat and helical worm
with smooth shaft nests
in the second section
consisting of the figure's
head and shoulders. The
third section, a nickel-
plated barrel torso jigger
stamped "PAT. APL. 1932"
holds the lower section,
a cork embedded in
cast steel cap-lifter feet,
weighted to stand,
stamped "PAT APL'D
FOR 1932", Bridgewater
patent, 1932. Nickel-plated
steel, cast iron and paint,
6" assembled. Made
in USA.

9

What's the Alternative?
OTHER MEANS TO THE SAME END

On February 4, 1976, an earthquake fractured Guatemala. Measuring 7.5 on the Richter scale, it caused a fissure of 230 km that zigzagged across the country and through the main runway of the Guatemala City airport. Thirty aftershocks later, a secondary quake of 6.8 toppled a massive Madonna from the second-story niche in the façade of a church in the outskirts of Antigua, against a backdrop of mountains collapsing across the Pan-American Highway. Twenty-three thousand people were killed; seventy-four thousand were injured and one-sixth of the population—that is one million people—were left homeless. There was no bread because the ovens, made of adobe, had collapsed. We made our way back from Flores to Guatemala City in the third stage of evacuation, after relatives of Guatemala City inhabitants and after a planeload of chicle (a plant, the resin from which chewing gum is made) had been airlifted out. By February 7th we had been evacuated to Panama.

I had spent the afternoon of February 3, the day before the earthquake, with Ivan and seven-year-old Jesse in the park of a quiet town called El Progreso, having flown into Guatemala City from New York City the previous day. We bought *helados* on hand-cut sticks from a vendor of homemade ice cream whose cart was an adapted tricycle. Jesse built ant mazes and bridges on the sandy ground around the bandstand. Ivan brought his daily journal up to date and I wrote picture postcards home and mailed them in the old post office.

The next morning we boarded a worn-down DC-4 and flew to Flores. From there, we were bussed to the partially excavated Mayan site of Tikal. We saw and climbed dramatic architectural vestiges of a symmetrical city that had been constructed between 600 BCE and 900 CE, half of which was being excavated; the mirror half was left buried. We didn't suspect that Tikal would soon become famous as an other-worldly location in George Lucas's *Star Wars* or that there would be an earthquake that night or that our postcards would never leave the downtown of El Progreso, which was swallowed up in the great fissure.

524 (at left) Cork extractor with a cast steel handle serving as a stop to three capped pins, topped by a cap-lifter and marked "U-NEEK" and "PAT'D" in raised letters on front and back. When the base of the apparatus is placed on the bottle lip, the pins are inserted into the cork by finger pressure applied to the pin caps; as the handle is turned, the cork is raised. Pulling the pins back up releases the cork, Brady patent, 1917. Steel, 2.75" closed, 3.5" extended. Made in USA.

The following is another account of the same event, by E. L. Krinitzsky and Samuel B. Bonis for the United States Army Engineer Waterways Experiment Station in Vicksburg, Mississippi.

"A reconnaissance examination was made of earthquake effects in soils resulting from the 4 February 1976 earthquake in Guatemala. The earthquake was caused by strike-slip movement along a discrete fault plane in the Motagua Valley with a length of about 200 km. The Motagua Valley is determined by a zone of active faults that date back to Cretaceous time or older. Several distinct faults are recognizable on air photos but others may have been obscured by alluviation. The valley is a zone of active faults. Although movement was along only one plane, the entire mapped length of the Motagua fault zone participated in the movement. Extensive landslides were induced in deposits of pumice ash. Liquefaction is a probable contributing factor to at least two of the larger landslides in which entire valleys were blocked with debris. At Puerto Barrios there is a suggestion that liquefaction occurred in sands at 70 to 100 ft below the surface."

These are two accounts of the same event, from two dissimilar viewing angles. Consider the disparate viewpoints of the child soldier guarding the airport, the Budget Rent-A-Car concessionaire, the nun in the convent orphanage, the Indian woman with an infant whose livelihood depended on selling her embroidered *huipils* in the market and the stoned hippies in the pick-up truck with a large jar of Skippy peanut butter on the dashboard who couldn't figure out what the traffic jam was about.

Each is a different route to the same end, informing via firsthand experience. The perspectives vary, but each discrete form refers to the same event: that's what earthquakes and opening wine bottles have in common. There's more than one way to release the wine. This chapter looks at other means, other points of view, other classes of uncorking tools that free the elixir without the use of a conventional worm. Bottle and barrel gimlets with tight *pointeaux* or turned tips, Champagne taps and prong pullers are historical alternative viewpoints about approaching the wine.

BARREL GIMLET

The barrel gimlet, or "coup de poing," with cast-steel plug-hammer handles provides a time-honored way to check barrel contents. The point would be used to make a hole in the side of a wine barrel and, deed done, the hammer used to bang in a small wood plug or bung, thereby resealing the hole. A less conventional use of the gimlet or the barrel anchor is as a cork pry.

525

BOTTLE GIMLET

The bottle gimlet, also called "forêt à bouteille," was used to pry the cork from the bottle by piercing the cork at an angle and levering the gimlet shaft against the bottleneck in times when corks were not so tightly fitted as they are now. This worked in much the same way that massive weights can be lifted and shifted with a crowbar.

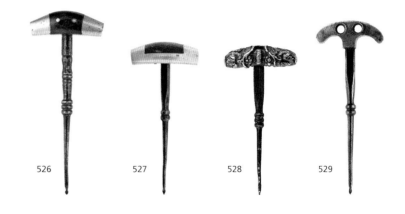

526   527   528   529

525   Barrel gimlet with cast steel handle, tapered turned steel shaft and turned steel pointeau tip. This gimlet was used to check barrel contents by penetrating the side of a wine barrel and resealing by hammering a small wood plug in the resulting hole, c. 1890. Steel, 4.75" high. Made in France.

526   Bottle gimlet (forêt à bouteille), with hammer-end handle, turned steel shaft, tight pointeau tip, c. 1880. Pinned horn and steel, 4.75" high. Made in France.

527   Bottle gimlet (forêt à bouteille), with an inlaid horn and brass handle with hammer ends, turned steel shaft stamped "GUINOT" with a tight pointeau tip, c. 1880. Brass, horn and steel, 4.25" high. Made in France.

528   Bottle gimlet (forêt à bouteille), with cast figural brass handle depicting laden grape vines, barrel and pitcher, tapered square shaft stamped "Guelon", turned steel tight pointeau tip, c. 1900. Brass and steel, 4.25" high. Made in France.

529   Bottle gimlet (forêt à bouteille), with a pierced shaped brass handle, tapered square shaft, tight pointeau tip, c. 1880. Brass and steel, 4.5" high. Made in France.

CHAMPAGNE TAPS

Champagne taps get to the elixir while leaving the cork in place. They are paired affairs, with a worm to penetrate the cork and a valve to control the flow. Both one- and two-piece mechanisms exist. The one-piece style features a long, smooth, hollow shaft with a short center worm perforated at the tip, and beneath the handle there is a simple turn valve and spout to regulate the flow of the bubbly. The two-piece style is comprised of a basic T or knob handle with long hollow needle that screws into a long, hollow Archimedean worm with a perforated tip and a valve and spout mechanism at the top. When assembled, the center spike is seen at the tip of the worm. Once the cork has been penetrated, with the valve in the closed position, the handle and needle may be unscrewed and removed. A quarter-turn of the valve handle regulates the flow of Champagne through the hollow worm and cork, which stay in place. Fully assembled, this type may also be used as a corkscrew.

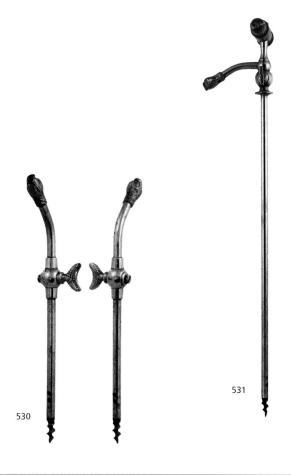

530

531

530   Champagne tap for a "demi" or half-bottle with a valve mechanism to regulate the flow of Champagne through a serpent-headed spout and a long smooth hollow shaft with perforations and a short center worm. After rotating the worm straight through the center of the cork, the shaft is pushed through until the perforations in the shaft are below the level of the cork and into the Champagne. When the fish-tail shaped valve handle is opened, Champagne is released through the spout; when the valve handle is quarter-turned, the flow is stopped, c. 1890. Nickel-plated brass, 7.5" high. Made in France.

531   Champagne tap with a turned wood handle screwed to the top of a shaft with valve mechanism to regulate the flow of Champagne through a serpent-headed spout and a long smooth hollow shaft with perforations, short center worm. After rotating the worm straight through the center of the cork, the shaft is pushed below the level of the cork and into the Champagne; when the key shaped valve handle is opened, Champagne is released through the spout, when the valve handle is quarter-turned, the flow is stopped, c. 1890. Wood and nickel-plated steel, 13.5" high. Made in France.

532   Champagne tap with a valve mechanism to regulate the flow of Champagne through a serpent-headed spout and a long smooth hollow shaft with perforations and a short center worm. After rotating the worm through the center of the cork, the shaft is pushed through until the perforations in the shaft are below the level of the cork and into the Champagne; when the valve handle is opened, Champagne is released through the spout, when the valve handle is quarter-turned, the flow is stopped, c. 1890. Nickel-plated brass, 12.5" high. Made in France.

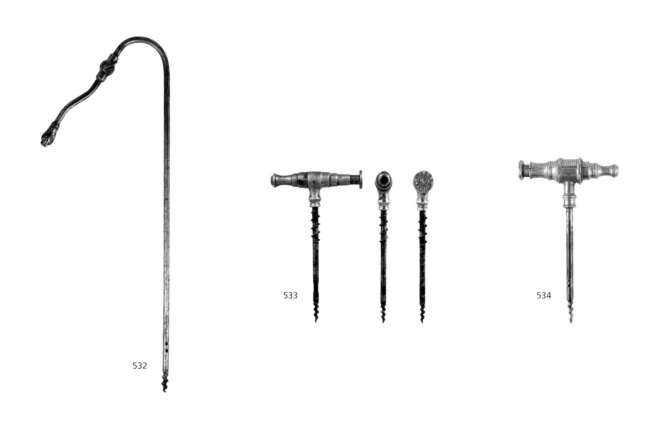

532

533

534

533   Champagne tap with a nickel-plated brass handle with a plunger stamped "Bte SGDG J.D. Paris"* on one end, which operates the spring loaded valve mechanism to regulate the flow of Champagne through a spout in the other end and a long, smooth, hollow, top-threaded shaft with perforations, short center worm. After rotating the worm straight through the center of the cork, the smooth section of the shaft is pushed below the level of the cork and into the Champagne. The top, threaded portion of the shaft is rotated into the cork; when the bottle is tipped and the plunger is depressed, the valve in the handle is opened and the Champagne flows through the spout end of the handle; when the plunger is released, the flow is stopped, J. Depagne patent, c. 1890. Nickel-plated brass and steel, 5.5" high. Made in France.

534   Champagne tap with a nickel-plated steel handle with a plunger on one end, which operates the spring-loaded valve mechanism to regulate the flow of Champagne through a spout in the other end of the handle and a long smooth hollow shaft, threaded at the top, with perforations, short center worm. After rotating the worm straight through the center of the cork, the smooth section of the shaft is pushed below the level of the cork and into the Champagne. When the bottle is tipped and the plunger is depressed, the valve in the handle is opened and the Champagne flows through the spout end of the handle. When the plunger is released, the flow is stopped, J. Depagne patent, c. 1890. Nickel-plated steel and steel, 5.25" high. Made in France.

* Bte SGDG stands for Breveté Sans Garantie Du Gouvernement.

535

536

535   Two-part Holborn-type patent Champagne tap with a turned wood handle and steel finger-pull assist, ending in a long spike. This mechanism is threaded to the top of the turned steel shaft which becomes a valve mechanism and a hollow Archimedean worm with a perforated tip. When assembled the center spike is seen at the tip of the worm. Once the cork has been penetrated and the valve is in closed position, the handle and spike may be unscrewed and removed. A quarter turn of the valve handle regulates the flow of Champagne through the hollow Archimedean worm, which stays in place, Wolverson patent, 1890–1900. This may also be used fully assembled as a corkscrew. Wood and nickel-plated steel, 7.25" assembled. Made in England.

536   Holborn Champagne tap with a turned wood handle and nickel-plated brass finger-pull assist shaft stamped "HOLBORN CHAMPAGNE SCREW" on front and back, the valve mechanism is on the shaft and connects to a hollow steel Archimedean worm with a perforated tip. Once the cork has been penetrated and the bottle inverted, a quarter turn of the valve handle regulates the flow of Champagne through the hollow Archimedean worm, which stays in place, Wolverson patent, 1890–1900. This may also be used as a corkscrew. Wood, nickel-plated brass and steel, 6.75" high. Made in England.

537

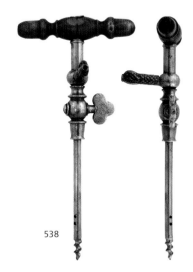

538

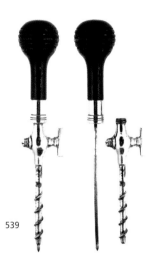

539

537 Champagne tap with nickel-plated brass finger pull handle and valve mechanism on the shaft connected to a hollow steel Archimedean worm with a perforated tip. Once the cork has been penetrated and the bottle inverted, a quarter turn of the valve handle regulates the flow of Champagne through the hollow worm; this may also be used as a corkscrew, 1890–1900.

Nickel-plated brass and steel, 5.75" high. Made in England.

538 Champagne tap for a "demi," or split bottle, with a turned acorn-tipped boxwood handle, screwed to the top of a long smooth hollow shaft with perforations and valve mechanism, stamped "Déposé JHP Paris" (J. Perille), to regulate the flow of Champagne through a serpent-headed

spout. After rotating the short center worm straight through the center of the cork, the shaft is pushed below the level of the cork and into the Champagne. When the key shaped valve handle is opened, Champagne is released through the spout; when the valve handle is quarter turned, the flow is stopped, c. 1890. Boxwood and nickel-plated brass, 7" high. Made in France.

539 Two-part Champagne tap with a turned wood round grip handle connected to a long spike by a turned threaded shaft onto which screws a hollow Archimedean tap worm with a nickel-plated brass valve. With the valve in closed position, the handle is rotated to cause the worm to penetrate the cork. Once the cork has been penetrated, the

handle and spike may be unscrewed and removed. A quarter turn of the valve handle regulates the flow of Champagne through the hollow Archimedean worm, which stays in place, 1890–1900. This may also be used as a corkscrew. Wood, brass and nickel-plated steel, 6.75" assembled. Made in England.

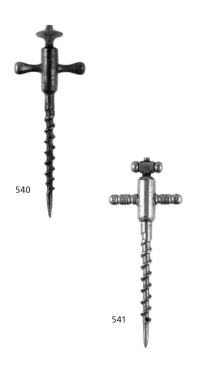

540

541

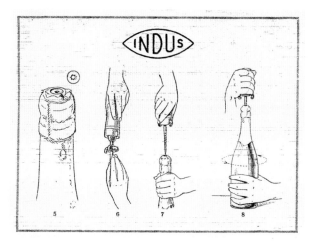

542

540 Champagne tap with a turned steel handle topped by a turned screw valve and connected to a hollow Archimedean tap worm. With the valve in closed position, the handle is rotated to cause the worm to penetrate the cork. Once the cork has been penetrated, the valve may be unscrewed and removed while the Champagne flows through the hollow Archimedean worm which stays in place, Sargent and Munger patent, 1871. This may also be used fully assembled as a corkscrew. Steel, 5.25" assembled. Made in USA.

541 Champagne tap with a turned steel handle topped by a turned screw valve and connected to a hollow Archimedean tap worm. With the valve in closed position, the handle is rotated to cause the worm to penetrate the cork. Once the cork has been penetrated, the valve may be unscrewed and removed while the Champagne flows through the hollow Archimedean worm which stays in place, "The Favorite" Williamson patent, c. 1900. This may also be used fully assembled as a corkscrew. Nickel-plated steel, 5" assembled. Made in USA.

542 Box and instruction sheet for champagne tap #543 on facing page.

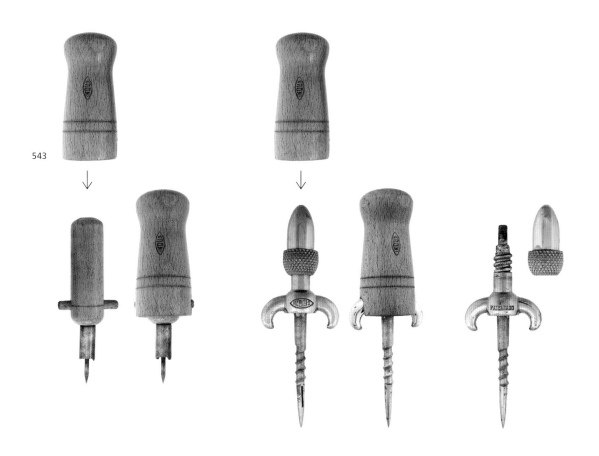

543

543   Champagne tap with a turned wood locking cap/handle for turning the cork perforator and the worm. The nickel-plated steel Champagne tap is stamped "INDUS' and "Patentado." After the cork is perforated, the worm (without the acorn valve) is placed into the wood locking cap and rotated through the perforation, and straight through the cork. The acorn valve is then screwed onto the worm. The worm is slotted to admit the Champagne through the hollow shaft when the bottle is inverted and the flow of Champagne is regulated by turning the acorn-shaped valve; Champagne is released through the spout, which is a hole atop the acorn. The entire bottle with the Champagne tap may then be inverted in a stand to dispense glasses of Champagne successively by turning the acorn valve, 1926. Wood and nickel-plated brass, locking cap 5" high, perforator 4.25" high, tap and valve 6" high. Made in Spain.

PRONG PULLS

Prong pulls with uneven legs, forced into the spline between the bottleneck and the cork, by rocking the handle, embrace the cork and with a twisting pull, extract it. Cork extractors and converging piercers were patented and sold but were neither improvements upon nor replacements for the corkscrew: they are the also-rans in the ingenuity contest. Their virtual disappearance as cork removal devices says it all.

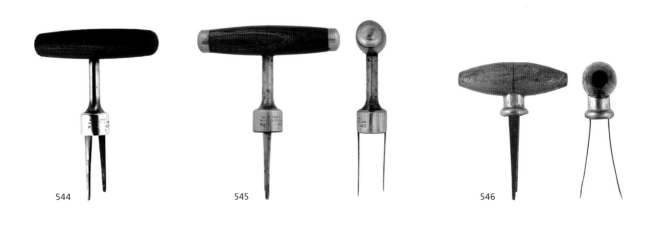

544   545   546

544   Prong pull with a simple turned wood handle, threaded smooth steel shaft with a brass collar stamped "Magic Cork Extractor Pat. March 4-79 May 10-92", stamped steel prongs, Mumford patent, 1892. Working the points of the prongs between the

cork and the bottle neck with a rocking motion until they reach the bottom of the cork, the cork may then be drawn by an upward pulling twist of the wrist. Wood, brass and steel, 4.5" high. Made in USA.

545   Prong pull with a turned wood handle with steel end caps, smooth steel shaft with collar stamped "MAGIC CORK EXTRACTOR Pat. March 4-79 May 10-92", stamped steel prongs, Mumford patent, 1892. Wood, brass and steel, 5" high. Made in USA.

546   Prong pull with a turned wood handle, steel collar and stamped-steel prongs, Converse patent, 1899. Wood and steel, 4" high. Made in USA.

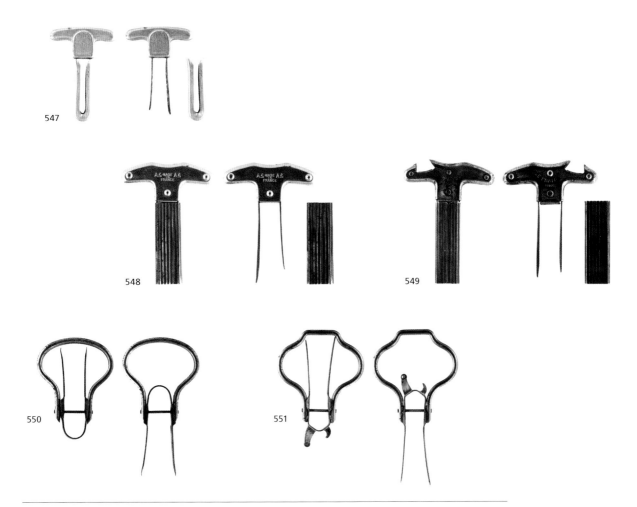

547 "Maro" prong pull and sheath, c. 1930. Aluminum and steel, 3.75" high. Made in Germany.

548 Prong pull and sheath, handle stamped "A S Made in France A S", c. 1920. Stamped steel, 3.5" high. Made in France.

549 "Le Pratique Paris" (with cap-lifter in handle) prong pull and sheath, c. 1920. Stamped steel, 3.5" high. Made in France.

550 Folding bow prong-pull with pinned locking pivot, compression of prongs releases the lock to open and close, Detroyes patent, 1929. Steel with traces of nickel plating and black paint, 2.75" closed, 4" assembled for use. Made in France.

551 Folding bow prong-pull with pinned locking pivot and cap-lifter with wheel foil cutter; compression of prongs releases the lock to open and close, Serre patent, 1934. Stamped steel, 3.5" closed, 4.5" assembled for use. Made in France.

After the 1930s, the twentieth century saw the rehashing of many of the corkscrew inventions of the last two and a half centuries, in contemporary materials. Reproduction corkscrews promise "a legacy of inspired uncorkings" as a corporate enterprise. The great flush of corkscrew ingenuity seems to have petered out except that the late twentieth century did yield up the Rabbit corkscrew and injector openers.

The Rabbit comes in a variety of colors and finishes; each model has a precision metal gear mechanism and ergonomically designed levers modeled on the ears of its namesake. The selling hype boasts twenty thousand independent laboratory uncorkings with one Rabbit (the Duracell Bunny comes to mind) and warrantees the critter for ten years. That's two thousand bottles a year. Quick as a rabbit or "faster than a speeding bunny," it "pulls the cork in three seconds," automatically ejecting it. I find it comparatively graceless and disconcertingly top heavy.

Injector openers come in a few configurations around a sturdy hollow needle with either an air pump or an aerosol cartridge. Once the needle penetrates the cork, air or gas (your choice at time of purchase) is forced into the wine bottle through the cork, building pressure to eject the cork with or without a POP (also your choice). The hand pump types force air in, boosting the cork

552   Cork extractor topped by a cap-lifter, cast steel handle serves as a stop to three capped pins, "U-NEEK" and "PAT'D" in raised letters on front and back. When the base of the apparatus is placed on the bottle lip, the pins are inserted into the cork by finger pressure applied to the pin caps. As the handle is turned, the cork is raised. Pulling the pins back up releases the cork. Brady patent, 1917. Steel, 2.75" pins raised, 3.5" pins extended. Made in USA.

553   Greely's cork extractor box for one dozen extractors, 1888. Printed paper, cardboard, 6" by 6". Made in USA.

554   Cork extractor with painted, turned wood handle affixed by a washer to a peened, tapered, flattened steel shaft (stamped "PAT MAR 8 88") with a curved and hooked tip. The tip is inserted between the cork and the bottle neck, then lifted, raising the cork from its bottom in a suctionless draw, Greely patent, 1888. Steel and painted wood, 3.75" high. Made in USA.

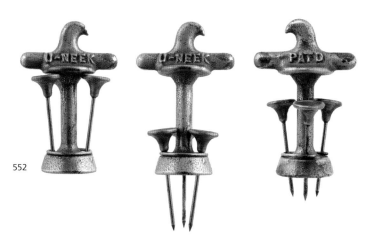

552

555 Cork extractor with ridged-tipped, grooved cast steel handle and a tapered squared shank and grooved shaft both stamped "M.Bte SGDG".* Cork removal is achieved by first inserting the slender hooked blade between the cork and the bottleneck then rotating the handle to enable the hook to catch the underside of the cork; pulling the handle raises the cork from its bottom in a suctionless draw, Mestre patent, 1874. Steel, 5" high. Made in France.

556 Cork extractor affixed through the turned wood handle stamped "DISSTON" by a brass washer and a peened, square, flattened steel shaft with a curved tip to be inserted between the cork and the bottleneck, then lifted, thereby raising the cork from its bottom in a suctionless draw, c. 1910.

* **Bte SGDG** stands for Breveté Sans Garantie Du Gouvernement.

out, like a bicycle pump in principle but smaller…The aerosol-cartridge types use propellants to force a burst of CO_2 into the bottle, popping the cork. With this device anyone might be bamboozled in thinking plonk is Champagne. "A fast, easy and fun way to open a bottle of wine!" There are sixty to eighty "POPS per refill" and the ad copy also says, "Simply insert the needle straight down through the cork, press once on the top of the low pressure propellant cartridge, and the cork is lifted out with a celebratory "POP"! What could be easier?…makes the perfect addition to your bar." Boasts and boosts aside, read the warning:

> Contents under pressure. KEEP AWAY FROM CHILDREN. Do not puncture, incinerate or store above 120 degrees F. Do NOT use on Champagne, Sparkling, or odd-shaped bottles; including square, rectangular, mixed, i.e., square to rounded. Misuse could cause fracture. A flawed bottle could rupture. If sprayed in eyes or on skin flush with warm water. If irritation occurs, see physician. Use only as directed. Intentional misuse by deliberately concentrating and inhaling contents can be harmful or fatal. Contains R-134A.

Thanks, I think I'll pass on propellent cartridge wine openers.

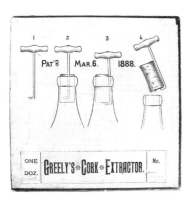

553

554

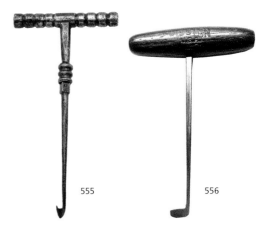

555   556

10 *In Vino Veritas*
THE CULTURE OF THE CORK

Alternatives to the corkscrew have been addressed, but what about the future of the cork itself in the evolution of wine-bottle closure? Cork variants in my friend Charlotte's cork collection are a testament to the occurrence of a revolution in the wine-bottle stopper world during her lifetime.

The same cork that is used for the core of baseballs has been sealing wine bottles for centuries. These days, the cork oak tree, a native of Mediterranean countries, is cultivated in Portugal, Spain, Algeria, Morocco, Tunisia, France, Italy and India and parts of the United States. The bark is first stripped when the tree is about twenty-five years old, and then again at intervals of ten to fourteen years. Cork is a renewable resource, but the length of time required for regrowth is at odds with present-day wine consumption. Since 2000 there has been a steady and inexorable shift from cork toward alternative closures. Waiting for corks to grow is no longer in the cards.

558

557 (at left) Toy figure of a European peasant drinking wine from a bota bag, c. 1948. Painted cast lead, 3" high. (Also on page 213.)

558 Group of wine bottle corks, 1982–2002. Printed whole cork, each 2" high.

First composite corks appeared. They looked and acted like familiar cork stoppers, but upon close examination, it was clear that they were made of bonded and compressed cork fragments. With so many adaptive plastics waiting in the wings, changes were quickly evolving. The first plastic corks masqueraded as the real thing. They were the color of cork, the texture of cork and were printed in the traditional way.

Plastic corks quickly took off and even evolved their own subculture of parody and uncorkishness. Sporting iconoclastic colors and witty, quizzical or poetic messaging directed at the person extracting them, they still stopper many wine bottles and the corkscrew still applies…for the time being.

559

As of 2020, all 50 states produce wine. All but Alaska grow grapes. As winemaking in the United States has come of age, centuries-old bottling and labeling formalities have been left by the wayside, to resurface at a later date with retro qualities. California has often led the way into brave new attitudes toward consumables, so it is not a surprise that the Golden State was on point in throwing tradition to the wind in the cork renunciation arena.

560

559 Composite corks, 1998–2004. Compressed and printed cork particles, each 2" long.

560 Bogle cork, 2004. Printed composite cork, each 1.75" long. Made in USA.

561 Plastic pseudo corks, 2002–2005. Printed plastic, each 1.75" high.

562 Plastic corks, 2002–2005. Printed plastic, each 1.5"–2" high.

561

562

TIN ROOF

*O*ur bottling of Tin Roof Sauvignon Blanc has been vinified in a "no-oak" style utilizing cold fermentation to enhance the lively flavors of the grape. The wine can be paired with delicate as well as highly flavored foods or is lovely all by itself.

There is an ongoing debate among "wine experts" questioning the viability of cork as a closure as "taint" or "off flavors" are becoming a frequent occurrence. We have bottled this Sauvignon Blanc with a "tin roof" to help ensure that the wine we have bottled is the same wine that you are about to enjoy. Removal is a simple process requiring no specialized tools, expensive equipment, cumbersome devices or fancy clothing.

Step 1 (figure 1): Twist top

Step 2 (figure 2): Remove

Step 3 (not shown): Enjoy

figure 1   figure 2

PRODUCED AND BOTTLED BY MURPHY-GOODE WINERY, GEYSERVILLE, CALIFORNIA, U.S.A.

563

GOVERNMENT WARNING: (1) ACCORDING TO THE SURGEON GENERAL, WOMEN SHOULD NOT DRINK ALCOHOLIC BEVERAGES DURING PREGNANCY BECAUSE OF THE RISK OF BIRTH DEFECTS. (2) CONSUMPTION OF ALCOHOLIC BEVERAGES IMPAIRS YOUR ABILITY TO DRIVE A CAR OR OPERATE MACHINERY, AND MAY CAUSE HEALTH PROBLEMS.

CONTAINS SULFITES

There are 101 great uses for cork - just not in a wine bottle. Cork taint, caused by the chemical TCA, spoils as much as 10% of all wine, giving it the odor of wet cardboard. Our T.O.P.P. screwcap keeps the wine in premium condition, from our winery to your glass.

corkamnesty.com
No Cork, No Taint.

read more, pull here

564

Enter the cork amnesty movement, proffering the aluminum screw-top, which is an effective seal, but consumers regard it as being for cheap wines. Cork taint, (caused by the presence of the chemical 2,4,6-trichloroanisole) it is claimed, "spoils as much as 10% of all wine, giving it the odor of wet cardboard." So far no one has suggested that the off-gassing of plastics (including the plastic liners of screw-tops) could be causing new synthetic corruptions. *Adieu* cork, *adios* taint; *vaya con dios* corkscrews. Inevitable change accompanies the inexorable march of time.

Corkscrews have had a three-hundred-year run of fascinating ingenuity, morphing through changes in format, fashion and hundreds of patents. As the age of printed books winds down, bookends are often seen propping CDs and DVDs. What will happen to corkscrews when there are no corks to pull?

563 Murphy-Goode wine bottle label questioning the viability of corks in preserving wine flavor, 2004. 4" high.

564 Anti-cork wine bottle neck label (back and front), Murphy-Goode Winery, Geyserville, CA, 2004. Each .75" x 4".

One answer is that more people will collect them. In the secondary marketplace corkscrew prices have moved along at a steady clip for the last fifteen years as collectorship grows. I visited the *Musée du Tire-Bouchon* (Corkscrew Museum) in Ménerbes, France in 2001, where one thousand examples were on exhibit. I'm sure they have more now. The online home for aficionados, corkscrewnet.com, lists nine international corkscrew societies that have formed in recent years. Sharing information about these compelling tools connects isolated collectors and brings more corkscrews to light.

Some of us scan the past searching for resonant objects that tell us about the times in which they were made. Along the way we are intoxicated by the improbable, uplifted by the prodigious richness of the world and enriched by the grandness of the spectacle. We are collectors. A good flea market or antique show is an unreserved venue for seeking and possessing. Good corkscrews are still affordable.

I feel at home in the topography of tools. When we use a tool, the ingenuity that its invention required doesn't seem surprising. The inconvenience of using its predecessor or any lesser apparatus doesn't pertain. With its cleverness and originality an invention becomes part of the lexicon of ordinary things. The brilliance of its conception is mute (integral but overlooked) and the new object joins the ranks of tools used to perform our ordinary rituals. This collection is artifactual proof that any tool is believable after it has been invented.

INDEX

ACKNOWLEDGMENTS

I owe a special debt to Jeremy F. Brooke for his all-nighters in caption hell and for his kind patience, steady acuity, expert technical support, hardcore dedication and supportive juggling skills.

My gratitude to André Burgos for sharing his corkscrew expertise, to William E. Rivers of the University of South Carolina for his *Bottle-Scrue* intelligence, to Clara Clack for her fine eye, to Will Lippincott for his bold confidence in my multi-flavored literary endeavors, to Deborah Aaronson for her editorial guidance and savvy, to Abby Kinsley for her generous counsel, and to Chris Hiebert, artist among book designers.

—Marilynn Gelfman Karp

I would like to thank, first and forever, Amie for sharing a life with me and Ike for perpetually providing a bright, wacko perspective and being my joy. Heartfelt gratitude to my parents, Sam and Sue, and sister, Becca, for steadfast support in my assorted undertakings. My deepest appreciation to Marilynn and Ivan for fostering the collector's spark and inviting me in, and to the Karp family for not only sharing their corkscrews with me but bottles of wine and Sunday dinners as well.

—Jeremy Franklin Brooke

PHOTOGRAPHY CREDITS

All corkscrews shown are from the Karp family collection.

Photography of objects in the collection

Carl Williamson
for all objects except as indicated below

Vivian Kamen
for objects #74, #87, #104, #115, #126, #128, #132, #175, #179, #182, #185, #189, #192, #199, #200, #204, #205, #208, #209, #213, #214, #219, #220, #221, #225, #226, #230, #234, #236, #239, #240, #242, #260, #269, #270, #281, #289, #296, #304, #314, #327, #339, #352, #353, #362, #372, #378, #379, #386, #388, #390, #406, #453, #457, #473, #475, #511, #529, #534

Jeremy Brooke
for objects #5, #6, #10, #131, #140, #159, #184, #195, #197, #215, #245, #338, #347, #348, #351, #395, #408, #421, #422, #423, #426, #427, #430, #432, #434, #435, #439, #440, #456, #470, #482, #485, #488, #490 and group, #491, #501, #505, #506, #507, #555

Marilynn Karp
for objects #2, #24, #67, #94, #100, #117, #167, #168, #169, #174, #228, #273, #280, #292, #312, #366, #409, #447, #465, #493, #500, #510, #515, #566

André Burgos
for objects #36, #121, #181, #183, #206, #244 (on page 89), #412, #428, #431, #535, #537

Amie O. Karp
for author photos, pages 224 and 225

Photoretouching

Jeremy Brooke, Chris Hiebert, Vivian Kamen, Marilynn Karp

Front and back cover
Mechanical closed frame corkscrew, Thomason V serpent variant, with recumbent lion and unicorn handle topped by the English imperial crown, c. 1830. See no. 348.

Spine
Figural eyebrow handle corkscrew with baby holding grape bunches, smooth shaft, bladed center worm, 1920s. See no. 11.

Interior design: CH Design
Cover design: Misha Beletsky

First edition

10 9 8 7 6 5 4 3 2 1

ISBN 978-0-7892-1377-8

Library of Congress Cataloging-in-Publication Data available upon request

For bulk and premium sales and for text adoption procedures, write to Customer Service Manager, Abbeville Press, 655 Third Avenue, New York, NY 10017, or call 1-800-Artbook.

Visit Abbeville Press online at www.abbeville.com.

MARILYNN GELFMAN KARP

Marilynn Gelfman Karp is Professor Emerita at
New York University, a fine sculptor, singular cook,
loving mother, proud grandmother, careful historian
and compulsive collector of extraordinary objects.
Her previous books are *In Flagrante Collecto*
(parsing the need to collect and examining the range
and breadth of objects of desire) and *I Married An
Art Dealer: Art, Enlightenment & Death with Ivan Karp*
(a memoir). She divides her time and her corkscrews
between New York City and a farmhouse in
Upstate New York.

JEREMY FRANKLIN BROOKE

Jeremy Franklin Brooke is Professor of Filmmaking
and Media Studies at the New School for Public
Engagement in New York City. He is a film editor
and screenwriter, an enthusiastic collector of arcane
objects and an inquiring mind whose compulsion
to master new media led him to develop the
information system used in *Uncorked*. He lives in
Manhattan with his wife, their son and Marty
McFly the Cat.